Praise for Fox Butterfield's

IN MY FATHER'S HOUSE

One of The Marshall Project's
Best Criminal Justice Books of the Year

"Perversely pleasurable."   —*The Week*

"A family portrait and a study in big ideas. . . . Posing difficult questions about mass incarceration, cultural marginality, and persistent communities of lawlessness."   —CrimeReads

"Based on an extraordinary research effort. . . . An outstanding book of sociology and criminology."   —*Kirkus Reviews*

"Fox Butterfield has written a spellbinding book, brilliant and bone-chilling. *In My Father's House* will change the way we look at what makes a criminal."   —Linda Fairstein, author of *Deadfall*

"A critically needed book, at once searing and poignant. Whether conservative or liberal, your assumptions about our criminal justice system will be shaken when you read it. With an academic's research, a journalist's eye for observation, and the fluidity of a novel, Butterfield puts a human face on the statistics and studies. . . . Every American who cares about a system that is costing us nearly $200 billion annually, and has 2.3 million Americans incarcerated, can't afford not to read it."   —Raymond Bonner,
author of *Anatomy of Injustice*

"Fox Butterfield somehow managed to find the most colorful family of outlaws in recent times, which makes for a very entertaining read. During my forty-four years behind bars, I saw ample evidence that criminality runs in some families, though I never met a prisoner who had so glamorous a view of his family's lawless exploits as do the Bogles. There's a lot of valuable information and insight in this book."
—Wilbert Rideau,
author of *In the Place of Justice*

Fox Butterfield

IN MY FATHER'S HOUSE

Fox Butterfield is the author of *China: Alive in the Bitter Sea*, which won the National Book Award, and *All God's Children: The Bosket Family and the American Tradition of Violence*. He was a member of the *New York Times* reporting team that won the Pulitzer Prize for its publication of the Pentagon Papers, and he served as a bureau chief for the newspaper in Boston, Saigon, Tokyo, Hong Kong, and Beijing—where he opened the *Times* bureau in 1979. Most recently he was a national correspondent for the *Times*, covering crime and violence. He lives in Portland, Oregon.

IN MY FATHER'S HOUSE

A NEW VIEW OF HOW
CRIME RUNS IN THE FAMILY

FOX BUTTERFIELD

Vintage Books

A DIVISION OF PENGUIN RANDOM HOUSE LLC

NEW YORK

FIRST VINTAGE BOOKS EDITION, SEPTEMBER 2019

Copyright © 2018 by Fox Butterfield

All rights reserved. Published in the United States by Vintage Books,
a division of Penguin Random House LLC, New York. Originally published in hardcover
by Alfred A. Knopf, a division of Penguin Random House LLC, New York, and distributed
in Canada by Penguin Random House Canada Limited, Toronto, in 2018.

Vintage and colophon are registered
trademarks of Penguin Random House LLC.

The Library of Congress has cataloged the Knopf edition as follows:
Names: Butterfield, Fox, author.
Title: In my father's house : a new view of how crime runs in the family / Fox Butterfield.
Description: First edition. | New York : Alfred A. Knopf, 2018. | Includes bibliographical
references and index.
Identifiers: LCCN 2017058454
Subjects: LCSH: Bogle, Bobby. | Criminals—Oregon—Case studies. | Criminals—Family
relationships—Oregon—Case studies. | Families—Oregon—Case studies. | Crime—
Sociological aspects—Case studies. | Criminal behavior, Prediction of—Case studies.
Classification: LCC HV6785 .B87 2018 |
DDC 364.3092/2795—dc23
LC record available at https://lccn.loc.gov/2017058454

Vintage Book Trade Paperback ISBN: 978-1-4000-3424-6
eBook ISBN: 978-0-525-52163-1

Author photograph © Paul Rich Studio
Book design by Maggie Hinders

www.vintagebooks.com

Printed in the United States of America
10 9 8 7 6 5 4 3 2 1

In memory of Sam Butterfield, beloved son,

gifted journalist, who died much too young

I the Lord your God am a jealous God, visiting the iniquity of the fathers upon the children to the third and fourth generation.

—Deuteronomy 5:9

Contents

A Note on Terminology

Many Americans use the terms "jail" and "prison" interchangeably, as they do with the words "parole" and "probation." This is often true of politicians, journalists and academic specialists, who should know better, as well as many ordinary people. But in the criminal justice system, the words have precise meanings and real differences, and misuse can create confusion. Jails are penal institutions run by cities and counties, normally for offenders who have either yet to be tried and convicted or for inmates sentenced to terms of a year or less. Prisons are run by states or the federal government and hold inmates already sentenced to terms of longer than one year. There is a much greater turnover of the inmate population in jails than in prisons, and inmates in prisons tend to have committed more serious crimes.

Probation is generally a less serious alternative to jail or prison, allowing the offender to remain in his or her home community under certain conditions, and is handed down by judges in courts. Parole usually means the offender has served a mandated portion of his or her sentence while incarcerated and has been released under specified conditions. The term "parole" derives from the French word *parole*, meaning the inmate has given his word or promise to behave in a law-abiding fashion. Offenders themselves often contribute to the confusion between parole and probation because, in speaking of their parole or probation officers, they refer to both by the shorthand "P.O."

The public confusion obscures the fact that while most Americans tend to focus on offenders in jail or prison, who now total

2.3 million, there are actually many more offenders on parole and probation, numbering 5.1 million, according to the Bureau of Justice Statistics, the research arm of the Justice Department.

Finally, because two-thirds of offenders on parole or probation commit new crimes within a few years, they are constantly being sent back to jail or prison, creating an enormous churn. Hence in practical terms, for the offenders themselves and their spouses and children, the effects of being placed on probation or parole are similar to being sent to jail or prison: the disruptions in their lives, the difficulty of staying in school, the loss of jobs and income, and particularly the insular, clannish behavior. So the homes where offenders live, often surrounded by other families like them, serve to perpetuate crime. These isolated, emotionally and economically strained communities help explain why crime often runs in families.

IN MY FATHER'S
HOUSE

Prologue

It Takes a Family to Raise a Criminal

The Oregon State Penitentiary sits incongruously in the middle of Salem, the state capital, next to a large park with fields for children's soccer games and rows of residential streets. Armed guards patrol the twenty-five-foot-high concrete walls of the maximum-security prison. When the penitentiary was first constructed, in 1851, Oregon was not yet a state and Salem had only a handful of settlers who had trekked on foot over the Oregon Trail, so as the population of Salem increased, the city grew around the prison, making it a familiar sight. The neighborhood came to be known as Felony Flats.

For Bobby Bogle, who had been locked up most of the time since childhood, the location of the penitentiary seemed an apt metaphor for his life. For him and his brothers, prison and life ran together. Sitting on the steel bunk in his cell and thinking back on his childhood, Bobby could remember only one Christmas when his father gave him a present—a heavy metal wrench in a plain brown paper bag presented with no explanation. Bobby was just four years old at the time and for a moment was puzzled by the gift. But he knew from listening to excited conversations around the dinner table that his father, known to everyone by the nickname Rooster, had served hard time in a Texas prison for burglary and took pride in his criminal record. So Bobby figured his father had given him a burglar's tool. Before dawn on Christmas day he snuck out of the house with his older brother, and they broke into the V & V Market, the little grocery store in the former migrant farmworkers camp where they lived on the edge of Salem. In the back of the store there were stacks of Coca-Cola bottles locked in a caged-in area. The wrench was big for Bobby's small hands, so he worked awkwardly as he used his present to break open the lock on the cage. Then the boys carried home their sodas for a Christmas celebration.

Rooster was elated. "Yeah, that's my sons," Bobby could still recall his father saying, years later, as if celebrating a school report card with straight A's or a Little League home run. "My father had been encouraging us to steal practically since I was born," Bobby told me. We were seated face-to-face in the penitentiary's visitors' room, where I was interviewing Bobby for an article I was writing for *The New York Times* as part of my beat covering criminal justice. "He taught us stealing was good, as long as we didn't get caught," Bobby added. "If we got caught, he would use the knife he always carried to cut off a tree branch to make a switch and then whup us till we were cut and bleeding." Bobby took the lesson to heart. In the Bogle family, crime brought respect. "So I wanted to go to prison from the time I was a young boy," Bobby explained, "to uphold our family honor and earn my stripes."

Bobby was wearing the standard-issue uniform for all Oregon inmates: dark blue denim pants and a lighter blue work shirt, both emblazoned in fierce orange letters with the label "Inmate, Oregon Department of Corrections." Bobby had been locked up almost continuously since he was around twelve years old, first in juvenile reformatories and later in a series of prisons. With all that incarceration, he had the cold-eyed convict look down. Bobby was short, five feet nine inches, but all the weight lifting he had done in prison yards for so many years made him look taller. His broad shoulders and thick chest seemed to belong to a much bigger man. His jaw was square, and his green eyes were always alert, on the lookout, as he had to be for self-preservation in prison. His salt-and-pepper hair was brushed back from his forehead and cut short on the sides. The gunfighter mustache drooping down around the corners of his mouth lent him an air of menace.

For Bobby and his five brothers and three sisters, childhood often meant accompanying their father, and their mother, Kathy, whenever Rooster selected targets for them to rob or burglarize. There were neighbors' houses to break into, chickens and cows to steal for food, gardens to loot for tomatoes and corn, and construction sites where they could pluck valuable lumber or metal that Rooster resold for cash to supplement his on-again, off-again job as an ironworker. One night Rooster led them to the Bonneville Dam on the Columbia River, ninety miles northeast of Salem, where they broke into the government-run fish hatchery and helped themselves to as many coho and Chinook salmon as they could load into Rooster's truck, later eating as much as they could and selling the rest to neighbors. Their mother served as the lookout, remaining in the truck while they were inside the fence, and then she drove the getaway vehicle.

One of Bobby's younger brothers, Tracey, recalled this period as a good time of madcap family adventure. Tracey Bogle was seven years younger than Bobby and was also locked up in the Oregon State Penitentiary. "We did it all as a family," Tracey said in a separate interview in the visitors' room. "We had pride in our family doing these robberies, so it was fun. We were a crime family."

Perhaps with more insight than he was aware of, Tracey observed, "What you are raised with, you grow to become." Despite a diagnosis of paranoid schizophrenia, Tracey was often the most articulate and analytical member of his family. "If I'd been raised in a family of doctors, I'd probably be a doctor. But I was raised in a family of outlaws who hated the law." His words made him sound like he was pronouncing an epitaph for his family. "The only law I knew was cops coming to arrest me or my brothers, breaking down our doors and taking me to court."

One of the happiest moments of his life occurred when Tracey was eight years old. He and Bobby managed to sneak into the attic of a bar one evening. They hid there until after closing time, then climbed back down the stairs into the deserted, darkened barroom and helped themselves to all the money in the cash register. They walked home to the trailer they were sharing with their mother at the time and dumped a sack of bills on her head. That woke her up and made her shriek with joy. Just telling the story made Tracey happy. He laughed so hard that tears rolled down his cheeks and his body shook with pleasure. It was as if he had somehow been transported beyond the high prison walls and the barbed-wire fence surrounding them and also transported back in time to that very moment in his mother's mobile home. This was his child-hood, the only one he knew, so it was fun even when it was painful.

As the boys grew older, they all dropped out of school. Bobby left in the seventh grade, and Tracey in the eighth grade. Instead of attending conventional commencement ceremonies, they gradu-ated to more serious crimes. Their favorite was stealing big-rig trucks, eighteen-wheelers running south from Salem in the Wil-lamette Valley to California on Interstate 5, a drive of 300 miles, or from Salem east to Boise, Idaho, on Interstate 84, a distance of 475 miles. When they started these capers, Tracey was so young and short that he could barely see over the steering wheel and his feet hardly reached the pedals. Semis were more valuable than cars, the boys calculated, because they carried much more gas and could go farther. One time they stole a semi from a truck park-ing lot in Salem and rammed it into the side of a gun store, right through the wall, and made off with a haul of guns. Another semi they stole was loaded with $100,000 worth of liquid sugar. That landed them in court, and they were both sent to the MacLaren School for Boys, Oregon's most secure juvenile facility, just off the highway between Salem and Portland. The brothers like to think they must have stolen three hundred semis altogether. Even allowing for youthful braggadocio, the number was probably large.

I first heard about the Bogles in 2002 from Steve Ickes, then an assistant director of the Oregon Department of Corrections. At the time, his office thought there were six members of the Bogle family who were in prison or had earlier been incarcerated. Steve arranged for me to interview a few of them behind bars, including Bobby and Tracey. I had previously written a book about four generations of outlaws, thieves and murderers in a black family, *All God's Children: The Bosket Family and the American Tradition of Violence,* and I was struck by a recent series of studies showing that crime seemed to run in certain families. I hoped to find a white family with a sizable number of inmates to illustrate this perverse legacy while removing race as a factor in the discussion. The Bogles seemed like a candidate.

Now, after ten years of research, I have found *sixty* Bogles who have been sentenced to either prison, jail or a juvenile reformatory, or placed on probation or parole—in other words, put under the supervision of the criminal justice system. These are only the ones for whom I could find official court, prison or police records. More than likely, the actual total is higher. Over the passage of years, court files often get lost or stored in some forgotten warehouse: in other cases, Bogle family women who went to jail may have used their married names and therefore are untraceable. Or, they may have had children who were sentenced to prison under the name of a husband or boyfriend whom I could not identify.

The figure of sixty might appear to be an outlier, some oddity out of *Ripley's Believe It or Not.* But the Bogles are something much more important, and commonplace—a dramatic example of findings by criminologists from around the United States and other countries that as little as 5 percent of families account for half of all crime, and that 10 percent of families account for two-thirds of all crime. Perhaps the most important of these studies was conducted on a group of 411 boys from South London, England, following them from 1961 to 2001, by a team of British criminologists led by David Farrington of the University of Cambridge. Half of all the convictions of these boys were accounted for by less than 6 percent of the families in the sample; 10 percent of the families accounted for two-thirds of all convictions. The longitudinal study, known as the Cambridge Study in Delinquent Development, also showed that having a father or mother who had been convicted, or an older brother or sister who had been convicted, was a good predictor of a boy's later criminal activity. Having a parent who had not only been convicted but was then sent to prison was an even stronger predictor of a boy's later criminal life.

A similar concentration of criminality was found in large, multiyear studies of delinquent boys in Philadelphia, Pittsburgh and Rochester by American criminologists. Another measure of how strongly crime runs in families comes from the Justice Department's Bureau of Justice Statistics. It has reported that roughly half of the 2.3 million Americans in jail or prison have a father, mother or other close family member, like a brother, sister or uncle, who has previously been incarcerated.

What criminologists call the intergenerational transmission of violence was first documented in a pioneering longitudinal study of five hundred delinquent boys in the Boston area in the 1940s by a husband-and-wife team of researchers at the Harvard Law School, Sheldon and Eleanor Glueck. The Gluecks found that two-thirds of the boys sent by a court to a reformatory had a father who had been arrested and half had a grandfather who had been arrested. Forty-five percent also had a mother who had been arrested.

Equally striking, all the delinquent boys in the Gluecks' study were white. In part, this racial makeup is a reminder that until the 1960s, at least, until the Second Great Migration of blacks from the South after World War II, most crime, including violent crime, was committed by whites. Our best-known outlaws until then were white: Jesse James in Missouri in the nineteenth century, Al Capone in Prohibition-era Chicago and Bonnie and Clyde in Texas during the Depression. They tended to be rural, white and poor, or ethnic white immigrants: Irish, Italians or Poles who belonged to gangs in this country's big cities. The common American stereotype today of young black predators with guns dealing drugs was a creation of more recent years, starting in the 1960s.

Michael Harrington, the social worker and Socialist Party leader, captured the spirit of the Southern rural, white poor who had moved into the big cities during the Depression or in World War II in search of jobs in his 1962 best seller, *The Other America: Poverty in the United States.* He called them "urban hillbillies," at a time before political correctness. "They are in the slums," Harrington wrote, using another term that has fallen out of favor. "They came up from the Appalachians to Detroit for war jobs, and stayed on.... They can be identified by their ninth-generation Anglo-Saxon faces, by their accents, and by the ubiquity of country music.... One could read the fates written on some of the children's faces. It was relatively easy to guess which boys might end up in a penitentiary, which girls would become pregnant before they were out of grade school."

The Bogles are a carryover from this older America, when crime was largely a phenomenon of disadvantaged whites. By examining what happened in their family, how they passed a malignant heritage of criminality on to their children and grandchildren and even great-grandchildren, it might be possible to get around race when thinking about the causes of crime, to disentangle race and crime and overcome one of our most deep-seated stereotypes. This is not meant to downplay the terrible racial disparity that arose as the war on drugs and the accompanying movement to toughen our sentencing laws resulted in a quadrupling of the U.S. prison population from the 1970s until it began to decline in the late 1990s in the past few years. This experiment with mass incarceration has given the United States the terrible distinction of having the highest rate of imprisonment in the world along with a racially skewed prison population. In 2014, the Justice Department reported that 6 percent of all black men age thirty to thirty-nine were in prison; the rate for Hispanic men the same age was 2 percent, and it was 1 percent for white men in that age group. It is also important to note that even now, if property crimes are included with violent crimes, 69 percent of all crimes reported to the police are committed by whites, according to the Uniform Crime Report, published annually by the FBI.

As I spent more time listening to the Bogles' stories and learning how many of them ended up with criminal records, I realized the Bogles also offered a way to refocus on the family as a cause of crime. Oddly, many criminologists have neglected this aspect of criminality in recent years, looking instead at such well-known risk factors as poverty, bad neighborhoods, deviant peers at school, drugs and gangs. These are real issues. But chronologically, a child's life and development begin at home with his or her family even before their neighborhood or friends or classmates can influence them. John Laub, a professor of criminology and criminal justice at the University of Maryland and one of the leading American criminologists, has suggested that scholars have avoided focusing on the family because the very mention of family suggests a possible biological or genetic basis for crime that could lead to charges of racism.

Tracey Bogle, though, had no such compunctions in trying to analyze his own descent into a criminal career. "Once you get in it, it is a really strong pull," he told me in another prison interview. "Sometimes I think it was the power of imitation, copying the behavior of my father and older brothers and uncles." Without realizing it, Tracey had stumbled into one of the main schools of criminology, known as "social learning theory," which holds that young criminals develop by imitating behavior they see around them through the same psychological process as any other behavior is learned. Tracey had never graduated from high school, much less studied criminology, so it was sufficient for him to repeat his family's view of how they became ensnared in criminal lives. "We just call it a curse, the Bogle curse," Tracey said. Both Tracey and Bobby and their brothers and cousins had come to believe that crime starts at home. They learned everything they needed to learn in their father's house. In other words, it takes a family to raise a criminal. And here lies the central thesis of this book: we talk about the importance of family values, and in doing so we tend to assume that these values are good, but family values can go off track and be bad, and the results, over generations, can be devastating.

As the criminal paterfamilias, Rooster Bogle not only took his children out to commit crimes with him; he even happily prophesied where this would lead them. Some days he would take his boys to a lake southeast of Salem to go fishing, their route taking them past another sprawling prison, the Oregon State Correctional Institution, which was surrounded by mounds of shiny razor wire. Rooster would gaze at the facility with something akin to a perverse nostalgia, as if he were looking at a great castle. On these occasions he liked to tell his oldest son, Tony, "Look carefully, because when you grow up, you guys are going to end up there." Tony took this not as a warning but as a challenge. Far from imposing and terrifying, the place looked downright inviting to Tony. He would look up at the guard towers and say to his father, "Let's go there right now." Later Tony made his father's prognostication come true, albeit in a different state and a different prison. In 1991, at the age of twenty-nine, he murdered a man in Tucson, Arizona, and was sentenced to life in prison. He is still there.

Bobby, Tracey and Tony had no idea about the total number of Bogles who have been sentenced to prison, or about when their family's ruinous criminal history began. "The past was kept back from us," Tracey said. "It was a secret." As boys, the only thing they knew were the stories Rooster told them. He traced the family history to his mother, Elvie, who he said was a gypsy from Germany who migrated to Texas. Not just any gypsy, Rooster told them, but the queen of the gypsies who worked in a carnival, sold moonshine and befriended Bonnie and Clyde during the Depression. "My dad said gypsies lived by stealing, so we would steal," Tracey recalled. Rooster personally gave each of his eight children what he said were gypsy tattoos, little blue dots under their left eyes.

But even what little the brothers thought they knew about their family, the stories their father told them, often were not true, and none of their older relatives who knew more, their aunts and uncles, their grandfather and grandmother, corrected Rooster's version. It was only years later, after the boys grew old enough to be sent to prison, that they learned the blue dots on their left cheeks were a mark convicts in state and federal prison in the 1950s and 1960s gave themselves so they could identify one another after they were released. Richard Hickock and Perry Smith, the two ex-convicts who murdered the Clutter family on their farm in Kansas, as recounted by Truman Capote in his best seller *In Cold Blood,* had the marks. It was another of Rooster's ways of branding his children and leading them to a long criminal doom. Oddly, one thing that no one in the family seemed to know was the origin of their name, Bogle; it is a Scottish word, meaning a goblin that, on behalf of the victims, sometimes causes mischief to those who have committed crimes.

Bobby, Tracey and Tony have each been incarcerated most of their adult lives. They had no way to track down their lost family history, so they urged me to find out what I could. Perhaps by going back in time, back into the Bogle family's memories, its myths, its brutalities, it might be possible to learn when all this began and how the criminal virus was transmitted. When we first discussed attempting this research, none of us knew that the Bogles could be traced to the hills of Tennessee during the Civil War or to a poor cotton sharecropper's farm near Paris, Texas, in 1920. This is their family story.

[I]

ORIGINAL
SIN

I'm here to say one thing. Jesse James was a good man.
I'd be thankful if you'd grow up to be as good a man as
Jesse James.

> —WILLIAM A. OWENS, quoting his grandmother
> in his memoir of growing up near Paris, Texas, circa 1910,
> *This Stubborn Soil: A Frontier Boyhood*

1

Louis and Elvie

The Carnival

In June 1920, twenty-one-year-old Louis Bogle left his log-cabin home in the farming hamlet of Daylight, Tennessee, to seek his fortune in Texas. Daylight was near the small city of McMinnville on the edge of the high Cumberland Plateau, and there was a grist mill and a creek running down a hillside to power it, but not much else. Louis had merely a few years of education in the one-room schoolhouse that was open only during the winter when farming came to a halt. Louis, Rooster's father, made the trip at the invitation of his uncle, Louis Harding. Harding himself had moved from Daylight to Texas only two years earlier to try his hand at selling Daylight's specialty, nursery-tree stock—young apple, pear and peach trees—and had already made enough money to buy a fine house in the new city of Paris. More important to Louis, Harding had also purchased a Ford Model T, the symbol of the new age of the automobile.

When Louis made his way to Texas, he was following a well-trod path. In every decade after the South's ruinous defeat in the Civil War in 1865, people had been moving to Texas from the states of the old Confederacy in increasing numbers, seeking cheaper land and new beginnings. They left signs behind in their abandoned homes: "Gone to Texas." It was a statement of fact, and a dream. Many of these Southerners headed for northeast Texas around Paris, where the long trail from South Carolina and Tennessee, from Georgia, Alabama and Mississippi, emptied into the flat prairies that marked the beginning of the West.

This area, just west of the Arkansas border and just south of the Red River, which separated Texas from the new state of Oklahoma, was familiar-looking land to these displaced settlers. There were piney woods, stands of oak trees and creek bottoms for water, with the land planted ever more intensively with white blooming cotton as time passed, just like at home. These settlers, "pore whites," in their own term, came at first by wagon or oxcart, on horseback or, as they said, "footback and walking." Only later could they take a train, as Louis did, over a newly constructed rail network from Nashville to Memphis, then on to Fort Smith, Arkansas, and Dallas. They shared a memory of defeat in the Civil War, lived on the edge of poverty and worshipped an Old Testament deity as Baptists or Methodists. By early in the twentieth century, perhaps three-quarters of the families in Texas were headed by people who traced their ancestry to the slave states. "So many Texans have come out of the South," two scholars wrote in 1916, "that Texas is predominantly Southern in thought and feeling." There were no cowboys around Paris; instead it was a center of the cotton business, one hundred miles northeast of Dallas.

Louis Bogle was infatuated the moment he stepped off the Gulf, Colorado and Santa Fe train from Dallas. Although Paris had a population of only twelve thousand in 1920, it was the biggest and by far the most modern city he had seen. For the first time he saw paved roads, like smooth polished floors, and handsome white houses with shade trees lining the streets. There were more automobiles than he could count. On weekdays people walking on the sidewalks wore better clothes than most had for Sunday back home. A large cottonseed mill worked at night making golden-yellow meal to feed dairy cows. The plant left an aroma over the city in the morning like fresh-baked bread, only more delicious. Scattered around the city were factories making candy, furniture and boxes: the newest was a Campbell's Soup factory, a sure sign that Paris had arrived. There was even a splendid new seven-story hotel, the Gibraltar, that dominated downtown. On the outskirts of town, behind a long fence, there were acres of green grass, and big shade trees and sprays of water turning slowly in the sun. Men were walking on it, but Louis could not tell what they were doing. It was the prettiest pasture he had ever seen. Later he learned it was called a golf course.

The city fathers had changed the name of the town from Pin Hook to Paris to make it seem more grand and progressive, but it was still part of the Old South. A few days after Louis arrived, he was swept up in a crowd, later estimated at three thousand people, who were rushing to the city fairgrounds to seek revenge against two young black brothers, Ervin and Herman Arthur. They were cotton tenant sharecroppers who had been working for a white landlord outside the city when, as U.S. Army veterans of World War I, they had decided to move out when the landlord demanded an exorbitant share of their crop. They were in the midst of loading their meager possessions on a truck when the landlord and his grown son, armed with shotguns, tried to stop them. "When the white folks started shooting, Uncle Herman showed them what he had learned in the war," a nephew of the Arthurs later recounted. The landlord and his son ended up dead. A sheriff had tracked the Arthurs down in Oklahoma and returned them to Paris, where on July 6, 1920, a mob used sledgehammers to break down the jail door and took the brothers to the fairgrounds. There they were chained to the flagpole, tortured, saturated with oil and set on fire. According to an account in the *Chicago Defender*, the black-owned newspaper, "Their charred, smoking bodies were then chained to an automobile and dragged for hours through the streets" of the black sections of Paris. Five men were indicted for murder, but the case was later dropped, and the records of the lynching destroyed in a courthouse fire. Louis would tell his family stories about that day for years, but his memories were more of the spectacle than any lessons learned.

Louis's uncle and his son, Charlie Harding, who was Louis's cousin and best friend, welcomed their newly arrived relative into the house they had purchased in Paris. His uncle said Louis could live with them, and they treated him to several sets of new city clothes, including a brown suit and a white dress shirt with a high, narrow, pointed collar topped with a stickpin for his tie. They also taught Louis to drive their new Model T around the city's streets. It was a thing as rare to Louis as a chariot of the gods dropped from the sky. To him all this was a miracle. For the first time in his life he felt like a success; in his mind he had money, a house, a car and, most definitely, a future.

Louis's favorite place in Paris was the S. H. Kress and Company five and dime store on Lamar Avenue. The curved-glass display windows and heavy bronze doors led into a long room of shiny glass-and-wood counters under bright hanging lamps. The counters were filled with buttons, men's hose, glassware and hardware. The air smelled of new, mercerized cotton cloth, candy in big glass bins and sweet, flowery perfume, unfamiliar yet delightful scents to Louis. Best of all were the salesgirls behind the counters. They were friendly with Louis, who was tall and slender, with brown hair and eyes and large protruding ears. Most of the girls were, like him, from poor farms in the countryside. Their families had moved to Paris so the girls could work at a place like the dime store—for seven dollars a week, far more than they could hope to make from farming. Most important, working at the Kress store gave them a better chance to find a husband. It was the best pickup spot in the city. If a girl did get married, though, she had to leave. Samuel H.

Kress, who owned the company, did not employ married girls. He thought it was bad for business, according to the principles of modern scientific management that he practiced. So a girl had to be careful in her choice; there were no second chances.

Louis was particularly taken with a short girl who wore her dark hair in marcelled waves, in the flapper fashion that had suddenly come into vogue. Her name was Elvie Morris, he learned, and she too was a country girl, born and raised on a cotton sharecropping farm in the crossroads village of Sherry, twenty-five miles east of Paris. Elvie, born in 1902, was three years younger than Louis. Her father had died in the influenza epidemic of 1918, with no land or house to his name, but her mother, Florence, making use of a small life insurance policy, had bought the two women new clothes and a modest house near Paris so Elvie could get a job at the Kress store. Florence and Elvie's self-improvement plan was to find a man with means to enable them to escape their life of poverty. Elvie had a clutch of new short flapper dresses and cloche hats, with their tight-fitting, bell-shaped tops decorated with large bows and ribbons. Elvie also wore bright lipstick, still frowned on in places like Paris, where the Baptist and Methodist churches had a strong influence. Louis was naturally quiet and reserved, but to his relief he discovered that striking up a conversation with Elvie was easy. She was open and direct and told Louis just what she thought. They were soon going out for Coca-Colas and then for rides in what he passed off as his car, his uncle's Model T. And when they visited his uncle's house, Louis did not hesitate to suggest he was part owner.

This embellishing was something that Louis had learned as a child in Tennessee from his mother, Mattie, from his grandmother Narcissa, and indirectly from his grandfather Carpenter. In 1866, when Narcissa was eighteen, she met Carpenter Harding, who claimed to be a doctor and a former Union Army cavalry officer. In fact, he was neither. But his stories made him appear to be an attractive match even though he was fifty-two. Carpenter and

Narcissa soon married. After the wedding, Narcissa discovered her new husband was a bigamist, with six children and a legal wife back in Indiana, something Carpenter had neglected to tell Narcissa. She also belatedly learned he had not served in the cavalry but was a private in the Thirteenth Indiana Light Artillery Regiment. As Louis himself heard years later from family stories, Carpenter was a confidence man, in the language of the time, or a con man in modern terms, the first of a series in the family. Despite these deceptions, Carpenter and Narcissa quickly had four children of their own, starting with Mattie, Louis's mother, and lived off their small farm. But Carpenter was old and suffered from dysentery he had contracted during his four years in the Army during the war, and he died of the disease in 1884.

For Narcissa, and eventually for Mattie, the most important thing after Carpenter's death was getting his Union Army pension, and Narcissa first applied for it to the War Department in Washington in 1887. Alone, with four young children, life would be hard without it. Carpenter's pension would have paid her $8 a month, plus $2 a month for each of her four children, a total of $16 a month, or $192 a year.

Union Army pensions were like a golden ticket, the first large-scale, nationally funded welfare system in American history. Between 1880 and 1910, Union Army pensions were the largest item in the federal budget, except for payments on the national debt. More than half a million men above age sixty-five and more than three hundred thousand widows and orphans were receiving payments from the federal treasury that averaged $189 annually.

Given the amount of money involved, Civil War pensions had become a big political issue, with many Americans in the late nineteenth century regarding them as a source of corruption and dependence, like Ronald Reagan's twentieth-century claims about "welfare queens." So Washington had to be careful in making the awards, and the War Department opened a routine investigation of Narcissa's eligibility. That Narcissa was from Tennessee, a state that joined the Confederacy, was not a problem because Carpenter had been a Union soldier, an investigator from the War Department concluded. Nor did he say Narcissa was disqualified because Carpenter was still married to his wife in Indiana at the time of his wedding with Narcissa. Narcissa was "perfectly ignorant on that point at the time of her marrying," the investigator wrote.

However, a special federal examiner sent from Nashville to Narcissa's home found a more troublesome issue. Narcissa candidly admitted to local gossip that she had been "intimate" with a neighboring farmer, John Melton, in Carpenter's last year and that she eventually gave birth to a son fathered by Melton. The affair contravened a law passed by Congress in 1882 meant, in the words of the commissioner of pensions in the Department of the Interior, "not to grant a pension to those widows who have dishonored the memory of their soldier husbands by adulterous acts." In 1897, after an astonishing ten years of investigation, the filing of dozens of affidavits and the taking of depositions from twenty of Narcissa's neighbors, the commissioner of pensions himself denied her claim to a pension. "The open and notorious adulterous cohabitation" of Narcissa and Melton "bars her claim to support from her husband's pension," the commissioner concluded.

This was a serious blow to Narcissa and her family. Narcissa and Mattie, convinced they could prevail, reapplied to Washington for the pension almost annually until the outbreak of World War I in 1914, each time adding new emotional appeals by neighbors and Narcissa's four children. All these applications were rejected. Con games were practically a way of life in the household where Louis grew up. Even Louis's father, a poor, illiterate farmer named James Bogle, exaggerated his wealth, tricking Mattie into marrying him before deserting and divorcing her. Louis knew almost nothing about his father; all he could do was use his imagination to conjure him.

.   .   .

Louis and Elvie had grown up living in homes made of rough-cut logs or boxing planks, without glass windows to keep out the cold in the winter or screens to deter the mosquitoes in the summer, leaving them subject to bouts of malaria. Leaves from mail-order catalogs papered the walls, and through the cracks in the boards the winter winds blew strong enough to make the coal-oil lamps smoke. The floors were dirt, and when it rained, mud. Water was hand-drawn from wells. There was no electricity. Farming meant plowing behind a mule, if you were lucky, or pushing the plow yourself if you couldn't afford a work animal. Their diet was corn bread with an occasional piece of pork fat and a few greens from the garden. In Paris, life was suddenly different for Louis and Elvie. They lived in a city and in a house that seemed like a mansion to them. They went driving fast in what Elvie believed was her new boyfriend's shiny Model T Ford along the country dirt road that led to her old home at the crossroads in Sherry. The road was like a trench cut through a high canopy of solid trees: post oaks, pin oaks, red oaks and sycamores. Going with Louis gave Elvie, for the first time, a sense of what an exciting time they were living in. "Bootleg liquor, cigarettes, bobbing your hair as a gesture of emancipation, it all went to your head," William Humphrey wrote about his mother in Sherry who was the same age as Elvie. "As the song they were singing that year went, 'How you gonna keep 'em down on the farm after they've seen Paree?'" For Louis and Elvie, Paris, Texas, might as well have been Paree.

Louis offered to show Elvie how to drive. But she was a natural and hardly needed instruction. Elvie explained that her uncle, Charles Morris, her father's older brother, in addition to being a cotton farmer also ran the general store, which included a small space for the post office in Sherry. Once a week it was his duty to go the seven miles into Clarksville, the nearest town, and fetch the mail, which he would hold for the forty or so families to collect.

To speed up his trips, Charles bought a motorcycle with a one-cylinder engine and a sidecar for the mail. Elvie, about thirteen at the time, begged her uncle to teach her to drive the motorcycle and let her go into Clarksville for the mail in his place. Everyone in her family was afraid she would get herself killed on the narrow, rutted dirt track, and driving a motorized vehicle was considered unladylike in a small Baptist community at the time. But she was already displaying the bravado and willingness to take risks that would determine so much of her life.

By now, Louis and Elvie were in love. Elvie was also pregnant, something they did not advertise. They were married in Paris on April 2, 1921. A photograph of Louis, apparently taken for the wedding, shows him in his brown suit and white shirt and dark tie with an almost architectural pompadour, his hair piled so high that it looks as if it were pulled upward and glued in place by someone with a mischievous sense of humor. Even the hair cannot hide his projectile ears, sticking straight out. Until the end of their lives, Louis and Elvie would say they fell in love the first day he walked into the Kress store and spotted her, thinking of themselves just like the characters in the hit song made popular by Bing Crosby, "I Found a Million-Dollar Baby (in a Five-and-Ten-Cent Store)." The song, however, was not recorded until 1931, ten years after they met. This lie became part of a pattern. When the facts of their lives were not convenient, they embellished them. It was a trait they would pass on to their own children, like dark hair and big ears.

Louis and Elvie's dream life ended as fast as it began. After the wedding, Elvie moved into the house owned by Louis's uncle in her belief that her new husband was part owner. But northeast Texas had just fallen into a sharp economic recession, with the price of cotton and land dropping by half in a year, and on top of that much of the crop was lost to a boll weevil infestation from

Mexico. With the demand for his fruit trees drying up, Harding decided to move back to Tennessee. So a few months after the marriage he sold the house in Paris and took his own grown son, Charles, and the Model T back to Daylight. For him, it was a business decision. For the newly married couple, it was a personal disaster. Elvie was confronted with Louis's boasts that had turned into deceits. How could they support themselves, especially with a baby on the way? Their first child, John Bogle, arrived in early December, eight months after they were married.

Louis had no real job skills or trade. In Tennessee he had worked part-time as an assistant to a mason and as a wallpaper hanger. Elvie, of course, could not go back to work in the Kress store now that she was married. The only available jobs for women in Paris were as teachers, nurses or store clerks. Black women worked as servants. Most white women in Texas still lived and worked on farms, but that was the last thing Elvie wanted to do. She was only nineteen, but she had been in rebellion against that life of poverty, backwardness and boredom as long as she could remember. Her earliest memories as a child were of being tied to a stake among rows of cotton where her parents were working to keep her from wandering into the woods, where there were snakes and scorpions. Her toys were the dirt and a stick to dig the dirt with. Elvie's father, James Morris, known as Jim, was a sharecropper of unprepossessing appearance: short, of medium build, with blue eyes and black hair. Each year he contracted with the biggest landowners in Red River County, the Lennox brothers, who let him live in a small unpainted house in Sherry and farm twenty-five acres of land. In exchange, he had to turn over half his cotton crop to them after the harvest. Every year, Morris thought he would make a big crop and be able to clear enough money to buy his own land and house, but each September, after the harvest, he found he had only enough cotton to sell to buy food for the winter and seeds for next spring. The Red River County tax records show that from 1895, when Jim began living in Sherry, until his death in 1918, he never owned any land to pay taxes on. In 1905, soon after Elvie was born, the tax records show, his entire net worth was set at $135—for a horse, a mule, a cow, a wagon and some tools.

Elvie had learned that cotton is a man-killing crop. As soon as the land is dry enough to be worked in the spring, it must be broken with the plow. Soon the days are long and hot, and the earth is baked hard. The plowshare must break through this rocklike earth, and then the seeds are sown. When the cotton plants are a foot high, they must be thinned with a hoe, every other plant being chopped out. Picking time came in late August or early September. Grown-ups and children strapped on knee pads and dragged long canvas sacks down the middle of the rows, picking two rows at a time, pulling out the lint and getting their fingers pricked by the pointy burrs. They worked from before daybreak until dark, under a broiling sun. After just one day of picking, the farmers and their children had aching backs and raw, bleeding hands.

So Elvie knew she could not go back to cotton farming. She had gotten a taste of modern city living in Paris, and she enjoyed wearing the stylish new clothes that her mother, Florence, had purchased for her. Elvie also had a wanderlust, a yearning to travel and try new things, as well as a strong will and daredevil streak that she got from her mother and her father's mother, Sarah Morris Hardin.

Her mother had been born in Tennessee, the daughter of two schoolteachers who, like so many Southerners, made their way westward after the Civil War. Perhaps because of her parents' status as schoolteachers, Florence seemed dissatisfied with her life as the wife of a poor cotton sharecropper, whom she had married in 1894. In photographs taken at the time, she has a dour, unhappy look. Four years after Elvie's birth, Florence deserted her husband and daughter, moving to Wichita Falls, one hundred fifty miles to the northwest. There she rented a room in a boardinghouse and worked as a wrapper in a candy factory. Florence told people she was unmarried and had no children. She also claimed to be twenty-eight when she was actually thirty-four. More prevarications.

Taken by themselves, these were only small fibs, but a serious pattern of deceit was emerging. Family members heard stories that Florence had been seen bringing men home, in some cases for money. Her sister-in-law at the time said, "Florence was a loose woman," and reported that Florence had responded to the allegation by saying, "I've been accused of being loose, so I might as well do it. If you're going to wear the name, then you might as well bear the blame."

In May 1910, Jim Morris filed for divorce from Florence on the grounds of abandonment in the Red River County district court. It was swiftly granted. But for Florence, being unmarried in her mid-thirties in Texas may not have turned out so well economically, or maybe she missed her daughters, so she came back to Sherry, and in December 1912 she remarried Jim Morris in Clarksville. Elvie was delighted her mother had come home after an absence of six years.

Soon after Florence had deserted her family in 1906, Jim's mother, Sarah Morris Hardin, arrived from Arkansas and moved in with Jim and Elvie to help out. Sarah was a lively, picaresque woman with a generous spirit who never shied away from adventure or difficult situations. At fifty-nine, though having given birth to nine children of her own, she remained vital and energetic. Sarah had been born in Georgia, moved to Alabama and late in the Civil War married a neighboring farmer, Lofton Morris. They soon had four sons, including Jim.

About 1875, for unexplained reasons, Sarah packed her four sons and all her belongings into a wagon and began a long trek to Arkansas. Perhaps her husband had died; perhaps she simply left him. There is no historical record. Records do show that at some point in her journey she met up with another Alabama farmer headed west, James Hardin, and they joined their wagon teams together. According to the story passed down in the family, Sarah and James got married during the trip, but it would have been a common-law marriage because Hardin had abandoned his wife, Elizabeth Barnes Hardin, in Alabama, along with four of his seven children. He never divorced her. The recombinant family found land it liked in northeast Arkansas and settled into a new life as Mr. and Mrs. James Hardin. Like Louis Bogle's grandmother, Elvie's mother and grandmother took what came their way and embellished when they had to.

Recent historical research has found that the lack of stability in these marriages, as well as the easy breaking of sacred vows, was more widespread among poor whites in the rural, sparsely populated upcountry South in the nineteenth century than Americans today presume. There were so few law-enforcement officials or ministers in this spread-out population that marriage and divorce were governed more by an "informal public" of family, kin and neighbors than by the niceties of the rule of law, according to Nancy Cott, a professor of history at Harvard who is a leading authority on marriage in the United States. Common-law marriages, desertion and what Cott calls self-divorce were widespread. There was also a sizable amount of adultery and bigamy among poor whites in the nineteenth-century South, Cott wrote in her book *Public Vows: A History of Marriage and the Nation.*

In Arkansas, as time passed, the new neighbors of Sarah Morris and James Hardin accepted that they were legally married, and the census of 1880 showed what a large family they had. In addition to the couple, there were three of Hardin's sons, four of her sons and a ten-month-old son born to James and Sarah in Arkansas. Eventually, they would have two more children together. Most of this big family remained together, unquestioned, until James Hardin died in 1891. Then, in an ending like something out of a Jane Austen novel, one of Hardin's sons by his previous wife showed up and took Sarah to court. He proved that his father had never divorced his mother and therefore that his father's marriage to Sarah was invalid. As a consequence, a judge ruled that Sarah and her children were not entitled to inherit anything from Hardin. Sarah was left with nothing. It was a few years after this debacle that Sarah moved to Texas to live with her son Jim Morris in Sherry.

For Elvie, having her grandmother around was fun. Sarah loved to dance, in a community where the Baptists thought dancing was a ticket to Hell, and she liked to organize square dances in people's houses, with a fiddler and someone to play the guitar and a banjo. Sarah taught Elvie to dance, and told her tales about life on the plantation in Alabama before the Yankees came and burned it down. Actually, there was no plantation in Alabama, only a small farm, but it made Elvie dream of a better life than being a cotton sharecropper. It made her dream of fine things and faraway places. Sarah also warned her about "the laws," the sheriff and the judge who would take your property away, as had happened to her. The moral of the story, Sarah said, was that a woman had to be strong and do whatever it took to survive.

In 1921, after Louis Bogle's uncle abruptly sold his house in Paris, it was Elvie who came up with a solution, drawing on what she had learned as a girl. That October, Elvie and Louis went to the biggest local event of the year, the annual visit to Paris of the carnival, held at the city fairgrounds. There were trained lions and elephants, and "mechanical and electrical riding devices sufficient to satisfy the whims of every youngster in Northeast Texas," *The Paris Morning News* reported on October 14, 1921. One of them, the paper said, "is surely sensational, that is, a regular hair-raiser." It was known as the motordrome, or Wall of Death, an invention of the past few years in which a motorcycle rider went faster and faster around a thirty-foot wooden circle that was banked in almost perpendicular fashion so that the motorcycle's centrifugal force propelled it higher and higher, clinging to the inside of the wall. Spectators climbed the outer wall of the wooden dome and looked over the top at the riders inside. When the riders reached the top, some spectators would reach over and put money in their outstretched hands, a tough feat for the riders, who had to take one of their hands off the handlebars and controls to accept the money. It was dangerous; some riders were badly injured or killed doing it. Elvie was instantly enthralled.

The carnival that came to Paris was run by the Great Patterson Shows, a major national company that traveled with its own collection of thirty railroad cars for the wild animals, performers, mechanics and equipment. Elvie sought out a manager to ask about a job. As it happened, one of their motorcycle riders was ill, or drunk, and they offered Elvie a chance to show what she could do. They gave her a uniform of tight horse-riding breeches, tall riding boots and an aviator's leather helmet, and she was off. She sped up the steep wall on her first try, reaching the open top, and was rewarded with handfuls of dollar bills. Elvie, a tomboy at heart, was ecstatic. It was as if she had been made for this. There was the fast driving, the danger and the sense that she was in charge. The carnival provided a fulfillment that farm life, school and what little she knew of church did not. She was following her grandmother's dictum: be strong and do what it takes to survive. At the end of the week, when the carnival prepared to move on to its next stop, in Louisiana, Elvie was offered a job for five dollars a week plus her tips, and a chance to sleep in a railroad car. As a bonus, they offered to make Louis a mechanic for an additional few dollars a week. If Elvie worried about the effect of driving around the motordrome on the baby she was carrying, there is no record of it.

The new jobs in the carnival were a godsend to Elvie and Louis, and they paid no heed to warnings from Elvie's family and friends that the people who worked in carnivals were a shifty lot. "Carnies," they were called, disreputable folk who were said to be dirty and decadent and often in trouble with the law. People in Clarksville, near Elvie's home in Sherry, were still talking about a young woman who was found murdered while working at a carnival there just two years earlier. Her family did not know she was working in the carnival, and when her father came to collect her body, he discovered that her two younger sisters were also employed there, so he took them home too. People in Clarksville had a saying, "When the carnival comes to town, lock your door." Many families in Clarksville would not even let their daughters into the motor-drome or other sideshows in a carnival. It just wasn't proper.

Elvie's friends also cautioned her about gypsies who were said to work in carnivals. Gypsies didn't bathe, they drank too much and they stole, her friends said. Elvie, however, had already made several friends among gypsy women who worked in the carnival. They too were adventurous, outsiders who were living a little on the edge, and she enjoyed it when they told her her fortune. Early on, she let one of the women give her a tattoo, a crudely drawn butterfly on her right arm at a time when respectable people did not etch permanent markings on their bodies. Elvie said it was a gypsy moth. As the years passed, Elvie would tell her children, and then her grandchildren, that she herself was a gypsy. In fact, she confided, she was a queen of the gypsies. She too was now embel-lishing, but it suggests how she thought at the time. Life on its own was not glamorous. Therefore, make it up. Create your own pres-ent. Erase your past. Devise a fable that summoned your dreams.

Elvie and Louis began drinking heavily with their new gypsy friends and others working in the carnival, going to parties in their railroad-car homes and staying up all night. It was another form of emancipation, in Elvie's eyes, freedom from the restrictive conven-tions of the small-town South in which she had been raised. Elvie had even more freedom because the carnival was always traveling, moving by rail once a week to other towns in Texas, Oklahoma, New Mexico or Louisiana, and as far away as Colorado and Utah. The carnival shut down only in the winter, when it was too cold to operate. Elvie and Louis would return to Paris then to visit their relatives and friends.

When she did go home, Elvie's relatives began to worry about her. They noticed she was not keeping her hair combed or her clothes clean, and when she stayed in their houses, they saw she wasn't keeping her room clean either. One of Elvie's aunts described her as slovenly and lazy. Those were the polite words she used in public. In private, her aunt began to call Elvie "trash." Working in the carnival was rapidly changing Elvie and Louis, making them coarser, putting them on the margins of society. Elvie had had the same kind of rudimentary education as Louis, though both could read and write. This, like being raised in poverty, didn't separate them from their contemporaries. It was true, though, that their family life was not stable. Their parents and grandparents had gone through a tangle of divorces, desertions and bigamous relationships. Hence they did not have the strong social bonds, the human capital, to draw on when times got tough. Now, working in the carnival, they were in danger of slipping into a white underclass.

In 1920, the same year Louis arrived in Paris, Prohibition went into effect. Since Paris had been the center of the Temperance Movement in Texas, the police and officials in the city were under intense pressure to enforce the wildly unpopular new law. Many Texans, including wealthy people in their new country clubs and poor white tenant farmers, would not obey the law against the production, sale and consumption of alcohol. As Randolph B. Campbell, a leading historian of Texas, has written, Prohibition was "surely one of the greatest incentives to lawbreaking in the history of the United States." Suddenly stills were everywhere in this big state with lots of empty space to hide illegal activity, and there was good money to be made in running a still, driving moonshine into towns and selling it to thirsty customers. Elvie used her driving skills to transport moonshine from stills in the countryside into Paris. Several times she was stopped by suspicious sheriffs' deputies, but she always managed to toss the mason jars full of home-brewed whiskey on the road, breaking them and scattering the whiskey so there was no evidence of a crime.

Louis was less fortunate. On January 13, 1923, he was arrested and charged with making and selling "spirituous, vinous and malt liquors and medicated bitters capable of producing intoxication" to three farmers outside Paris. Testimony at his trial in the Lamar County courthouse indicated he had a pretty good business going. Louis was found guilty of a felony on May 3. The jury sentenced him to two years in the state penitentiary in Huntsville. But because so many people were being convicted on similar charges and the state's prisons were overflowing with inmates at what Texans thought was an exorbitant cost to taxpayers, the district attorney gave the jury an option: if Louis had no previous convictions, they could suspend his sentence. The foreman filled in a slip for the judge. "We further find that the defendant has not been convicted of a felony in this state or any other state and we do recommend that his sentence be suspended." Louis was the first member of the Bogle family convicted of a felony, but he was free to go.

That same May, a grand jury in Paris handed down seventy-two other indictments for felonies and forty-five for misdemeanors, many of them for liquor being served in private homes or for illegal home poker games involving both men and women. The grand jury concluded with a warning: "There seems to be an unmistakable drift toward making the home an incubator of crime, when it should be the cleanest and holiest place on earth. After a while it will be as common to raid a private house as it has been to raid a bootlegging joint. God save us from the day, but it is on the way."

Elvie and Louis were too busy trying to eke out a living to worry about where society was headed. The income they earned from the carnival was small, and unreliable, and when the show closed for the winter there was no money at all, so they were becoming dependent on what they could make from selling moonshine or other petty crime. On July 20, 1925, Louis was arrested and indicted for a second felony, stealing a large quantity of brass from a house in Paris. He was taken to the county jail by the sheriff and released after posting bail of $800. Where he or Elvie got the money is unknown. Trial was set for October 20, but on that very day the trial was canceled when the victim suddenly recanted his earlier statements to the police and said he would not testify that the brass was "taken without his consent." For a second time, Louis had narrowly escaped.

Elvie and Louis were living such a precarious existence that they ultimately could not take care of the person closest to Elvie, her mother, Florence. From a surviving family photo, it is clear that after Elvie and Louis joined the carnival in 1921, Florence had gone back to Wichita Falls, where she had earlier lived after she deserted her husband; there is no explanation why. One photo, dated 1925, shows Elvie in a middy-style sailor's dress, with a jaunty scarf knotted around her neck, standing next to her mother and Louis in Wichita Falls. Louis is wearing a black stovepipe hat and a small bow tie. It looks like a normal family reunion, all their expressions benign, but Florence had begun to suffer from peculiar behavior that became increasingly severe, and somebody, presumably her daughter, had her committed to the new Texas state mental hospital in Wichita Falls. Elvie later told her children that Florence had gone insane.

Under Texas law, Florence's official diagnosis cannot be released, even to members of her family. But her death certificate, issued by the Vital Statistics Unit of the Texas Department of State Health Services, records that Florence died on April 22, 1927. She was only fifty-one years old. Dr. Liza Gold, a clinical and forensic psychiatrist who is a professor of psychiatry at Georgetown University and specializes in the history of psychiatry, believes Florence likely had an underlying mental disorder that today might be diagnosed as schizophrenia or bipolar disorder.

Louis and Elvie were too poor, or too busy, to take care of funeral arrangements for Florence. She was buried by the state hospital's staff in the potter's field on its grounds. The grave was unmarked.

By the time Florence died, Louis and Elvie had begun raising a family. All of their eventual offspring would be exposed to a host of risk factors for falling into a life of crime themselves—poverty,

neglect, alcoholic parents, little education and parental involvement in crime—and Louis and Elvie would now become the role
models for their children. In what may have been a coincidence,
or perhaps was a sign of something more fateful, Louis's mother,
Mattie, would later also be committed to the North Texas State
Asylum in Wichita Falls. She died there in 1960. Her diagnosis
also is not known. But the major mental illnesses, particularly
bipolar disorder—what used to be called manic depression—can
be heritable, so later generations of the Bogles may well have been
at risk for emotional disorders as well as criminality.

2

Charlie and Dude

Growing Up Criminal

Elvie gave birth to the Bogles' first child, John, on December 8, 1921. The carnival had shut down for the winter in early November when it became too cold for crowds to come out. Elvie and Louis had gone back to Paris and rented a small, rickety, unpainted shotgun house close to the Paris and Mount Pleasant Railroad depot, right next to the tracks. A big, redbrick Speas Vinegar plant near their house cast a sour odor over the neighborhood. The Bogles had no running water or electricity. The house was in one of the city's poorest sections, but it was all they could afford. The landlord, anxious not to let the house stand vacant, because a vacant house could not be insured, let them have it rent-free that first winter, on the condition that they keep it clean and tidy. On the front porches of nearby houses stood cast-off furnishings that once belonged inside, like an old settee, and in the weed-grown backyards the inhabitants threw bottles, old bedsprings and battered chamber pots. The smell of privies hung in the air, along with the whistle of the locomotives and the clanging of the trains' iron wheels on the tracks. The Bogles and all the branches of the family that conjoined together in Elvie and Louis, like most Americans, had always been farmers, living in isolated rural villages. Now, as America rolled into the 1920s, the Bogles were living in a city, just as a majority of their fellow Americans were becoming urbanized. But the Bogles were not able to enjoy the blessings of this new city life. They were disadvantaged, much like Michael Harrington's "urban hillbillies."

Other children soon followed John's arrival. Lloyd Douglas Bogle, quickly dubbed Dude within the family, was born in February 1924. Next came Charles Lindbergh Bogle, called Charlie, in 1928, the year after the famous aviator became the first man to fly solo across the Atlantic. Elvie and Louis were dreaming big with their choice of the name, but reality was much more down-to-earth.

Each new child meant a new mouth to feed and another body to clothe, requiring money that Elvie and Louis often didn't have, especially when the carnival was closed for the winter. Elvie cooked the same food every day, corn bread and beans, the boys remembered later, though she varied the way she prepared the dishes. They had meat only on special occasions. As they got bigger, Dude and Charlie supplemented their meager diet by hunting in the woods and fishing in ponds. Dude was genuinely crazy about fishing, catching catfish and perch in his bare hands, sometimes selling a fish or two for a nickel or a dime to the African American families who lived nearby. Their father made no secret of his scorn for what he called "colored people," but the boys, growing up in poverty and surrounded by black families, didn't much care about a person's race. At Christmas, there was not enough money for a tree or real presents, although their father usually managed to scrounge some candy or fruit, which he would put in one of his socks and hang from the fireplace mantel. The boys wore overalls that fastened in the back, the workingman's outfit of the time, but they had no shoes. Family photographs that survive from the 1920s and 1930s show each of the children with bare feet well into their teens.

Not long after Charlie was born, the stock market crashed, followed by the Great Depression, but the Bogles hardly noticed. They had never seen a stock certificate, and they didn't have a bank account. To them, Wall Street was a bunch of rich Yankees far away who deserved whatever happened to them. Businesses were laying people off, but at first that was mostly in Northern factories. Of greater concern was the dry spell that had begun and would turn into the Dust Bowl. It was not so much the parched lawns or the early shedding of the leaves from the trees, which made the streets of Paris shadeless by midsummer. It was the farmers' problems that concerned them, as the cotton came up stunted and the summer's corn looked just like the shriveled cornstalks left standing in the fields from the previous winter. This meant people were making less money and likely would skip coming to the carnival.

In 1914, the Texas legislature had passed a compulsory school attendance law, as part of a progressive effort to modernize the state. So Louis and Elvie registered the boys with the Paris school department, as required by law, but then when the carnival started back up again in the spring, the boys dropped out of school, if they were going at all. The surviving records of the Paris school district show members of the family registered every year from 1930, when John was eight, until 1941, when the family moved briefly to Wichita Falls and then to Amarillo, in the Texas Panhandle. John managed to make it to eighth grade; Dude dropped out in fourth grade. Charlie never went to school, even though he was registered as attending. He was born with a severe speech defect that he was embarrassed about, and remained illiterate all his life.

The records also show that the Bogles were renting a different house, on a different street, every year during the 1920s and 1930s. When they could not meet the rent, they moved. Life was chaotic for the children. All these moves, and all the time spent away from Paris in the carnival, might help explain why the city truant officers never took action against the boys—or against Louis and Elvie—for their poor school attendance, but the family suspected the local officials just didn't care about poor people. The federal census taker did manage to find the Bogles in 1930 in Paris. As was often true, they had a little embellishment for him. Louis said he was a veteran of the Great War, though the war had ended before Louis was drafted.

Despite their lack of education and the lack of books in their houses, the boys were growing up fast. Elvie and Louis remained "on the show," as the boys termed it, working in carnivals until the mid-1930s, when still more children arrived. Until then, each spring Elvie found a carnival that would hire them, but with the Depression and fewer customers the carnivals got smaller, paying even less. During the carnival season, from March to October, the family now lived out of a truck and a trailer they pulled behind them; big railroad cars were too expensive for the smaller carnivals.

Elvie continued to ride in the motordrome, on her own motorcycle, an Indian brand machine with what people termed a suicide clutch, meaning she had to take her hands off the handlebars to switch gears. Both Dude and Charlie thought of their mother as a daredevil and tomboy, which were good things in their young eyes. "She got so good at riding that she could get to the top of the open drome and reach up and take a customer's hat away on one pass and then put it back on his head when she came around again," Charlie told me, smiling at the recollection. The thrill of riding so fast and dangerously seemed to offer a sense of fulfillment to his mother, he thought. It was providing relief from their impoverished lives. "Mom liked the carnival pretty good," Charlie said. Elvie also worked in a sideshow called "the Hot Chair," designed to look like an electric chair, in which sparks of electric current appeared to come out of her hands and arms. "You could see it, and I imagine she could feel it," Charlie said. For a period Elvie also worked as a snake charmer, until one day several boys stuck a pin in the snake wrapped around her chest and the creature began squeezing her hard. It took four men to kill the snake and free Elvie.

Elvie and Louis continued to augment their tiny pay by making and selling moonshine, despite their earlier close calls with the law. Louis ran the still somewhere out in the woods; it was practically in his blood, the family said, because Daylight was in the middle of Tennessee corn whiskey country, near where the modern Jack Daniel's headquarters would be built. Elvie was in charge of driving the home brew into town and selling the mason jars to carnival customers or, in the off-season, to people in Paris. The boys didn't see anything wrong with their parents' activities. "It was the Depression" was how Charlie figured it. "People did whatever they could."

Elvie and Louis also continued to drink heavily, with a big party in someone's quarters at least once a week. Louis supplied the whiskey and played the banjo for dancing, a talent he had learned at home in Daylight. The favorite topic of conversation was outlaws, the heavily armed and homegrown gangsters who were robbing the banks that foreclosed on plain folks' homes. Texans were not that long removed from the violence of the frontier or the Lost Cause of the Civil War, and they still believed that the dictates of honor required a personal, physical response to insult, no matter how slight. Dispossessed by the Depression and driven from their land or homes, many men felt helpless when there was no work, and they turned to their guns. As William Humphrey wrote in his memoir, the times "turned desperate men into desperadoes and a sympathetic public followed their exploits in the papers and secretly cheered them on." Jesse James was the archetype, but Elvie and Louis particularly admired Clyde Barrow and Bonnie Parker, their contemporaries, who had grown up on small cotton sharecropper farms east of Dallas, not far from Paris. One time Pretty Boy Floyd stopped by their house in Paris and asked if he could hide out for a few days, Charlie and Dude recalled later. Floyd, officially Charles Arthur Floyd, who lived in Oklahoma, robbed as many as thirty banks over a twelve-year period, and in 1933 reportedly shot five men, including an FBI agent, in a massacre in Kansas City. After he was killed by the police in Ohio in 1934, twenty thousand people turned out for his funeral in Sallisaw, Oklahoma. Charlie remembered that when Floyd left the Bogles' home, he gave Elvie money to buy shoes and food for her boys, the first shoes he ever had. "Maybe us kids thought he was so good, that's why we turned out the way we did," Charlie said many years later, after his own series of crimes and prison sentences.

For many years, Charlie kept on the living-room wall of his double-wide trailer home a fading nineteenth-century black-and-white photograph of a slender, handsome young man who he believed was his uncle. The caption under the picture, written by one of Charlie's nieces, describes the man as "John Hardin, mom's uncle," meaning Elvie's uncle. In fact, Elvie did have an uncle named Hardin, her father's half brother, whom Charlie would later visit from time to time as he grew up. But the uncle was Will Hardin. The man in the photograph was John Wesley Hardin, the most notorious nineteenth-century outlaw and gunfighter in Texas. Hardin nearly stabbed a schoolmate to death as a boy, and shot and killed his first victim at age fifteen. He later murdered the city marshal of Waco, Texas, escaped repeatedly from local jails, stole horses and, by the time he was captured and sent to prison in 1878, claimed to have killed forty-two men. After serving seventeen years in the new state prison at Huntsville, Hardin was pardoned, became a lawyer and moved to El Paso. There, on August, 19, 1895, after having an affair with the wife of one of his clients, Hardin was shot dead by a gunman he himself had hired to kill the jilted husband. Hardin made the mistake of failing to give him the promised payment.

Charlie's favorite part of all the stories about the man he thought was his uncle took place in Abilene during a cattle drive. Hardin was staying in a hotel and got mad at a man in the room next door who kept him awake by snoring. So Hardin fired a number of shots through the wall. The snoring stopped; he had killed the man. Wild Bill Hickock was marshal of Abilene at the time and came rushing over to the hotel to see what the gunfire was about. Hardin, realizing he would be in trouble and being only half-dressed, ran onto the roof of the hotel and jumped into a haystack, where he hid for the rest of the night. The next day he stole a horse and made his escape out of town.

Charlie loved to hear his parents tell stories about these outlaws, and he began to identify with them. For the Bogle family, it became part of their mythology. It didn't matter to Charlie and his brothers whether John Wesley Hardin was actually their uncle. In his later teenage years and his early twenties, after Charlie left home, he always dressed like a Western badman, with a black Stetson hat, black shirt and black pants. "I liked to look that way, like an outlaw," Charlie said.

Consciously or unconsciously, Charlie was imitating the risky behavior of his parents, their friends and their supposed relative. This was the same kind of imitation that Tracey Bogle would later identify in himself, copying the actions of his father, Rooster. In fact, imitation forms the basis for social learning theory, one of the main schools of modern criminology. It holds that delinquent behavior is learned through the same psychological processes as any other behavior. Children learn how to behave by fashioning their behavior after examples that they have seen around them, starting at home with their family. Behavior is also learned when it is reinforced or rewarded. It is not learned when it is not reinforced.

This sociological theory of criminal activity traces its origins to a French judge in the nineteenth century, Gabriel Tarde, who served fifteen years as a provincial judge and then was put in charge of France's national statistics. After a careful analysis of these numbers, he came to the conclusion that "the majority of murderers and notorious thieves began as children," often because of a lack of education and food in their homes. Tarde came to believe that criminals were normal people who learned crime much like others learned legitimate occupations. At the center of his theory was what he called "the laws of imitation." In his view, individuals copy patterns of behavior much the same way they copy styles of dress.

Tarde was a pioneer in the then new field of criminology. The discipline "criminology" was given its name by an Italian professor of law, Raffaele Garofalo, in 1885. The study grew out of a reaction against the vaguely defined system of law, justice and punishments that existed in Europe before the French Revolution. Some crimes were specified; some were not. Those criminal laws that were written often did not indicate the punishment. Due process, in the modern sense, did not yet exist. In this vacuum, an Italian legal scholar, Cesare Beccaria, undertook a study of European prison systems, which he published in 1764 under the title *On Crimes and Punishments.* In his small book, Beccaria offered a blueprint for an enlightened justice system and concluded that the crime problem could be traced not to bad people but to bad laws. The book earned Beccaria the reputation of being the "father of modern criminology." There would be many other theories on the causes of crime and schools of criminology.

In Paris, Texas, while Charlie and his brother Dude were still boys, they began copying their parents and the outlaws they heard about by embarking on their own petty criminal acts, often as a way to make money and survive. "In East Texas in those days there wasn't no jobs," Charlie said decades later. "You just went out and did things. If you got caught, you got caught." Sometimes the brothers climbed aboard parked trains loaded with coal and took a bucket or two back home, or to sell. Charlie loved to go to the motion-picture shows in the ornate theaters downtown but usually didn't have the dime it took to buy a ticket. So one of the brothers would climb a tree to get on the roof of the theater, then open a trapdoor and come down and open the back door to let the rest of them inside. "If we didn't like the show, we'd leave and sneak back in later, just to have something to do, and to show we could do it," Charlie said. Their favorite movies were Westerns, with the Cisco Kid or later John Wayne. Since Charlie could not read, the movies were not just entertainment; they were his form of education.

Dude went fishing almost every day they were in Paris, often in ponds that belonged to farmers where it was illegal to take fish. Eventually some of the farmers reported him to the sheriff. He got caught and arrested and tried in the county courthouse downtown in 1939, when he was fifteen. He was sentenced to ten days in the Lamar County jail, where adult criminals were kept, exposing him to more hardened offenders.

Charlie had begun stealing money left out for the milkman on his daily rounds, and he too was arrested, at age thirteen, and sent to court. He was sentenced to work for a farmer outside Paris for a year, for a dollar a day. Charlie had to live in the farmer's house and help with the corn and cotton crops. Charlie had not grown up on a farm, so he hated the hard, hot work. One night, after Charlie had lived there for six months, the farmer went into Paris in his truck and his wife climbed into bed with Charlie. "She said, 'It's cold. I'll get into bed with you to keep you from getting cold,'" Charlie recalled. Charlie was disgusted. "She must have been sixty years old," he said. It was her age that put him off, not the thought of having sex. So Charlie got up and walked out the door. The farmer was too embarrassed to report Charlie's escape to the sheriff, and that was the end of his punishment for stealing the milkman's money.

About this same time, in the mid-1930s, Louis decided to take his wife and children for a visit to Daylight to see his mother and relatives. Louis and Elvie must have sold a lot of moonshine, because they bought a big touring car with an open canvas top for the trip. That didn't mean they weren't still poor. Along the way, they stopped more than once to eat at a soup kitchen. It was what they could afford. In Daylight, they stayed in an old house with Narcissa, Louis's grandmother, and Mattie, his mother. Louis and his boys made a lasting impression on his relatives in Tennessee, one that offered a glimpse into how badly they had been living and how far they had sunk since joining the carnival.

"To me, they were heathen," said one of Louis's nieces, Mae Smotherman, who had lived on the same farm as Louis growing up and later moved to Nashville. "We all noticed how vulgar the children talked and how bad their table manners were," the niece said. "They told dirty jokes and just wolfed their food down, like animals." They slapped some of their older women relatives on the backside, which the relatives took as rude, offensive behavior. "We had always been taught to avoid people like that, and now here they were in our house, and they were our relatives," Smotherman added. "We wondered what went on in the carnival that made them like that." Smotherman was also fascinated that Louis and Elvie had tattoos, something she had never seen before. Louis tried to recruit her to come back with them to Texas and join the carnival, but her mother, Lula, Louis's sister, said no. After Louis and Elvie left, Lula told the others that something had happened to the boys to make them "mean." It was the strongest language Lula would allow herself to speak. She also posed the question of what kind of parents Louis and Elvie had been to raise kids like that. It was as if they didn't have parents at all, she suggested to her own children. They did have parents, of course, and the boys were simply copying them. They had no positive adult role models: no teachers, no sports coaches, no ministers.

Back in Paris after their trip, John, the eldest boy, was arrested one evening in 1938 and charged with stealing a truck. He had been "fooling around downtown too much," Charlie said, so the police had become aware of him. John insisted he was not the driver who took the truck, that it was another boy, and that he had been framed. John was taken to the county jail and then put on trial. As a Southern and conservative state, Texas had been slow to adopt the system of separate courts for juveniles that had been pioneered in Chicago in 1899 and then spread rapidly across much of the nation. In these progressive family courts, the accused were to be defined less by their offenses than by their age. It was the children's welfare that the new courts were to protect. This paternalism brought a whole new set of courtroom practices. The key figure was the judge, who was tasked with getting the whole story about the child in the same way that a doctor tries to discover the nature of a patient's illness. Punishments were deliberately kept mild, since children's personalities were thought to still be in the process of formation, making them more open to rehabilitation. Judges were required to be lenient in sentencing, handing out only the least restrictive alternative. Texas, however, did not establish a full juvenile justice system until 1943, after John's trial, so he appeared before a regular judge. The only special protection for juveniles in Texas at the time was that the proceedings were confidential; the records of his case were sealed, and remain so even to this day. According to Dude and Charlie, John was not given a lawyer to defend him. That reform too would come later. The judge sentenced John, at seventeen, to what amounted to a maximum-security facility: two years in the Gatesville State School for Boys.

Gatesville is in the scrubby, arid plains of central Texas, not far from Waco and today close to the huge Army base at Fort Hood. When it was opened in 1887, with 767 boys, Gatesville was considered a humanitarian triumph, the first state reform school anywhere in the South. Reformers at the time believed that separating delinquent boys from hardened adult criminals would help them change their lives. A combination of schooling and light farmwork was seen as contributing to their improvement. Gatesville was supposed to be different from the state's prison system, which had grown up after the Civil War largely as a series of big, tough work camps where convicts were routinely whipped and sometimes worked to death raising cotton, corn and sugarcane in settings like those of slavery. Unfortunately, Gatesville itself soon developed a reputation for ruthlessness. Given its size—twelve hundred acres of sandy cropland—and the small sum of money the legislature appropriated for it, the facility's officials felt it necessary to make a profit on the crops the youthful inmates grew. Some boys went to school for part of the day and then went out to the fields; others labored from sunup to sundown. Idleness wasn't tolerated. Beatings by guards, sexual assaults and long stretches in solitary confinement were normal. In 1974 a federal judge finally ordered Gatesville closed after finding its operations constituted cruel and unusual punishment that violated the Eighth Amendment to the Constitution.

When John arrived, an assistant warden told the new inmates that they stood a 90 percent chance of later being sent to the state's adult penitentiary. It was not an auspicious beginning. The yards were well manicured, and the white-painted offices, classrooms and living quarters were uniformly positioned around a pristine parade field. Life at the school was conducted in strict military style. Each morning, John discovered, the boys were mustered onto the parade ground for inspection, followed by calisthenics and then drill practice. The guards enforced discipline through use of a thick leather strap called "the bat." John was the tallest of all the Bogles, six feet two inches, but he was gentle in disposition and, unlike his brothers, did not relish fighting. Still, a guard called him out one morning and administered twenty-five lashes with the heavy strap. It tore the flesh off his back and his haunches. John wanted to get up, but several other guards held him down. He screamed, but the beating continued, until, bleeding profusely, he passed out. John never found out why he was beaten, but it seemed to be a warning to him and the other boys, who were required to watch. Escape was impossible, John learned from his fellow inmates: the land around Gatesville was too vast, with few trees for cover to hide, and the guards had a stable of hunting dogs to track down any would-be escapee. John served twenty-one months.

When he came home to Paris, he told his parents and brothers about the harsh and violent discipline at Gatesville and swore he would go straight, which he did. Dude and Charlie scoffed at his stories and said they would not be deterred. In early 1942, just a few months after Pearl Harbor, the Army began building a large new training base on the north side of Paris, Camp Maxey, in honor of a local Confederate hero, General Samuel Bell Maxey. Newly drafted soldiers began to flood into Paris on weekend passes, by bus or taxi, heading for a host of recently opened bars downtown. The soldiers, who ultimately became members of the 99th or 102nd Divisions that fought in the Battle of the Bulge and in Germany, were a good source of income for Charlie. He would carry his shoeshine box into a bar, offer to shine a soldier's shoes and then pull out a pint jar of moonshine. He would buy the homemade brew for fifty cents and resell it for a dollar. Charlie didn't see anything wrong with what he was doing. He was very fatalistic for a fourteen-year-old.

Charlie was also aware that he was following in his parents' footsteps by selling moonshine. "I was taking after my daddy and mommy," he said. "They'd done it, so I did it."

There were prostitutes in the bars, and pimps, and Charlie got to know them too. Charlie was tall for his age, and ruggedly built; eventually he would fill out to six feet tall and two hundred pounds, with broad shoulders. He had blue eyes, dark wavy hair and prominent, almost menacing eyebrows. He looked at least five years older than he was. "I knew about gals from when I was four-teen, shining shoes in the bars for those GIs," he said. "The gals would fool with me, and take me home with them.

"My friends then were all gangsters who were also selling and drinking moonshine," Charlie recalled. One friend, Jay, worked in a small carnival and took Charlie into bars to drink. Jay was much older than Charlie, about thirty-five, and worked as a pimp when he was in Paris. Charlie looked up to him. "He was smart," Charlie said, and "I learned a lot from him." If someone said something to

Jay to which he took offense, he would "hit that man down." More than ten years later, when Charlie ended up at the state penitentiary at Huntsville, Jay was there too, serving a life sentence for murder.

About this time, in 1942, Charlie and Dude began going into bars "to clean them out," Charlie said. They both enjoyed fistfights and had quick, nasty tempers. Both brothers ended up with lumpy noses caused by too many punches and broken bones. By now Paris was getting too small for Charlie, and he was restless. "I wanted to get away," he said. During his fourteenth year he left home, "hanging freight trains," in his expression, sleeping in boxcars. "I was booming around." He went first to Tennessee and then to New York, and soon after that headed for California, where his goal was to join other poor, jobless Americans picking fruit. But the train he was riding stopped one night in Amarillo, where he found work for a while as a salesman in the Panhandle Fruit Company. Charlie was part hobo and part outlaw, only fifteen years old, too young to join the military and fight in World War II.

His brother and closest friend, Dude, was already eighteen and enlisted in the Army in Paris in October 1942. He was assigned to the Army Air Corps, the precursor of the Air Force, but his upbringing quickly caught up with him when he was sent to Kansas for basic training. The very first week, he got into a fight with another recruit, using his fists and a knife. This was the start of a pattern. After basic training, Dude was sent to India and Burma to fight the Japanese and was wounded by Japanese shrapnel. He served until the end of the war, though he was never promoted above the rank of buck private.

"I loved to fight," Dude remembered. "I was always fighting. So they wrote me up each time I had a fight, and they had a record on me." Dude, who, like Charlie, had dark curly hair and prominent eyebrows, was not bitter about the lack of promotions. He took it as a matter of pride. All those fights showed how tough he was. In his later years, he always kept wartime photos of himself in the trailers where he lived. One picture showed him standing next to a B-24 bomber, dubbed the "Yellow Fever," with sharks' teeth painted on the nose of the plane to make it more fearsome-looking to the Japanese. In another photo Dude was shirtless next to some palm trees, his arms raised and fists extended in a boxer's pose. That was the man he was—the fighter.

After Charlie and Dude were gone, Louis and Elvie left Paris for Amarillo. They were convinced by word from Charlie that there was work to be had on the construction of the new Amarillo Army Air Field. By now Elvie and Louis had three more children: a boy, improbably named Elvie, after his mother, but always called Babe; a daughter, Peggy; and the youngest, Dale Vincent Bogle, who was known in the family as Rooster. He was born in Wichita Falls in 1941 during a stopover his parents made on their way to Amarillo. The family may have been poor—in their last days in Paris and then during their sojourn in Wichita Falls and the beginning of their time in Amarillo they all lived in one big tent—but they had a strong sense of family loyalty, like a clan. Much as they may have looked dysfunctional to others, the Bogles held what amounted to mandatory family meetings every morning, wherever they lived. The family was like church for Louis and Elvie and their children: a place where they belonged, where they had something to believe in, a refuge where they all were accepted and forgiven, no matter what they did. They could tell one another about their latest escapade breaking the law, boast about it or laugh about it, and no one would report them to the police. Louis and Elvie never went to church. They were too busy "on the show," Charlie explained. And, he said, "they didn't agree with the church." The churches in Texas, whether they were Baptist, Methodist or Church of Christ, would have made them feel uncomfortable, even disreputable. Holding on to one another was simpler and more satisfying for the Bogles. This closeness, though, had the unintended effect of reinforcing the examples that Louis and Elvie set. It meant that the children had a crimped sense of values and aspirations. Instead of picking up bad habits from what criminologists now call "deviant peers" at school—their classmates—the Bogles were their own deviant peers.

When Dude came home from the war at the end of 1945, with no additional education, job skills or self-discipline, he returned to his vagabond life of petty crime, which quickly began to escalate. He was arrested in Topeka, Kansas, in 1946 for vagrancy; arrested and jailed in Paris in 1947 for burglary; and indicted for carrying a gun and committing another burglary in Portland, Oregon, also in 1947. After the last incident, an Oregon judge sentenced him to a year on probation and ordered him to return to Texas. Instead, Dude went looking for Charlie, who was working in a logging camp on the Oregon coast near Tillamook. Charlie had picked up his own minor charges in the late 1940s: an arrest for being drunk, another for stealing a woman's pocketbook and an assault. As time passed, Charlie was more and more frequently breaking into stores and bars in Oregon and in Washington State to get food or beer, though he wasn't caught in these cases.

When the two brothers ultimately got together, they "hung" a freight train and then hitchhiked into the small town of Chelan in central Washington, in the Cascade Mountains. Chelan is in the Wenatchee Valley, the self-proclaimed apple capital of the world, with enormous orchards of apple and pear trees nestled between a deep blue lake and the high evergreen-covered mountains. The brothers stayed in a cabin for migrant farm laborers imported to pick the fruit trees, and on the evening of September 4, 1947, after getting drunk at a tavern with some local young women, found themselves in front of Weimer's Jewelry Store in Chelan. In a later signed confession to the police, Charlie said he went to the back of the store and let himself in by pulling a fan out of the wall, thereby opening a hole to crawl through. "I was the only one that went in,"

Charlie said. "I took about two watches and two charm bracelets and some lockets."

The police did not catch him that fall, and he left town. But he made the mistake of coming back to Chelan in July 1948 in search of work. The police recognized him this time, or so they thought, and he was arrested and charged with second-degree burglary. On July 21, 1948, the Chelan County Court sentenced Charlie to fifteen years in prison. He was taken to the state prison at Monroe, Washington, where his sentence was later reduced to fifteen months for good behavior. In fact, Charlie and Dude both said later, it was really Dude who broke into the jewelry store, but Dude did not go back to Chelan in 1948, and the two brothers looked so much alike that the police arrested the one they found. "I had to take the rap for Dude; it saved him a trip to the pen," Charlie said. He was following the Bogles' code of family loyalty.

Charlie's Washington State prison records reveal how tough life had been for him. Prison officials described him as illiterate, totally unable to read or write, with a serious speech impediment. The Washington authorities requested an investigation into Charlie's circumstances at home in Amarillo before they considered whether to reduce his sentence. A long typed response came back from Mabel Ray, the director of the county welfare board in Amarillo. "The Bogles live in a very small shack-type house, built in one of the less desirable residential districts at the edge of the city," Ray wrote. Louis worked in an automobile junkyard, and he had spent his time building their "low, squatty, little house" with what he could salvage from the junkyard, she said. It was made entirely from old battery crates, painted white. It was just about the poorest house she had ever seen in Amarillo, and it was her job to visit the homes of poor people. "Mrs. Bogle states that, for many years, they were show people," Ray added. "Part of the time they lived in tents, sometimes they lived in converted boxcars, and occasionally, they stayed in hotels, but they were never any place very long and, as a consequence, none of the children have any education to speak of, and Charles has absolutely none. Mrs. Bogle stated that Charles had had this speech impediment since birth and that he had always been extremely sensitive about it. She stated that he had never been able to get away from the feeling that people were criticizing him and if they could not understand him the first time he became stubborn and refused to answer."

Elvie also advised Ray that "her mother had died in a mental institution at Wichita Falls, Texas." Lastly, Ray reported that "the Bogles have never belonged to any of the churches and do not attend church nor Sunday school here." Because Charlie could not read, his entertainment had been mostly movies. But Louis told Ray that since "they were having quite a struggle, they could certainly use Charles's additional contribution to the budget" if he was released from prison. Overall, it was a bleak but candid assessment.

Charlie was released after serving only eight months, and in April 1949 he made his way back to Amarillo. Meanwhile, Dude had drifted back to Kansas, where he had done his basic training. He met an attractive woman in Liberal, Kansas, and they went out together for a period of time. One day Dude gave her money to go shopping with him. At the store, the woman accused him of taking the money back and they argued. Perhaps Dude had been drinking. Pretty soon some of the people in the store came to her aid and called the police. She told the officers that she was only sixteen years old and that she and Dude had been sleeping together. By Kansas law, she was underage. Dude was arrested and charged with statutory rape. At trial, Dude pled not guilty. "I didn't think I was guilty of anything—she was willing to have sex with me," he said. "I didn't know what statutory rape was. I was still a dumb kid." Dude was found guilty in August 1950 and given an odd sentence, one to twenty-one years, in the state prison at Lawrence.

Out of all this, Dude found one consolation. In the days before handguns became so common and armed robbers and drug lords replaced burglars as big-time criminals, burglars were seen as the criminal elite in the eyes of convicts. It required impressive skill to break into a safe. Burglaries also tended to net large amounts of cash. Dude used his time in the Kansas prison to make friends with burglars, and they, in turn, taught him how to crack a safe. It was a craft he would soon put to use when he was released after serving just twenty-one months. Prisons are supposed to deter inmates from committing more crime by showing them the painful price of being locked up. Deterrence is the theory behind the whole criminal justice system. But neither Dude nor Charlie had been frightened by their first prison stays. "They didn't show me anything," Charlie said about his Washington State prison experience. And now Dude was heading back to Amarillo to rejoin Charlie and his family and whatever adventure they could find.

3

A Burglary
by the Whole Family

After Charlie got out of prison in Washington and Dude came home from prison in Kansas in 1952, Louis and Elvie were united with their children for the first time in years. They were all living in adjacent houses in Amarillo in the flat, dry, windswept Texas Panhandle, where the Great Plains to the north merge into the southwestern desert. The relentless wind was what people remembered about the place. "There is nothing between us and the North Pole but a barbed-wire fence" was the local saying. The Bogles were as poor as ever—Louis earned a mere thirty dollars a week working in the automobile junkyard, and the shack of a house he had built out of used battery crates was stained with leaking acid. At least the acid kept out the roaches, the family joked. The house had no running water, no indoor plumbing and no electricity. Elvie had given up riding her motorcycle in the carnival because of her advancing age and ever-increasing family. Their youngest child, Rooster, had arrived unplanned in 1941, when Elvie was already forty. Their neighbors in "The Flats," the poorest section of Amarillo, puzzled over how Louis and Elvie had been able to buy four plots of land on Spruce Street for one thousand dollars apiece from a local postal worker.

If Paris looked like the Old South, with its sharecroppers hand-picking cotton on their hands and knees, Amarillo was the modern western Texas of popular imagination, with wide open spaces flat to the horizon in all directions, the views broken only by new grain elevators and rapidly spreading oil derricks. There were good jobs for men willing to work hard. Amarillo was the center of a thriving beef-cattle industry, with ranches of thousands of acres, and there were enormous irrigated fields of wheat, sorghum and cotton that were all now harvested by machines. The Army Air Corps had built a large airfield in Amarillo during World War II to take advantage of its dry climate and flat, hard terrain to prepare crews to fly B-17 bombers to pound the Germans and, later in the war, to man the big B-29s that firebombed Tokyo. The Defense Department also built a major factory in Amarillo to make artillery shells and bombs, the Pantex Army Ordnance Plant. In the 1950s, with the advent of the Cold War, the Air Force expanded the air base to accommodate the Strategic Air Command's giant new B-52 bombers that were ready to strike the Soviet Union. And the Pantex plant was retooled by the Atomic Energy Commission to manufacture nuclear weapons. Route 66, then the main highway between Chicago and Los Angeles, cut through the center of Amarillo, and trucks roared by day and night. There were truck stops at either end of the city, and motels and steak houses for hungry travelers. Amarillo, in fact, was the fastest-growing city in the fastest-growing state at the time. So it offered opportunity. But something was holding the Bogles back again.

The Bogles' closest neighbors when they arrived in Amarillo in 1944 were Margaritte Garcia, her husband and their two young sons. They lived in a tiny, low-ceilinged home directly across the street. Mrs. Garcia was a descendant of the early Mexican elite, Spanish by blood, who had trekked up from Mexico City to found

Santa Fe in what is now New Mexico before the Pilgrims landed at Plymouth in 1620. She took an immediate liking to Louis, whom she found to be decent, quiet and hardworking, "without a bad bone in his body," she said. But Elvie, in her words, was "mean" and "plain spoken," or tough and vulgar.

One time Elvie confided in her, "Unless I want something real bad, I keep my husband at bay," meaning no sex. "He knows where his bread and butter is coming from. After I keep him away long enough, he will do anything I want." In Mrs. Garcia's view, "Elvie was real bossy. She managed the money and was in charge of everything."

The Bogles' source of income was an enigma to the Garcias. Mr. Garcia had a steady if low-paying job in a warehouse for forty-five years, and he volunteered at the Maverick Club for Boys while Mrs. Garcia cleaned houses and babysat. All they knew about Elvie was that before coming to Amarillo she had ridden a motorcycle in the carnival and wore a helmet and riding breeches. "She never worked a day the entire time she was in Amarillo," Mrs. Garcia said. "She was always at home during the day, and you should see the way they ate. Big roasts and coffee all the time. They set a real good table."

One day Mrs. Garcia saw Elvie pulling piles of brand-new girdles out of boxes. "I said, 'Elvie, where in the world did you get all those girdles?'" Mrs. Garcia remembered. "Elvie said, 'Oh, that's one of my lawsuits,' and she just about died laughing." Elvie said she and a friend would go to work in a store for three or four days, maybe a week, "then we'd pop something and claim our backs was hurt and get a settlement." Elvie said they were helped "by a shyster lawyer." In this case, the store had paid off the resulting court settlement in merchandise, the girdles. Elvie was continuing the scams she and Louis had been doing since soon after they first met. Only now they were doing them on a serial basis. Elvie had become a grifter.

When Louis built the battery crate house, Elvie was initially thrilled. "This is the first actual house I've ever had that is mine," she told her neighbor. But soon she was complaining about it all the time, Mrs. Garcia said. "It just isn't nice enough for me," Elvie kept saying, according to Mrs. Garcia. So Louis built a larger house in the adjacent lot out of wood he salvaged from the junkyard. The roof was tar paper and the sides were gray vinyl and it too had an outhouse. But it had four bedrooms, practically a mansion in their neighborhood.

Rooster was only three years old when the Bogles settled in Amarillo, and it was clear to the Garcias that Elvie held out much hope for him, her youngest child, whom she called "the pick of the litter." Officially, Rooster was born without a name. His Texas birth certificate shows that Louis and Elvie had a son born at 8:50 a.m. on October 12, 1941, in Wichita Falls. The space marked for "Full Name of Child" was left blank. This was not so unusual. But when Rooster found out about the omission, he believed either that Elvie was not his mother or that his parents were trying to hide something. As Rooster got older his doubts about his legitimacy got worse, and he became obsessed by that empty space, family members recalled. They thought this perceived slight may have started a brooding suspiciousness in Rooster that could turn into instant anger, rage and violence. It was not until fifteen years later, on November 22, 1956, that Elvie herself went back to Wichita Falls and petitioned the county clerk to give her youngest child an official name, Bobby Vincent Bogle.

In the meantime, he had decided to give himself a name, Dale, which he used at school. Within the family, he was always called Rooster because from infancy "he got up before the chickens wanting his bottle and so woke up his older brothers who had to babysit him," according to his first wife, Kathy.

Later Rooster would boast to boys in his neighborhood that the nickname had another meaning. "They call me Rooster because I get all puffed up when I get in a fight," he told one boy with whom he would have a fight that almost killed him.

The earliest surviving school record for Rooster is his second-grade report card from Mrs. Heinemann's class at Garland Elementary School in Amarillo. It shows he earned a Satisfactory in art, physical education and music—perhaps partly a product of his proficiency on the guitar, which his father had helped teach him. He was given an Unsatisfactory in arithmetic, study habits and promptness. For his full second-grade year, in 1950–51, Rooster missed almost half of the school days and was tardy for about a third of the classes he did attend. It was an early indication of Rooster's lack of interest in education.

As was true for his older brothers, Rooster's parents did not make him go to Sunday school or church, nor did the family belong to any community organization such as the Maverick Club for Boys, where Mr. Garcia sent his two sons to help keep them out of trouble.

As he grew up, Rooster was always slight and short, and at age seventeen was only five feet eight inches tall and weighed a mere 120 pounds, this in a place where men grew tall and strong. Rooster was sensitive about his size. Charlie and Dude, of course, were big, and he liked to listen to their stories of going into bars and knocking other patrons out cold with their fists. "He wanted to be a Bogle," Charlie recalled years later. "He wanted to be like us, only tougher, and begged us to teach him to fight," Charlie said. Charlie and Dude gave him lessons. Always hit first, they counseled him, to keep the element of surprise, and since you are smaller, carry a weapon you can conceal. This led Rooster to walk around with a three-inch-long piece of pipe cased in adhesive tape to make his fist stronger and increase the chance of a knockout punch. It was his homemade version of brass knuckles.

By the time Rooster was in seventh grade, at James Bowie Junior High, Mrs. Garcia's two boys began to keep their distance from their neighbor, though they had played together when they were younger. Phillip Garcia, who was two years older than Rooster, recalled that he had become "wild," or violent, and liked to fight. "It got so bad that I wouldn't have anything to do with him," Phillip said. "In fact, I wouldn't have been caught dead with him. If I did meet up with him, I was afraid I might have been killed."

Dennis Lindvay, another boy in the neighborhood who was in Rooster's seventh-grade class, decided "to play with him as little as possible because he always got in fights." Lindvay, the son of a salesman for Llano Cemetery, only a block down the street from the Bogles' homes, was slight himself and was as shy, polite and cautious as Rooster was pugnacious. "I never in my life saw anybody as tough as Dale, and I never saw Dale lose a fight," Lindvay said. "Dale was like a professional boxer, the way he fought with his fists. He was very skilled and aggressive." Lindvay began to think of Rooster as "the world's youngest professional fighter. Nobody ever lasted long with him. When the younger boys went down, their older brothers would come out and fight Dale, and they would lose too."

Having Rooster in the neighborhood and in his class had unexpected benefits, Lindvay added. "The hoodlums from the other side of town had always beat up on us, but with Dale around, even though he was so skinny, as soon as they insulted him, he knocked them out," Lindvay remembered.

When it came time to elect a class president in seventh grade, "Dale said we should keep out the popular kids and make sure we got a boy from our side of town for a change," Lindvay said. Lindvay had never been a class leader, but he was Dale's pick to be class president. "In the end," Lindvay said, "even some of the good kids joined in, out of fear of Dale and of getting beaten, and so I was elected. I was shocked. It showed how much power and influence Dale had."

Rooster had been getting into trouble with the law by the time he turned fifteen. He broke into vending machines to steal soda and candy. He also carried a .22-caliber pistol, which he used to shoot out the numbers on pay telephones, turning them into slot machines that disgorged their coins. One time the police caught him breaking into a store downtown, and Rooster said, "You can't do anything to me," according to another classmate, Jimmy Wilson, who was with him. "You can't take me to jail, I'm too young," Wilson recalled Rooster saying. "The cops said, 'Sure we can,' and they put him in jail for a few hours."

By that time, Rooster had become well known to the police. E. N. Smith, a former Amarillo detective, said Rooster had a juvenile record that ran to a dozen pages for thefts, fighting, assaults and driving a stolen car. Rooster's first wife, Kathy, who grew up in the same impoverished Amarillo neighborhood, said he had once forced a girl into a car he had stolen, effectively kidnapping her. Even though the girl reported it to the police, Rooster managed to get off without being charged with a crime, Kathy recalled. Rooster himself claimed that another time, when he had been drinking heavily, a teenager kicked him in the head over and over until Rooster beat him to death. In Rooster's telling of the episode, the police found the body but he was not arrested because people were too scared of him to snitch.

Mrs. Garcia, observing from across the street, saw a pattern of behavior emerging. "Rooster was always in trouble, but Elvie actively defended him and denied he did anything bad," she said. She thought Elvie was actually encouraging Rooster's growing delinquency. His mother may have identified with her son because she too was short, five feet three inches tall, Mrs. Garcia said. In any case, Elvie "spoiled him rotten. She bought him fancy leather cowboy boots with pointed toes and black leather pants." The more Rooster stole and the more he got in fights, the greater the gifts, Mrs. Garcia said. When Rooster wanted an expensive new Cushman Eagle motorcycle, Elvie went to a store and bought it for him.

His mother "only pretended to discipline Rooster," according to his second wife, Linda. One day he broke another neighbor's window, and when the woman complained to Elvie, she said, "I'll take care of him." His mother then went inside and took out a book, saying, "I'm going to hit my hand real loud, and when I do you scream."

"Rooster was her pride and joy; whatever he wanted, he got," Linda said. She believed Elvie was indulgent and permissive. Today such behavior would be recognized as enabling, reinforcing negative behavior by making it possible and then explaining it away. Elvie was almost a textbook example of an enabler.

To compound the problem, Rooster's father "never opened his mouth" about the mounting number of delinquent acts, Mrs. Garcia said. But one time, when Elvie went on a long car trip to California, apparently to sell moonshine—one of many such trips family members said she made—Louis lost his patience and took out his belt and whipped Rooster. When Elvie returned home and discovered what had happened, "it almost caused a divorce, she was so angry," Linda said.

The poor supervision exercised by Elvie and Louis over Rooster and their lack of consistent discipline fit in with the findings of another major school of criminology, what is known as "social control theory." This school grew out of work done by sociologists at the University of Chicago as they watched crime rates soar in Chicago in the 1920s and 1930s with an influx of Eastern European immigrants, the growth of bootlegging during Prohibition and the rise of urban gangs led by the Mafia. Chicago itself became their laboratory. To them, social control meant social bonds, the informal ties that can produce conformity to society's rules. Good parents, a good education, religious beliefs and stable jobs all help create what these criminologists called "social capital," which holds society together. The more a person is involved in conventional activities and the greater his or her ties are to their parents and spouses, the less likely a person is to break the law, the theory held. It was a valuable supplement to social learning theory, the notion that young criminals are made by imitating the behavior of their parents or older siblings.

A more recent and comprehensive iteration of social control theory, by Robert J. Sampson of Harvard and John H. Laub of the University of Maryland, offers an eerie explanation of much of what was happening in the Bogle family. The two criminologists reexamined the pioneering work by Sheldon and Eleanor Glueck in Boston. In analyzing the Gluecks' data, the professors found that "the largest predictor of delinquency" was the mother's supervision. Poor supervision by both the mother and the father, inconsistent discipline by parents, and alcoholism and criminality among parents all turned out to be important factors in the origin of juvenile delinquency and later adult crime, the professors concluded in their book, *Crime in the Making*. Both alcoholism and family criminality were critical because they made it harder for fathers and mothers to properly supervise and discipline their children. Instead of focusing on race or neighborhoods, or poverty and prisons as a cause of criminality, Professors Sampson and Laub wrote, "our research suggests that family life is far more important in understanding persistent criminal behavior in the early adolescent years." For their research, Sampson and Laub were awarded the Stockholm Prize in Criminology in 2011. It is the highest international honor in the field of criminology.

Elvie and Louis's lack of supervision and erratic discipline also affected John, Dude and Charlie. They had grown up in an even more chaotic family environment, while their mother and father were working in the carnival. They lived in trailers when the show season was on, traveling from city to city, or in rented houses for a few months in the winter and later in a tent that they pitched whenever they moved. Their mother was often absent, busy riding her motorcycle. Their living conditions were crowded. The Boston study found that frequent moves and crowded housing also made it harder for parents to provide good supervision and discipline for their children. The Bogles were hardly an organized crime family; they were more of a disorganized crime family, a dysfunctional family, even if the boys were close to their mother and father. The boys all ended up with criminal records, and in Amarillo, Dude and Charlie themselves directly contributed to Rooster's first criminal conviction.

At the beginning of his ninth-grade year, in September 1957, Rooster already had a number of girlfriends. They were attracted by his combination of charm and toughness, a persona that reminded some of the girls of James Dean, the brooding young actor whose film *Rebel Without a Cause* had been an enormous hit two years earlier. Rooster was not an athlete—he didn't even like sports, which required teamwork—but he was quick with his fists and also his feet, which he used to kick opponents in the groin. He often practiced his kicking by dropping a can from his hand, then trying to kick it before it hit the ground and propelling it as high as possible.

Rooster began going out with Kathy when she was only eleven years old. He made her feel good by giving her attention, something she got little of from her alcoholic, impoverished parents. One night Rooster snuck her out of her bedroom window and took her for a ride in a Ford his mother had bought for him. Kathy never forgot that Rooster drove while hanging on the outside of the door, below the window, to escape detection by the police, who he said were looking for him. She was impressed that he smelled of leather, the black pants that Elvie had purchased for him.

At the time, Rooster had another girlfriend, Margaret Presley, but he got tired of her and dumped her, and she became the girlfriend of Rooster's friend and chief rival in their class, Jimmy Wilson. Both boys were born in Wichita Falls before moving to Amarillo, and both of their families were "dirt poor," Wilson recalled years later. On the evening of September 5, 1957, a rainy night, Presley had a party at her house to which Rooster was not invited. Rooster learned about it and thought she was betraying him by taking up with Wilson, so Rooster broke into the house while the party was going on. "He slammed her up against the wall and grabbed her by the neck and choked her, and tore off the chain I had given her and slapped her in the head," Wilson recalled. Wilson challenged Rooster to "take the fight outside." They agreed to meet at an abandoned house nearby where bootleggers made moonshine. Each boy named his second. Rooster's was another school friend, Pat Dunavin.

Rooster arrived for the fight on his new Cushman Eagle motorcycle. Wilson was walking. Wilson was several inches taller than Rooster and at least twenty-five pounds heavier. In keeping with his habit, Rooster hit Wilson first, Wilson later told the police, with the short metal pipe concealed in his hand. The blow opened a big cut over Wilson's right eye that required a number of stitches to close. Wilson meanwhile had picked up what he claimed was a stick, but that the police said was a two-by-four piece of lumber that was four feet long. He cracked Rooster on the side of his head, instantly knocking him unconscious. That ended the fight.

Dunavin thought Rooster had just passed out. "So I picked him up and put him on my motor scooter and drove him to my house," Dunavin remembered. He then got a wet rag from his family's bathroom and tried to bring Rooster to. "It was my mother who figured out it was a much worse injury," Dunavin added. "She called an ambulance, which took him to the hospital."

Rooster arrived at the Northwest Texas Hospital in Amarillo in critical condition with a fractured skull. The next morning he underwent surgery that lasted four hours. He remained unconscious for three days, and even after he regained consciousness he was partially paralyzed on his right side and was unable to speak for a month.

Jimmy Wilson was arrested as a juvenile, put in jail for several days and initially feared he might face execution. When Rooster was finally released from the hospital and regained much of his ability to speak, Wilson was sentenced to eight years' probation.

The fight had long-term consequences for Rooster. He had a hole the size of a silver dollar in his skull and would need more brain surgery. He suffered from epilepsy and for years into the future took a combination of phenobarbital, used for treatment of seizures, and Sodium Dilaudid, a narcotic painkiller. Dilaudid is highly addictive, and its effects may intensify with alcohol. Rooster's speech remained impaired, and he never went back to school after the fight, so his education stopped at eighth grade.

His personality changed too. He became even more impulsive and more paranoid, according to Kathy, and he began drinking even more, though he was only fifteen at the time of the fight. Long after Rooster was injured, doctors and other researchers would find that traumatic brain injuries can cause precisely these types of changes in personality and behavior, making people who suffer them more impulsive, more paranoid and, in some cases, more prone to violence. One group of people who have suffered these effects are professional football players with repeated concussions. They have developed chronic traumatic encephalopathy, or CTE, a degenerative brain disease that can lead to impulsivity, disinhibition and poor judgment. This condition can be confirmed only by posthumous exams of their brains, and CTE was not known about in Rooster's day. Nor did doctors at the time have the sophisticated brain scans and magnetic resonance imaging tests, MRIs, that exist today. So how much of Rooster's later behavior can be attributed to the brain damage he incurred in the fight must remain conjecture.

Despite, or perhaps because of, the brain injury, Rooster was ready for more adventure only a year later. Charlie and Dude had just the ticket. Dude wanted to try out the burglar skills he had learned in prison in Kansas, and he came up with a plan to break into the safe inside the Bogles' neighborhood grocery store, Scivally's Affiliated Food Store. The store was a plain-looking cinder block building with a large eight-hundred-pound Mosler safe sitting on a raised, enclosed platform three steps above the main floor. Tom Scivally, the owner and manager, used the platform as his office; it was also a good vantage point to keep track of what was going on in the store. Dude knew from shopping there that most of the customers cashed their weekly paychecks in the grocery on Fridays or Saturdays, since few of these working-class people had bank accounts. They worked for the Santa Fe Railroad, whose tracks ran nearby, or did construction jobs or worked for the city. Tom Scivally was happy to cash their checks because they bought their food from him; cashing payroll checks was good for business.

Dude invited Charlie to help with the burglary, but Charlie turned him down. He was married now, with a wife and four young children to consider, and he was trying to be an ironworker. Dude instead enlisted two other men with petty criminal records, Fred Box and Donald Ray Branham. At eleven p.m. on the night of Sunday, December 7, 1958, Box broke a window in the back door of the store and crawled inside. He then unlocked the door and let in Dude and Branham. When Dude and his friends tried to lift the steel and concrete safe, they realized it was too heavy to get down the steps and out the back door, which faced a dirt alley. Dude decided to go fetch Charlie, who was both strong and handy. If anybody could wrestle the safe down the steps, it was him.

This time Charlie agreed. He brought some two-by-fours, and he figured they could work the safe down the steps. Charlie also offered his old Mercury sedan. After the four men got the safe down to the main floor, they used a dolly they found in the store to roll it to Charlie's car, which he had parked in the alley. They drove it to Llano Cemetery, less than a block from where the Bogles lived, and put it in an area where workmen had dumped dirt they had recently dug up while creating new grave sites. Then, in their excitement, the four men got drunk. They started singing and shouting so loudly that the police heard them and arrested them for public drunkenness and disturbing the peace. The men were put in jail for the night. The police didn't yet know about the burglary and had not seen the safe in the graveyard.

The story of the missing safe was played at the top of the front page in both of the city's newspapers for several days. Scivally estimated the burglars had made off with close to $20,000 in cash and checks. The detective assigned to lead the police investigation, E. N. Smith, said it was one of the biggest burglaries in the city's history. It also made for a "miserable Christmas" for Scivally and his family. "It could have bankrupted us," he said later. "It was a big blow. We were sleepless for a few nights." But they soon figured out that they had enough receipts and other documentation to make an insurance claim for some of the cash and checks.

The police were skeptical at first that the burglars would be savvy enough to get the safe open, unless they were part of a gang of professional burglars from Dallas. Lieutenant Eli Leflar told *The Amarillo Globe Times* that the type of safe was one of the toughest to crack. It had what the Mosler company called an internal burglar-resistant chest, with a tube of double-thick steel encased in concrete, and it was also equipped with a self-locking device that would activate if someone tampered with the safe. "If the burglars don't know what they are doing, or can't find a safe-man who does, they may never get that thing open," Leflar told the paper.

When the Bogles got out of jail the next day, they decided to move the safe to a more discreet spot. They needed a bigger vehicle for the safe, which had caused Charlie's car to sag badly, so they borrowed a truck from Rooster's older sister, Peggy, and then stopped by their parents' house, where Rooster lived. As soon as he saw the safe, Rooster announced, "I'm coming with you." It was a fateful decision, made, as was often the case, on impulse. Rooster had just made himself a criminal.

The newly enlarged group drove fifteen miles northwest of Amarillo to an isolated, middle-of-nowhere place up a draw on some sandy ranchland. There were low bushes and hills that made good cover. The men worked on opening the safe for three days, using an acetylene torch they stole from a Santa Fe Railroad workshop to cut through the top. They rigged a canvas cover and several tarps to hide the flame just in case anyone came by. It took so long to burn through the Mosler's protective walls that the metal looked like it was burning, so the men poured water on the safe to keep the money inside from catching fire. When the burglars finally broke through, they discovered that the water had soaked the cash. More important, they found that bits of molten metal had dripped inside burning pinhole-sized openings in a number of the bills.

The five men then drove back to Louis and Elvie's house in Amarillo and hung the wet bills to dry on clotheslines they strung inside the small house. This sight did not escape Elvie's attention. "The boys weren't smart enough to figure out how to divide up the money, so they gave the task to Elvie," according to A. B. Towery, who was married to Rooster's sister, Peggy.

Elvie first sat down at the kitchen table and counted the money. The cash portion came to $5,700. She gave each of the five men, including Rooster, $900, and she dealt herself $500, all that was left of the bills that were not too badly burned.

At this point the police still didn't know who the burglars were. Over the next few weeks, however, bills with pinholes in them began surfacing in bars and stores around Amarillo. The big break in the case came when a young woman bought a fake fur coat with some of these telltale holes, Detective Smith said. The police picked her up and interrogated her. Faced with arrest and going to prison as an accomplice, she said the money had come from Dude.

Seven weeks after the robbery, the police arrested Charlie, Dude and Rooster and the two men who had helped them. Smith also arrested Elvie and took her to police headquarters for questioning. "She was hard as nails," Smith said, "a tough old woman, and she never told us a thing." In fact, Elvie insisted the police had it all wrong. "My boys would never do something like that," she told the detective.

Given Elvie's denials, Smith brought Charlie, Dude and Rooster into the room and announced that there was enough evidence to charge their mother and their sister, Peggy, as accessories. Elvie would have to go to trial and faced a prison sentence. Smith was an imposing figure, a tall, dark-haired man with big hands who spoke with the twang of the small farming town in the Texas Panhandle where he was born. His parents and neighbors were "all God-fearing Christians, who believed in hard work and an honest living," he liked to say. So the Bogles' behavior offended him. He was also astute enough to see that the Bogle sons loved their mother. His threat to charge Elvie and Peggy worked. The three Bogle men quickly agreed to plead guilty if the charges against their mother and sister were dropped.

On April 3, 1959, Dude was sentenced to three years in the state penitentiary, as the principal in the burglary; Charlie received two years as an accessory; and Rooster was initially handed a much more lenient punishment of five years of probation. He would need to be careful, however. If he violated the terms of his probation, the judge warned him, it could be revoked and he would also be sent to prison. For Smith the case was a career booster. He later rose to be chief of detectives in Amarillo and then became a police captain. A. B. Towery, Peggy's husband, began calling Elvie "Ma Barker," after the legendary leader of a gang that consisted of her four criminal sons. They committed a series of robberies and murders in Missouri and Oklahoma from 1910 to the 1930s. Peggy did not appreciate the comparison. She later divorced Towery.

Rooster did not heed the warning. Less than a year later he left Texas without permission from his probation officer and went to New Orleans for Mardi Gras. He compounded his trouble by getting caught shoplifting by the New Orleans police. They shipped him back to Amarillo, where he was arrested and put back in front of a judge, who sentenced him to five years in the penitentiary.

A report by a psychologist for the Texas Department of Corrections soon after Rooster arrived at the penitentiary at Huntsville, in April 1960, found that Rooster had an IQ of only seventy-seven. He was still suffering from epilepsy incurred in the fight with Jimmy Wilson, his speech was still impaired and the psychologist "was impressed that he is mentally defective, mentally dull at best." A separate report by a prison psychiatrist said Rooster showed no hallucinations, thought disorder or psychosis. "His general information is poor and his calculations are poor, even considering his eighth grade education," the psychiatrist wrote. Moreover, he cautioned that Rooster's police record showed he had a pattern of "anti-social behavior which began some years before his skull injury." As if to confirm Rooster's propensities, within a week of being admitted to Huntsville he was sent to solitary confinement for fighting with another inmate.

A few weeks later, a medical exam revealed that Rooster had indeed suffered a skull fracture "with a defect in the left parietal area." Damage to the left parietal lobe can result in difficulty writing, or trouble with math or language. It can also cause an inability to perceive things normally, including people, objects, shapes or sounds and smells. Dr. M. D. Hanson, the medical director of the Texas Department of Corrections, reported this news in a letter to Elvie on May 16, 1960. But he also had some good news for her. As a result of Rooster's physical and mental condition, he had been classified "Third Class," which in Texas prison terms meant that Rooster would be exempt from being sent to one of the state's notorious prison farms and would remain at the main prison at Huntsville.

Charlie was not so fortunate. He was assigned to Eastham, the most brutal and terrifying of all the state's prison farms, where inmates clad in white uniforms worked on thirteen thousand acres of swampy river bottomland near Houston. They labored raising cotton under the supervision of guards mounted on horseback and armed with shotguns, Charlie remembered. "You had to call them

'Boss,'" Charlie said. "You couldn't fall behind in picking cotton or they would whoop you." At night the Eastham inmates were housed in crowded dorms with double and triple bunks that were run by building tenders, usually the biggest and strongest convicts with reputations for cruelty. Clyde Barrow, the outlaw, had helped give Eastham its reputation. It was at Eastham in 1931 that Barrow killed a building tender who had repeatedly raped him. A year later, still at Eastham, Barrow cut off his own left big toe and part of another toe, leaving him with a permanent limp, in an attempt to get out of the punishing fieldwork under the hot Texas sun.

Charlie spent eighteen months confined at Eastham. After that, Charlie said in his laconic fashion, "I changed. I couldn't do it no more. They showed me something."

AND THEIR CHILDREN AFTER THEM

So that you, your children and their children after them may fear the Lord your God.

—Deuteronomy 6:2

4

Rooster and His Boys

On to Oregon

Getting released from prison was becoming a familiar ritual for the Bogles, like celebrating a birthday or graduating from high school in many families, except, of course, that the Bogles were seldom able to enjoy such happy passages of ordinary American life. So after Charlie, Dude and Rooster served their time in three separate Texas prisons, the Bogle brothers once again looked forward to coming home to Amarillo and being together with their extended family. The question was, Could they escape their family's already building heritage of scams and crime, what some of them were beginning to sense was a family curse that ensnared them?

Charlie was intent on going straight. In his first week at home in 1960, though, he realized it would not be easy. He got pulled over almost every day by police in cruisers who knew his car by sight. "If there was any kind of break-in, the law was always looking at me," Charlie said. It happened so often that Charlie and his brothers imagined the police had created a new category of crime,

"Driving while Bogle," they called it. It was an early form of what today would be called profiling. Charlie was also easy for the police to recognize, a big man with dark curly hair, a high forehead, his family's characteristic protuberant ears and heavy eyebrows that gave him a passing resemblance to Bela Lugosi.

One night at a dance hall a man accused Charlie of sticking him up while Charlie was riding on a motorcycle. "But I can't even drive a motorcycle," Charlie protested to the police. They took him to the city jail anyway and held him for three days on suspicion of robbery.

That was it for Charlie. "It was time for me to get out of there and make a fresh start," he decided, even though he wanted to be near his parents and brothers. He had a destination in mind—the fertile, green Willamette Valley in western Oregon, nestled between the Cascade Mountains with their snow-covered volcanoes and the Pacific Ocean. In the 1840s and 1850s, the Willamette Valley had been the hoped-for destination of many of the pioneers on the Oregon Trail. They had heard it described as the Promised Land, or as a New Eden, in the words of Hall Jackson Kelley, the Harvard-educated promoter of settlement in what was then known as the Oregon Country, claimed by both the United States and Great Britain. After reading the journals of Lewis and Clark, who had made that first, epochal journey down the Columbia River to the Pacific in 1805, Kelley wrote to newspapers across the East Coast, "The word came expressly to me to go and labor in the field of philanthropic enterprise and promote the propagation of Christianity in the dark and cruel places about the shores of the Pacific." The Oregon Country, Kelley wrote, was a land with "sublime and conspicuous" mountains, a "salubrious" climate, a place "well watered, nourished by a rich soil and warmed by a congenial heat."

Charlie knew about the Willamette Valley because he had already wandered through Oregon several times in earlier years of bumming around and committing petty crimes. Once, on his way home to Texas, he ran out of gas and out of money just north of Salem. He earned some cash there by signing up to pick strawberries during the harvest. He stayed in a migrant farmworkers' camp on the northeast edge of Salem called Labish Village. It was a collection of cheap, unpainted barracks with wooden platforms for beds and only scratchy old blankets to sleep under, with no sheets or pillows. Charlie liked the big fields around the camp with their rich, black volcanic soil and ripening crops of mint, onions and strawberries. He heard tales of catching enormous salmon and plentiful trout in the Columbia River. Charlie, of course, loved to fish. Charlie met a welder in a workingman's bar outside Salem, and he invited Charlie to come along for lessons. Charlie quickly showed an aptitude for welding, and his new friend said he could make good money as an ironworker. Charlie made a mental note of the place. It might make a good new home someday.

With the police in Amarillo repeatedly picking him up, Charlie packed his wife and four young children into the family car, an old two-tone, brown-and-black Ford, and headed back to Salem. It was a 1,700-mile drive from Amarillo, almost the same distance as the 2,000-mile route of the Oregon Trail from Independence, Missouri, to the Willamette Valley. The last section of the drive for Charlie, in fact, was nearly identical to the original Oregon Trail, following the newly completed Interstate 84 across southern Idaho past Boise, then heading north in Idaho before crossing the Snake River into eastern Oregon and cutting northwest through the Blue Mountains until reaching the mighty Columbia.

As a teenager Charlie had hopped freight trains all across the West, from Texas to California and up to Washington, but he had never seen anything like the three-thousand-foot-deep canyon of the Columbia as he turned his family's car west and headed downstream, toward Portland, one hundred miles away. It was a vast, desolate stretch of dun-colored cliffs, marked by multiple long, dark horizontal bands, or striations. They had been left by enormous flows of molten basalt lava that coursed down the Columbia River bed fifteen million years ago.

An early emigrant on the Oregon Trail, Harvey Kimball Hines, first glimpsed the Columbia on September 13, 1853, at a point near where Charlie, driving his family, saw it. Hines was struck by how some force of nature "had worn and ground" the basaltic rock away, leaving a smooth path down to the river. "It was our first view of the mighty river toward which we had been looking and journeying so long. We stood and gazed upon it, and felt the thrill of the successful explorer in our hearts as when the goal of hopes attained rises to the vision."

Looking down the Columbia, with his wife and four children, Charlie too had a vision, like the pioneers: make a new life in the Willamette Valley, free of his family's troubles.

Rooster was a different case. Prison had not chastened him or made him less defiant or pugnacious. When he was released from the state penitentiary at Huntsville on May 26, 1961, he was given a bus ticket back to Amarillo and told that he would be on parole for three years. The conditions of his parole were clear: he needed to get a job, stay out of trouble and report regularly to his new parole officer in Amarillo, Roy Crumley. Rooster went back to living with his mother and father as if he had never been sentenced to prison, and he showed no interest in finding a job or checking in with his parole officer. In Crumley's first "Progress Report" on Rooster, dated June 26, 1961, he noted that Rooster was not working and that "his mother seems to be over protective of him." Elvie was trying to check in with Crumley on Rooster's behalf, despite the officer's warning that "Bogle must do the parole, himself, contact this office, instead of her trying to telephone, make arrangements for various permissions and making excuses for her son." In Rooster's first month out, Crumley also reported, he had already been arrested for driving a stolen car and on suspicion of taking part in several burglaries. Rooster was back in the comfort zone of his family, and his mother was again enabling him, not supervising or disciplining him. It was not an auspicious start for Rooster's parole.

At the same time, Rooster had gotten back together with Kathy Curtis, one of his girlfriends before the burglary. That August, Crumley gave Rooster permission to marry Kathy. He was nineteen. She was fourteen.

Kathy's family was even poorer than the Bogles. Her father was an alcoholic house painter and musician who played the steel guitar at neighborhood house parties in exchange for liquor. Her mother, who had only finished third grade, was a part-time bartender and drugstore counter clerk who supplemented her meager income by cleaning houses. When Kathy went to fill out an application for a marriage license, her mother had to sign it on her behalf.

Kathy married Rooster on September 2, 1961, at the Pentecostal church where she had been baptized. She was wearing a fuchsia satin evening gown, really a repurposed prom dress that belonged to her aunt Lucille Curtis, the most prosperous member of the family, whose father was a car salesman. When the preacher reached the part of the ceremony where he asked Kathy, "Do you take this man to be your lawfully wedded husband?," she stammered out, "I take this man to be my awful husband." The preacher laughed and said, "Katherine, it's lawful." But Kathy's words were an omen of things to come in her life with Rooster, slapstick-funny before it became sad, violent and destructive.

Rooster and Kathy moved into the tiny house made from old battery crates that Louis had built next door to the Bogles' main house. Crumley reported all that fall that Rooster still did not have a job, and judging by everything Crumley could see, was not even looking for work. "Doubtful that subject will ever hold a steady job," the parole officer wrote on December 5, 1961. So Elvie made a decision for the family. She and Louis would move to Oregon to live near Charlie, who had gotten his first good job as an iron-worker, and Rooster and Kathy would go with them. Elvie dipped into the cash reserves she had accumulated from her scams and bought an old yellow school bus. The family piled all their possessions inside it, and those that didn't fit they tied on the top or lashed to the sides. "They looked like a bunch of hillbillies," remarked Margaritte Garcia, their neighbor.

In January 1962, Rooster found a job as a mushroom processor at West Foods, Inc., in Salem. He worked for thirteen days, wrote his new Oregon parole officer, Leonard McHargue, "at which point he slipped and purportedly injured his back." Elvie filed an insurance claim on Rooster's behalf, the latest of her scams, and nine months later Rooster received a settlement of $928 from the food company's insurance firm. Rooster immediately used all the money to purchase a used 1955 Chevrolet Bel Air. His parole officer ordered him not to drive it, because he didn't have the money to buy insurance.

In the spring of 1962, with Rooster still not working and Kathy seven months pregnant and homesick for Texas, the family drove back to Amarillo for a few weeks. On their way back to Oregon, Elvie hatched another scheme. As their car was passing through Boise, Idaho, they drove very close to a truck and then deliberately sideswiped it. Kathy was not injured, but Elvie told her, "Lie down and say you're pregnant and having a miscarriage." "What is a miscarriage?" she asked. Elvie explained it to her. They drove to a nearby hospital to establish a record and then filed an insurance claim with the trucking company. The case eventually went to trial, and the Bogles pocketed a $10,000 settlement negotiated just before the jury reached a verdict. Kathy and Rooster's first child, Melody, was born a month after the accident, in good health.

Throughout Rooster's three years on parole, his parole officers in Amarillo and Salem grew increasingly frustrated by his lack of effort to find a job. A few days after Melody was born, for example, McHargue wrote that "subject states that most of his free time is spent at home playing records and practicing on his guitar. He wants to start a band in this area and hopes to have his friends from Texas come here so they can start the band and play in Salem. The subject's major problem remains steady employment."

A few months later, in October, McHargue toughened his language, though he had no real leverage. "Subject has no prospects for employment. Writer is doubtful he would work if he had a job. Appears all the subject wants to do is to play the guitar." His hobbies are "loafing, fishing and playing the guitar." His mother "watches over him and makes excuses for him" by letting him, his wife and the baby live at home with her, rent-free, McHargue reported.

Equally annoying to the parole officers was that Rooster was drawing county welfare money in Salem for himself, Kathy and their baby even though he was unwilling to do the work legally required to earn it. "Too lazy to work for welfare," McHargue fumed. In December 1963, McHargue reported that Rooster went to the Oregon State Medical School in Portland and had a free operation to place a plastic plate in his skull to cover the hole still left from his fight with Jimmy Wilson. One of the last entries in Rooster's parole file noted the birth of his second child, Tony, on February 7, 1964. Then, given the limited power of parole officers, McHargue had to close Rooster's file when the state of Texas officially declared he had finished his parole that June. He was still unemployed.

The failure of the parole officers, in Texas and Oregon, to make Rooster get a job and try to make him a better citizen reflects both a weakness in the criminal justice system and a lack of understanding about the role families can play in perpetuating crime. Parole officers tend to have caseloads that are too big to allow them to spend more than a few minutes a week or month to supervise, no less investigate, the newly released offenders they are charged with monitoring. They are the poor stepchildren of the criminal justice system, with the bulk of the money going to build and run the most expensive part, prisons. Moreover, at that time the little academic research that had been done on how crime tends to run in families had received scant attention outside of some universities' criminology departments. So Rooster's parole officers had never looked into the rest of his family and were unaware that his father and mother, as well as his older brothers and sister, had themselves been arrested for crimes and that Rooster was at risk of being infected by their behavior.

Rooster himself had found other things to do. Less than four months after being released from parole, he was arrested for having sex with a fourteen-year-old African American girl in Salem. He was still married to Kathy and by now had three infant children. Exactly what happened between Rooster and the girl is unclear because most of the records in the case were destroyed in a fire in the Marion County Courthouse. Rooster told his second wife, Linda, a friend of the girl, that he had snuck her out of a window in her family's house and taken her to a party where they got drunk and had sex. Initially, Rooster was charged with statutory rape when the girl's mother went to the police. But after he was arrested, on October 7, 1964, he agreed to plead guilty in exchange for a lesser charge of contributing to the delinquency of a minor. The one document that survives, the sentencing document, records that in January 1965 Rooster was sentenced by Judge George Duncan of Marion County to a year in jail, with the sentence to be suspended.

Rooster's sexual proclivities would leave a deep stamp on the lives of his first and second wives and all his children.

It was around Christmas that same year, 1965, when Rooster met Linda, then Linda White, another young woman who took his fancy, the sixteen-year-old offspring of two migrant farmworkers who had moved to California during the Depression from their homes in small towns in Arkansas and Oklahoma. They were Okie fruit tramps, by their own description. In the 1960s they heard about the bountiful fruit pickings in Oregon, so they had moved north to the Willamette Valley. Their son, Tommy, was scheduled to get out of the Oregon State Penitentiary at the end of December after serving a sentence for stealing a money-order machine, and they wanted to celebrate his release. So Linda's father planned a party and hired two young men from the neighborhood who played the guitar to provide the music—Rooster and his cousin, Michael Bogle, the son of Rooster's uncle John, who years earlier had been sent to the Gatesville School for Boys in Texas. They all lived in Labish Village, the migrant farmworkers camp where by then Rooster's parents had somehow managed to buy two houses. Tommy White, when he emerged from prison, had the same small blue tattoo under his left eye that identified him as a convict.

Linda was pretty, very shy and smart even though she had dropped out of school after the ninth grade, largely because her parents could not afford decent clothes for her and she was ashamed to be seen in school with her worn-out, hand-me-down outfits. Her father had put Linda to work in the fields at the age of three, along with her five siblings, and every sunset she had to turn in the tickets she earned from picking flats of strawberries or pounds of beans, fifty cents for a flat of berries, made up of twelve boxes.

Her father, who had ascended to the job of row boss, took the cash earned by each of his children "and bought him a gallon of wine every night," Linda remembered. The Whites lived in the workers' wood shacks or, during some winters, in chicken coops a farmer lent them. They never had running water or electricity, and the only toilets were outdoor latrines. Linda's mother cooked the same meal every day: biscuits made from baking powder, flour, salt and water. She put water on the biscuits for gravy. Linda didn't remember ever having milk, and they seldom enjoyed even a small helping of meat.

When Linda first met Rooster at the party, she "couldn't stand him," she recalled. "He was a real show-off and thought he was God's gift to women." Rooster was still very thin, only 125 pounds, and wore his fancy shirts unbuttoned to the waist, an Elvis Presley look. Rooster kept coming by her house and invited her to parties with him where there was live music, dancing and a lot of drinking. This was excitement Linda had never enjoyed before. She was still a virgin. Rooster was now making an impression on Linda. "He had a deep, strong, commanding voice and a persuasive way about him," she recalled. He was also the smartest man she ever met, even though he could barely read and never picked up a book or newspaper.

Her parents opposed her spending so much time with Rooster, who seemed to have no skills or prospects of a decent-paying job, so Rooster came up with a plan. He told her to sneak out of her house at night after her parents were asleep, and he picked her up in his car and drove her fifty miles north to Portland to the house of a woman he knew. They stayed there for four days while the police in Oregon launched a large manhunt for Linda, who was presumed to have been kidnapped. Her parents appeared on television to appeal for information, and Linda had the odd sensation of seeing her photograph shown on television. Rooster decided she had to go home to her parents, but he told her she should call them first to extract a condition for her return: that she could continue to see Rooster. Her parents reluctantly agreed.

After Linda and Rooster got back to Salem, she met his cousin Michael Bogle, who dropped a bombshell. Did Linda know that Rooster was married to Kathy, with three children and a fourth on the way? "I didn't like it, but I was a stupid kid," Linda said. "So I kept on seeing him."

Rooster and Kathy were living in a small house next to his parents that they had bought for him. Melody was four years old, Tony was two and Bobby was one. Linda's father now threatened to press charges against Rooster. So Rooster piled Linda and Kathy into his

Chevy Bel Air, the car he had bought with the insurance money for his phony back injury. They headed the 1,700 miles southeast to Amarillo, where Rooster promised Linda he would divorce Kathy and marry her. "I was so young and ignorant, I believed him," Linda said. Kathy was so naïve that she seemed oblivious to what was going on.

After five days of partying and drinking in Amarillo, and no sign that Rooster was taking the necessary legal steps to get a divorce or marry Linda, they all got in Rooster's car and headed back to Salem. "It was just a big con job," Linda later realized. "Rooster never had any intention of divorcing her or marrying me."

When they returned to Salem, Kathy surprised Linda by inviting her to move in with her and Rooster and their children. "That way I'll see more of Rooster," Kathy explained, "because he won't be out so much at night chasing after you." Elvie gave her approval of the novel arrangement. "To his mother, Rooster could do no wrong, so whatever Rooster wanted, she gave him," Linda said. Elvie would put fresh money for gas on the hood of Rooster's car almost every day, and there were new clothes, food for his family and lots of beer and wine to drink. Rooster still wasn't working and both Louis and Elvie were effectively retired, but a puzzled Linda didn't ask where the money came from.

Linda did not stay long, however. "It was horrible," she said. The house had three bedrooms, one for Rooster and Kathy, one for Linda and one for Rooster's three children. Rooster would go back and forth at night between Kathy and Linda, drinking heavily until he passed out drunk. Some nights he wanted to have sex with both women at once, and on many nights he got so drunk he started beating them with his fists, leaving them with swollen black-and-blue eyes. Linda moved back to her parents' place after four months of this treatment.

Yet she kept seeing Rooster. She was in love with him. Their first child, Debbie, arrived in April 1970; their second child, Tim, was born in April 1972. In the meantime, Rooster and Kathy kept having more children too: Michael in August 1966, Vickey in September 1967, Glen in December 1968 and Tracey in November 1972.

Family life was becoming chaotic to the point of being dysfunctional, or worse. The drunken beatings continued. Linda suffered three broken noses as well as assorted cracked ribs and chipped teeth.

"When he was drinking, he'd get mean," Linda said. "One night he pushed me down on the floor and stood on my back. He said, 'I'm going to take you to the edge of death. If I stand on your heart, I can make it stop.'

"He started bouncing up and down on me till I couldn't hardly breathe," Linda recalled. "I was passing out."

Rooster finally got off her and said, "How does that feel to almost die and then be brought back?"

Rooster was a strict, if volatile and unconventional, father to the boys, whipping them with his belt or switches he cut from trees in the yard. Tim recalled that there were days he could not go to school because the whippings left large welts and cuts on his arms, legs and back, and he was ashamed to take off his shirt in gym class. Rooster forbade the children to play with any kids outside the family, either at their own house or at their friends' houses. Later the boys decided Rooster did not want anyone outside the family to learn about his drinking. Whatever the reason, the boys did not have to find a gang at school to learn deviant behavior; their deviant peers were right there in their own home, their own family.

When Rooster caught any of the boys with a cigarette, he made them all smoke a pack or two of cigarettes, one right after another, until the boys threw up and their noses and throats burned. "Are you ever going to smoke again?" Rooster then asked them.

Rooster had each of his boys learn to box and even built a ring near their house where he staged tournaments and bet on his boys. Rooster kept the money when they won. He thought he was making them tough, as he had been, and instilling discipline.

He gave them wine to drink when they were as young as six or seven years old. One time he made Tony get drunk and then ordered him to box his much larger father. Rooster forced Tracey, the youngest boy, to drink such large amounts of beer that he became an alcoholic as a teenager, an addiction that contributed to his criminal proclivities.

There were no birthday parties or celebrations of Christmas that any of the brothers could recall. "Rooster thought presents and toys were stupid," Tracey said. Perhaps because Rooster did not read very well, there were no books or newspapers in the house, and he did not go to parents' nights at the schools his children attended or help with his boys' homework.

Rooster talked all the time about his criminal exploits, all the fights he had won, how he thought he had killed a man in a fight in Amarillo, and particularly about the burglary and his time in prison at Huntsville. He made himself sound like a really big-time criminal, like Clyde Barrow or John Dillinger, the boys thought.

"Those talks really impressed me," Tony remembered years later, sitting in a prison in Arizona where he is serving a life sentence without parole for murder. "They made him important in my mind. It made me want to do something to impress him. Maybe that's what made me a criminal"—the social learning theory of criminology in action.

Rooster showed six-year-old Tony how to steal bicycles and took him to a shop that would buy the stolen bikes without asking any questions. Rooster also went with Tony to steal cows from a farmer's pasture and then sold them.

As the children got older, Rooster began taking the whole gang of them, often with Kathy and Linda along too, to burglarize a neighbor's house or garage for items to sell for cash. The family's biggest caper was their break-in at the salmon hatchery at the Bonneville Dam on the Columbia River east of Portland.

Rooster needed the cash he made from these crimes because he was still not working full-time. At Charlie's encouragement,

Rooster learned to weld, spending time on job sites with Charlie and Dude, who had already gotten their ironworker union cards. Charlie had done so well as an ironworker that he was hired to work on the construction of the World Trade Center in New York in the late 1960s, and he kept a black-and-white photo of himself on top of one of the towers in his Salem trailer home. Eventually, Rooster learned enough to pass the state test and get his own iron-worker certificate.

Rooster took a special, if unorthodox, interest in his boys' sexual education. Despite having Kathy and Linda in his house, Rooster often cruised the local bars looking for women to pick up and take to a motel for the night. When Tony was about thirteen, Rooster started the practice of bringing one of his sons to join him and the woman he had picked up at the motel to initiate them into sex. Rooster went first and then told Tony to climb up on the woman while he watched. A couple of years later, when Bobby was thirteen, it was his turn, and his father brought him to a motel to have sex with a redhead named Ginger. The next year it was Michael, who was in the seventh grade. It was in a motel in Reedsport, on the Oregon coast, where Rooster was working at the time, and he had rented the motel room and already had picked up a woman, Daisy Mae, who owned a nearby bar. When Michael walked in at four a.m. as instructed, Rooster was having sex with her. He got off the woman and ordered Michael to climb right on in his place. "I was scared and embarrassed, and I cried," Michael said. "The woman was fifty or sixty years old, older than my mother, and very heavy. It was disgusting. And my father was there watching. It was also a school night, so I had to leave the motel early in the morning and go straight to school." A few years later, Michael was arrested and sent to prison for having sex with a fifteen-year-old girl. He claimed he didn't know her age and thought she was eighteen. It was statutory rape, nonetheless, and the crime made Michael a registered sex offender, an unhappy legal status that followed him wherever he moved for years to come.

Rooster was also giving his boys sex lessons at home, unknowingly. Bobby had drilled a small hole in his father's bedroom wall so he could observe what was going on. At night he could often hear a lot of moaning and crying and shouting coming from the bedroom, and sometimes he could see his father having sex with his mother, or Linda, and sometimes he watched as his father beat one or both of the women. "Watching all that, it kind of stimulated me, but it also messed me up," Bobby said. "I had seen my dad beat them up all the time and I had watched him having sex with them, sometimes both at once, so I thought sex was part of their punishment." One day Rooster caught him peeking through the wall and made Bobby wear women's panties around the house for everyone to see.

Tracey, the most articulate and thoughtful of the boys, tried to sum up what had happened in his family. "We really didn't have a childhood," he said. "Rooster tormented us, he tortured us, and we were the product of that." Since he has been in prison for most of his life, Tracey has had a chance to read. "I've learned about the importance of nurturing," Tracey said. "But there was no nurturing going on in the Bogle family." His dad, Tracey said, "had a heart of stone. He never told me he loved me, or cared for me. Not once. He was always beating me or criticizing me." This is the power an abuser holds. He exerts such dominance that those under his sway feel powerless to resist. Rooster had anointed himself to this position, a master manipulator, oblivious to the law and living in an empire of his own making.

The boys did not have toys, because Rooster didn't like toys, and they didn't play sports, since Rooster did not like sports. "So our only game was stealing," Tracey said. "Rooster taught us to steal stuff, and it was for him. That was the fun thing in our lives, stealing. It had a very powerful effect on us, and there was a domino effect. It started with Tony, and then it was passed on to Bobby, and next to Michael, Glen and me and even to Tim. We copied each other."

Perhaps because Tony was the eldest, or more likely because Elvie had taken a liking to him, making him her new pet in place of his father, Rooster was particularly hard on Tony. When Tony was around the age of six, Rooster taught him to drive a motorcycle. Later, he lined up a series of automobile tires back-to-back and made Tony jump the motorcycle over them. When Tony mastered that trick, Rooster put fifty-gallon oil drums under the tires and made Tony jump the double height. He didn't always succeed; when he failed, Rooster would cut out a switch and whip him.

Rooster had a .30-30 rifle, and he ordered Tony to stand sideways with matches between his teeth as he shot the wooden sticks out. Sometimes Rooster did this trick when he was drunk, and Tony got scared. Other times, Rooster put the matches in his own mouth and ordered Tony to shoot them out. That made Tony even more terrified. "What if I missed and killed my dad?" he once said. But while sitting in his prison cell in Arizona, years later, Tony came to believe he would have made all their lives easier if he had just shot his father. It was an astonishing insight into how tortured and tormented Tony was.

Where Rooster was a harsh and inconsistent disciplinarian, Kathy was lax, a parody of permissive parenting. Linda said later she thought that Kathy had married so young that she never really grew up. She was like a child with her own children.

In Tracey's memory, "My mother wasn't very responsible. She was going through her hippie phase, sitting around smoking marijuana or doing acid. The house was always full of other young people, friends of hers who were younger than her, and they called me the bartender. My job was to pass out pills and drinks. I didn't like it."

In academic terms, the Bogles had created a family where there was both social learning—imitation of criminal behavior—and almost no social control, the learned values and bonds that could inoculate a family against deviant behavior.

To make matters worse, in 1972, when Tony was eight, Linda

gave birth to her own second child with Rooster, Tim Bogle, and at Kathy's invitation Linda and her two children moved back in full-time with Rooster, Kathy and their seven children. Rooster and Kathy now had one bedroom, Linda and her two children had the second bedroom, and Rooster and Kathy's seven kids slept in the third bedroom.

Not surprisingly, Tony, as the eldest, was the first to get in trouble—in first grade. Rooster had been taking karate lessons and began teaching Tony, age six, some of his new moves. That first year, Tony often brought a pet rat to school, named Charlie, whom he had found in a big mound of garbage that accumulated behind the Bogles' house that they called "Mount Bogle." One day the teacher noticed something that appeared to be crawling up Tony's chest inside his shirt. "Take that thing out and put it in a trash can," she ordered him. Tony said, "No way, I'm keeping him on me."

Then he got down in his karate stance and kicked the teacher "real hard in the leg," just like his dad had shown him, Tony said.

The school called the police. The principal told Rooster that Tony could not come back to school until Rooster took him for counseling. Rooster refused. "My boy did nothing wrong," he told the principal. Eventually the school relented and let Tony come back to class.

Meanwhile, at home, Tony was exhibiting other signs of troubling behavior. One day he told his younger brother Glen to sit on the family's push lawnmower, holding on to the wheels with his hands. Suddenly, Tony swerved the lawnmower sideways and Glen lost his grip, with the fingers of one hand getting caught in the cutting blades. Four of his fingers were cut off. Rooster came out and found the severed fingers and drove Glen to the hospital. A doctor was able to sew several of the fingers back together, but he never fully recovered the use of that hand.

Tony had also begun to set cats and dogs in the neighborhood on fire, one day setting so many of them on fire that the field they were playing in caught fire. Tony laughed uncontrollably.

If Rooster had taken Tony for counseling he might have learned that cruelty to animals, particularly setting cats and dogs on fire, is a classic sign of childhood antisocial behavior, which in turn can lead to psychopathic behavior or adult antisocial personality disorder. That is a big step toward criminality. Such behavior is also a sign of a child having been abused.

Tony's cousin, Tammie Bogle, the daughter of Rooster's older brother, Babe, remembered the incident with Glen on the lawnmower for years. When Tammie grew up, she became the religious member of the family and worked as a counselor with newly released prison inmates. The behavior exhibited by Tony and his brothers bothered her. "I remember Tony pushing Glen on the lawnmower and thought he was not all there," Tammie said. "Those boys didn't play normal. They talked real loud and were abusive to each other, picking on each other and always hitting each other or putting one boy in a headlock," Tammie said. "It was as if Rooster had trained them to live out his childhood fantasies. It was how they learned to get attention. It was typical of a dysfunctional family."

In sixth and seventh grades, Tony became hyperactive in school, unable to sit still, what would be called attention deficit disorder today, and a doctor put him on Ritalin. He didn't do much homework and had failing grades. One of his teachers in seventh grade reported he had told her his father had two wives in their house, "My mother and my other mother," as Tony explained it.

Tony was taken to Juvenile Court in Salem and sent to a foster home in seventh grade. He soon escaped. After his return home he was caught burglarizing houses in the neighborhood, taking after his father. He was taken back to juvenile court in front of Judge Albin Norblad. Norblad, a gray-haired man with a square jaw, silver-rimmed glasses and a deep, raspy voice, was a former prosecutor who thought of himself as a no-nonsense, law-and-order Republican. Appearances, however, could be deceiving with Norblad, because under his black robe he usually wore blue jeans and when he went home he paddled his canoe or fished on a stream near his house—a typical Oregonian who loved the outdoors.

Judge Norblad was already getting to know the Bogles. He had first had Rooster in his courtroom for bringing a woman from a bar to a motel to have sex with one of his boys. Years later Norblad didn't remember which boy it was, but the very nature of the case made a deep impression on him. He never heard of anything like it, before or afterward, and in his career he handled more than one hundred thousand cases. His experience had worn away some of his crusty conservatism, making him more mellow, flexible and pragmatic.

The Bogles were one of four families whose trials he had presided over in which there were four generations of defendants. He had tried Rooster, and now here was Tony, and he instinctively knew there would be more Bogles before him in court, which there were. "With a family like that, I've become convinced that whatever we do has little effect, because the adults have permeated their kids with their values through their everyday example. It's like an infection," Norblad said. "With these families, we always lose." Just locking up members of families like these would only be a waste of taxpayer money, he had concluded. It wouldn't change them. That would require something else, maybe finding a way to separate them from all their relatives so they could not infect one another.

Unfortunately, Judge Norblad didn't know how to do that; it wasn't on the menu of the criminal justice system at the time. The normal tools used by probation and parole officers or by prison officials to try to change offenders' criminal habits, like mandatory drug testing, parenting classes and job training, had little effect on the Bogles, and forcibly separating family members from one another after they had served their time in prison would be unconstitutional. In recent years, however, Norblad's suggestion, of finding a way to separate families like the Bogles, has now been put into practice in several widely scattered programs, with good results.

The first of these came about by accident, after Hurricane Katrina pulverized New Orleans in 2005 and destroyed large chunks of the city's housing, especially in poorer areas. A young criminologist then at the University of Texas, David Kirk, observed that Katrina offered a surprise opportunity, what he called a natural experiment. Because a significant proportion of state prisoners in Louisiana came from New Orleans, and because many of them were black and poor and had their housing destroyed by Katrina, many inmates had nowhere to go after their release. Kirk interviewed some of the inmates from New Orleans and compared them with a sample who could and did go back to their old homes. Those who did not return to their homes were 15 percent less likely to be rearrested and sent back to prison over a period of one to three years after their release than those who did go home, Kirk found. Eight years after Katrina, he looked at these men again, and while the differences between the two groups narrowed, those who stayed away were still rearrested less, especially those who had been sent to prison only once. "Those that moved away were making a break from all their social networks, providing new opportunities for supervision and social support and creating a turning point in their lives," said Kirk, who is now an associate professor of sociology at Oxford University in England. One man who succeeded by moving away from New Orleans after Katrina had been a "big-time drug dealer and gang leader who was sent to prison for murder but after his release moved to Texas," Kirk said. He has now married and has a whole new social network. He has reversed his life course and has stayed out of prison.

Kirk was so struck by the results that in 2015 he started an experimental demonstration program in Maryland to see if state prison inmates from Baltimore who volunteered to move to a suburban county after their release showed evidence of lower rates of recidivism—committing new crimes and being sent back to prison—than those who returned home to Baltimore. Getting inmates to agree not to go home after their release presents many problems, in particular because of constitutional protections. Unless they are sex offenders, subject to strict legal restrictions, no one can dictate where newly released inmates go to live.

Kirk ultimately devised a financial incentive for newly released offenders who volunteered to move out of Baltimore—housing subsidies provided by the state of Maryland. With the cooperation of the Maryland Department of Public Safety and Correctional Services, Kirk recruited volunteers from four Maryland prisons and offered them housing subsidies. Half were assigned to move to Prince George's County, Maryland, a suburban area forty miles from Baltimore, and the other half were a control group who went back to Baltimore, where they had lived prior to being incarcerated. Kirk called it the MOVE program, the Maryland Opportunities through Vouchers Experiment. Ultimately, thirty inmates were included in a pilot program. Those who consented to move to Prince George's County received $1,230 a month for six months, a figure pegged to the U.S. Department of Housing and Urban Development's established fair-market rent for private housing in the area. Kirk thought the cost a bargain, considering that the national average daily expense for an inmate in prison is $100.

Kirk acknowledges that both the small sample size and the short passage of time do not allow statistically valid conclusions yet. He is very encouraged, however, that none of the participants who moved away from Baltimore has been rearrested or sent back to prison, while half of those who stayed in Baltimore have been rearrested. He is now preparing to expand the program in size and duration.

A similar effort was launched in Reggio Calabria, in the southern toe of Italy, a stronghold for a branch of the Mafia known as the 'Ndrangheta, where children as young as eleven or twelve have served as lookouts during murders, or taken part in drug deals and mob strategy sessions and received training in how to handle Kalashnikov assault rifles. The Mafia has recruited children for these tasks because if they are caught, they are subject to much less serious punishment than adults. After watching this go on for years, Robert Di Bella, the local magistrate and president of the area's children's court, decided to take a drastic step. He has separated children from parents convicted of mob affiliation and moved them to different parts of Italy into foster families to break the intergenerational cycle of criminality.

"Sons follow their fathers," Di Bella told *The New York Times*. "But the state can't allow that children are educated to be criminals," he said. Since 2012, Di Bella has sent about forty boys and girls, from twelve to sixteen years old, into this sort of witness-protection program. About a quarter of the time, mothers looking to flee the Mafia's grip have ended up going with their children. So far, Di Bella said, none of the children he has separated from their families has committed another crime. In 2017, the Italian Justice Ministry codified laws so that Di Bella's program can be applied nationwide to combat the Mafia.

In a country where close-knit families are still the norm, some Italians have expressed outrage at the program, with critics calling it "Nazi-like." Yet some fathers have written to Di Bella, he said, to thank him for his innovation. Many children have told him they finally feel free. Some mothers have even asked him to send their children into foster care to save them from a life of crime or risk being killed.

When Judge Norblad had Tony in front of him, though, these programs were still far in the future. So after hearing the facts of Tony's life, as much as anyone outside the family knew, he ordered Tony to be sent to the Oregon State Hospital in January 1978, at the age of thirteen.

It is important to point out that virtually all the boys who came before Judge Norblad, and all the members of the four families he dealt with that had four generations of criminals, were white.

Oregon is one of the whitest states, with blacks making up only 2.1 percent of its population. This was because of a quirk of history. Many of the early pioneers on the Oregon Trail in the 1840s and 1850s came from slave states, including Missouri, Tennessee and Kentucky, near the start of the trail, in Independence, Missouri. Pro-slavery politicians dominated the state's early legislature, and there was some sentiment to secede when Abraham Lincoln was elected president. However, because it was far away and isolated, Oregon needed federal government help, particularly against Native Americans. So when the state constitution was passed in 1857, a proposal to allow slavery was defeated, but the voters also overwhelmingly approved a clause to exclude free blacks from living in Oregon. The provision remained in the Oregon constitution until 1926.

The Oregon State Hospital, like the many other mental hospitals, or "asylums," as they were called, built in the 1800s, was a peculiarly American institution, founded on a progressive, utopian vision. It was thought that America could find a more humane way to treat the problems of stashing the aged and the poor and the mentally sick in the almshouses and jails that dated to medieval times—crowded, dark and desperate places that offered no treatment and no hope. For a few decades starting in the 1830s, the first American psychiatrists, known as "medical superintendents," were really architects more than doctors. They were in charge of building enormous new institutions in bucolic settings outside cities where, they confidently predicted, they could cure almost all kinds of troubled minds. Their supposed secret was the design of the institution itself, where a new environment would be created that corrected the unusual mobility and uncertainty of life in America that it was believed led to emotional difficulties. Curing insanity, in their view, was a "moral treatment." No surgery or medicine was required. This thinking reached Oregon soon after its statehood.

The design of the buildings was the key, as Thomas Kirkbride, the medical superintendent of the Pennsylvania Hospital for the Insane, wrote in his widely printed book, *On the Construction, Organization and General Arrangement of Hospitals for the Insane*. Every detail was critical: the size and location of the buildings, the right construction materials, the location of the water closets, the placing of the ducts and pipes. The philosophy was simple and straightforward, as David J. Rothman put it in his masterly book *The Discovery of the Asylum: Social Order and Disorder in the New Republic*.

"Create a different kind of environment, which methodically corrected the deficiencies of the community, and a cure for insanity was at hand," Rothman wrote about the work of the medical superintendents. The new asylums would "arrange and administer a disciplined routine that would curb uncontrolled impulses without cruelty or unnecessary punishment. It would re-create fixity and stability to compensate for the irregularities of society."

The first reported results from these new asylums were seemingly miraculous. The superintendent of the new Massachusetts asylum at Worcester reported in 1834 that "in recent cases of insanity, under judicious treatment, eighty-two percent of the patients recovered." In 1843, Dr. William Awl, of the Ohio Asylum, declared that 100 percent of his patients were cured. Of course, on closer examination, many patients seemed to be cured multiple times, improving the statistics.

The Oregon State Insane Asylum, completed in 1883, was carefully copied from Kirkbride's Pennsylvania Hospital. It was built on a grassy campus of 140 acres in the new city of Salem only a few blocks from Oregon's state capitol building and also near the new Oregon State Penitentiary. The hospital would eventually have thirty-one major Italianate buildings plus twenty-eight smaller cottages that housed a total of 3,474 patients.

Later in the nineteenth century, new treatments were devised as the architecture of the buildings themselves proved unable to deliver on the early optimistic promises. So the Oregon State Hospital, as it came to be called, performed lobotomies, electroshock treatments and, under the influence of the eugenics movement early in the twentieth century, more than 2,400 sterilizations for sexual deviance.

By the 1960s, these enormous state mental hospitals were passing out of favor, derided for their cruel treatments and warehousing patients for too many years far from their families—some of the same criticisms that the founders of the big state asylums had directed at the almshouses and jails that preceded them.

Promising new psychotropic drugs were suddenly seen as cures for schizophrenia and bipolar disorder and major depression, the major mental illnesses, and advocates for people suffering from mental illness began calling for shutting down the big state institutions and replacing them with smaller, more humane community-based facilities. Politicians, looking to cut state budgets, found closing the state hospitals a convenient target, and their number soon shrank rapidly. New community facilities were seldom built as replacements.

In the midst of this shift, the increasingly decrepit Oregon State Hospital allowed the filming of *One Flew Over the Cuckoo's Nest,* staring Jack Nicholson, inside its buildings, with some real doctors and patients appearing in minor roles. The movie was a huge popular success and won all five major Academy Awards in 1976, for Best Film, Best Actor, Best Actress, Best Director and Best Screenplay. Tony Bogle found himself a patient there just two years later.

Tony was assigned to what was called the Forty Ward, or the Adolescent and Youth Treatment Program, housed in McKenzie Hall, a two-story brick structure. The youngest twenty children lived on the first floor, and the oldest twenty lived on the second floor. In his first three weeks there, Tony managed to set fire to the building and smash a greenhouse next door. As a result, he was transferred to a security unit in a smaller cottage. He was testing the authority of the staff, as he had tested his father, to see if they were strong enough to deal with him. If not, he would show them he was in control. After two weeks in the special security unit, Tony was "not improved," according to the hospital's records, and he was discharged. His final diagnosis was "adjustment reaction of adolescence." This was a catchall diagnosis that basically meant Tony was a teenager having a hard time going through his growing pains. It could indicate Tony felt stress or sadness or a sense of hopelessness. Essentially the Oregon State Hospital just dumped Tony because he was too difficult.

Tony later explained to me that when his mother came to visit him on his thirteenth birthday, she brought a cake, and as soon as he blew out the candles on it the guards said it was time for her to leave. "I was angry," Tony said in an interview in prison in Tucson. "I felt abandoned."

A few months after the hospital let him go, Tony was arrested by the police in Salem for several burglaries. He was sent back to a medium-security juvenile facility in Salem called Hillcrest. While there, Tony often started fights and kicked and bit guards, and threatened to kill one guard.

That was too much for the facility. They took Tony back to Judge Norblad, who ordered him committed again to the Oregon State Hospital, in February 1979, at the age of fifteen. More of Tony's troubled history came out in records submitted to Norblad. They showed that Tony had a history of setting fires to kill animals, and that he had been described as "an extremely anxious child obsessed with a number of issues, particularly regarding his father." His father was described in the court documents as "coming from a carnival background," which was partly true, though Rooster was born after his parents had quit being in the carnival. Tony's father was also reported to have a prison record, a dependence on welfare and a history of alcohol abuse. Tony himself, according to a psychological evaluation by the Oregon State Hospital, suffered from "anxiety neurosis," meaning he had strong feelings of anxiety or fear. Tony made little progress at the hospital, his record shows, and after five months he escaped.

Tony was soon caught during another burglary and was sent back to Hillcrest, which did not want him. Judge Norblad returned him to the Oregon State Hospital, in theory to finish the program he had just run away from. That all these authorities were not strong enough to corral Tony only fed his growing sense of power.

Back at the Oregon State Hospital for the third time, in late 1979, Tony "showed no interest in working on his problems or relating to his treatment team," the hospital reported. This time his diagnosis was more specific and bleak. It was "anxiety neurosis with depressive features, and unsocialized, aggressive reaction of adolescence." In layman's terms, Tony was anxious, fearful and depressed, but also had an aggressive personality with a tendency to fight, and he might suffer from antisocial personality disorder as he grew to be an adult. This was tantamount to saying he was likely to become an adult criminal. After a mere two weeks, he was discharged again. "Unimproved," the hospital said.

When Tony went home this time, the family situation had changed. Rooster, often paranoid, had come to believe that Kathy was cheating on him with other men and had initiated divorce proceedings—ironic, to say the least. In the divorce, Rooster won custody of all the children except the youngest, Tracey, whom Kathy kept. Divorce in hand, Rooster packed Linda and the children into his car and drove to Reno, Nevada, where he and Linda got married in the Starlite Chapel.

After the divorce, Tony decided to spend a night at his mother's new house with his brother, Tracey, just like old times. Rooster unexpectedly showed up the next morning and found Tony arguing with Kathy. Rooster lost his temper, grabbed Tony and hauled him down to the Marion County courthouse to Judge Norblad, who was practically becoming a member of the Bogle family. "I can't keep him," Rooster said to the judge. "I'm done with him. I'm not taking him home."

As it happened, the police had been looking for Tony because he had been observed stealing mail from the neighbors' mailboxes, another trick Rooster had taught him. The best letters to steal, Rooster said, were those containing Social Security or pension checks, which could be cashed, or cards at Christmas, which often contained cash. This was a federal offense, so Norblad sentenced Tony to the MacLaren School for Boys, the toughest sanction he could impose.

MacLaren, as everyone called it, was Oregon's maximum-security facility for youthful offenders, set behind tall evergreens on a large 270-acre estate of grass fields and farmland close to Interstate 5, in Woodburn, seventeen miles north of Salem. Its campus was made up largely of small cottages designed to give its young residents a welcoming family feel. It was surrounded, though, by high fences of barbed wire with their tops facing inward and down to make escape harder. MacLaren had a reputation for brutality by its guards—and by fellow inmates—with boys often locked up in chains in cold and isolated conditions and subject to beatings. MacLaren's most famous inmate had been Gary Gilmore, a Portland native, who murdered two men in Utah and was executed there in 1977 after demanding his own execution by firing squad. Norman Mailer's best seller *The Executioner's Song* chronicled Gilmore's life, and his younger brother, Mikal Gilmore, wrote a poignant book, *Shot in the Heart,* that traced much of Gilmore's murderous rage to his stay at MacLaren. When Tony was sent there, MacLaren was in the middle of a class-action lawsuit that dragged on for ten years before the Oregon Youth Authority agreed to a number of reforms.

"When I arrived at MacLaren," Tony recalled, "it was totally out of control." Tony saw a boy who was in chains beaten by a burly guard for what seemed like an hour during his first day there. That night, Tony was assigned an upper bunk, unaware of what was about to happen. The first thing he knew was that something warm and wet hit him in the face, and then his blankets and sheets were pulled off and he was covered in a hot, milky substance. "The other boys were jerking off and spraying me," Tony said. "Some boys had saved up their cum in bottles and were tossing it all over me." It was Tony's introduction to MacLaren's tradition of "cum fights."

"The guards didn't do anything," Tony said. "They just left us alone. It happened to every new boy when they arrived." There were also guards having sex with the boys, sometimes in exchange for passes or for cigarettes, Tony said, and a few of the medical staff and a cook in the kitchen also had sex with the boys.

Tony got into trouble for hitting one guard over the head with a glass ashtray. The guard called for backup and a group of guards took turns beating Tony. "They sent me to the hole for a week for that," Tony said, using the prison argot for solitary confinement. He frequently ran away, only to be recaptured and put back in solitary.

Tony was discharged sometime in 1981 and went to live with his mother, Kathy, who by this time had moved to Kennewick, part of the Tri-Cities area of southeast Washington, a two-hundred-mile drive up the Columbia River from Salem. Tracey was living there too, as was their other brother, Bobby. Tony and Bobby went on a spree of forty or fifty burglaries, Tony said. The total is certainly an exaggeration, but the police eventually caught the brothers and Tony was sent back to MacLaren.

It was there in April 1982 that Tony was charged with the sodomy of a younger boy. Tony was surprised because he had only had oral sex with a boy who often had sex with other inmates. It was no different, in Tony's mind, than what went on every day at MacLaren, with the authorities turning a blind eye. But in this case, the boy, named Lee, had a steady boyfriend who took offense at Tony's interference in their relationship and reported Tony to the guards. Tony was taken to Salem, and because he had turned eighteen just two months before, he was put on trial in adult court. By coincidence, Judge Norblad had just been promoted from juvenile to adult court, and the case was assigned to him. "He tossed the book at me," Tony said. "'I've seen you too many times before,'"

Norblad told him. "I'm through with you. I'm sending you to the big boys' house." Tony was convicted of sodomy in the second degree, meaning deviant sexual intercourse where the victim was under fourteen, and he was sentenced to ten years in the Oregon State Penitentiary, Oregon's maximum-security prison. Tony had arrived on the big stage.

5

Bobby and Tracey

The Family Curse

Since Kathy had insisted in the divorce agreement that Tracey must live with her, in 1980 he moved into her small apartment in Kennewick. Kathy would go out to bars every night to pick up strangers to bring home, smoking marijuana and popping pills. Kathy, now thirty-four, still had a little girl's face, was slight and only four feet eleven inches tall, so she could pass for being ten years younger. Perhaps because of this, some of the men Kathy brought home were only a few years older than Tracey, who was eight. Kathy gave Tracey strict instructions never to call her "Mom" or "Mother" when any of these men were around.

One of Kathy's new acquaintances was a leader of a local motor-cycle gang. Another locked Tracey in the trunk of his car, so he and Kathy would not be disturbed while having sex. A third tried to drown Tracey in a swimming pool.

Kathy was changing houses every few months, when she ran out of money and could not make the rent. As Rooster soon discovered, this was in part because Kathy was cashing his court-ordered child-support checks at local liquor stores. The frequent changes in residence meant that Tracey often had to switch schools. "One day my mother dropped me off at a new school, but it was a holiday and the school was closed," Tracey said. "She had forgotten and drove off leaving me standing there. My mom was pretty irresponsible." Tracey did not remember the address of his latest apartment, so he walked around aimlessly, hoping for a clue. Finally a police cruiser stopped him and asked what he was doing. After he explained, the policeman took him to police headquarters and he was placed in temporary foster care.

After Rooster saw that his checks were being cashed at liquor stores, he and Linda began telephoning Tracey to find out what was happening. Tracey told them about his life, including how he had stepped on some glass and cut his foot, which was now swollen by a bad infection. When he asked his mother to take him to a doctor, Kathy said it would get better by itself.

Rooster and Linda sent Kathy a plane ticket to fly Tracey from Kennewick back to Portland, a short flight. "When we saw him get off the plane, he was like an orphan," Linda said. "The stewardess had him by the hand, and all he had was a paper bag with all his possessions. He was wearing a cheap plastic raincoat with nothing under it: no shirt, no pants, no underwear and no socks or shoes."

Rooster took Tracey to Judge Norblad, who awarded custody back to Rooster.

Looking from the outside, at this moment in time, one might be tempted to think that something like normalcy had settled into the Bogle household. Rooster, with his ironworkers' certification, had more frequent jobs. All the children except Tony, who was in prison, were living under one roof, at least most of the time. But in reality life for the Bogles was not only sometimes crazy and cartoonish; it was often violent or criminal.

Later that same year, 1980, Bobby wanted to visit his mother for his sixteenth birthday. She was now back living in Amarillo, her birthplace, and Kathy took him to a strip club, the Crystal Pistol. "Out came this stripper, who I didn't recognize at first," Bobby said. "Then my mom said, 'That's your sister, Melody,' and Mom nudged me. 'That's your birthday present.' Everybody thought it was very funny and they were laughing."

Bobby was embarrassed and offended. "I had never seen my sister nude," Bobby said. "And they had played a trick on me. I wondered why in the world would they want me to see my sister nude, and what kind of birthday present did they think it was."

On the drive back to Salem, Bobby and his mother quarreled in the car, and a few miles outside Salem, Kathy dropped Bobby off in the small town of Turner, without any money or way to get back to his home with Rooster. Bobby did the only thing he knew to do, what his father and older brother Tony had taught him—he burglarized a house. When that did not produce any cash, he broke into a local amusement park, the Enchanted Forest. That did get him some money—but the police caught him. Bobby soon found himself in front of Judge Norblad, who was becoming more and more convinced that the courts needed a new extralegal sanction to deal with families like the Bogles, something that could treat the whole family. But a program of that kind was still years away, so he sentenced Bobby to the MacLaren School for Boys, at the age of sixteen.

Over the past two decades, some psychiatrists and psychologists have, in fact, developed a new set of therapy programs to deal with families like the Bogles in much the way Judge Norblad envisioned, what might be called intensive in-home supervision for high-risk families. The programs act like probation, in that probation officers attached to a court offer programs to youthful offenders instead of a sentence to a reformatory or prison. In this major innovation, a highly trained team of clinicians goes to the family's home for three to five months to provide in-home counseling for both the parents and their children, or any other relatives who may be involved, including grandparents and siblings.

One of these innovative programs, called Multisystemic Therapy, was developed by Scott Henggeler, who recently retired as a professor of psychiatry and behavioral science at the Medical College of the University of South Carolina in Charleston. While he was getting his Ph.D. he was hired by the state of Virginia's Department of Pediatrics to work with antisocial children and was given some of the most difficult cases. After working with them for a while, and making little progress, Henggeler decided to visit the adolescents in their homes. "It took me fifteen to twenty seconds to realize how incredibly stupid my brilliant treatment plans were," he said. He realized that he needed to treat the children in the full context of their lives, to see them where they lived, with their families—their parents and siblings—and where they went to school. His central insight was to take therapy to the adolescents instead of taking the adolescents to therapy. "This meant our clinicians needed to go to their homes and families, to treat the whole family, and also to go to their schools, teachers, friends and any other close relatives they were in contact with," Henggeler said. Siblings can be particularly important because they may know things the parents don't, or may be starting to exhibit the same risky behavior and need to be treated too.

This is especially true for families like the Bogles, given how insular and clannish they are, Henggeler said. They are like a giant rogue iceberg, with most of the dangers hidden out of sight below the waterline, and only a small portion showing to outsiders. Getting inside their secret patrimony, their family myths, with their endless history of abuse, violence and disappointments, would be key to understanding why any of the individual Bogles had such difficulty making good choices, he said.

"Where you get the biggest bang for the buck," Henggeler added, "is when you decrease the activity of the most antisocial member or members of the family. And if you focus on the most troublesome member, the parents are usually involved. The key to getting good outcomes, to stopping the most chronic and violent offenders, is to get the parents to be more effective parents."

In most families Henggeler has worked with, "you sell the family to accept the therapy by persuading them it is a way to get their kids out of trouble and to stay out of prison," he said. "The parents usually love their kids, and we teach the parents how to make the therapy work to help their kids." In some very troubled families, Henggeler said, the clinical teams may take a different path. "In those families we try to identify the most pro-social member of the family, even if it is a grandparent not living in the home, and then try to forge a bond between them and the kid to make the therapy work."

Multisystemic Therapy, or MST, as it is often called, now has 535 locations in thirty-four states and fifteen countries. The clinicians that MST employs work in teams of two to four people per case and are specially trained social workers or psychologists. Henggeler estimated that they have worked with two hundred thousand families since the program began in 1996. Randomized clinical trials have found that when measured three years after MST therapy, the adolescents who have undergone the program have an average decrease in arrests of 42 percent, Henggeler said, a very high figure in the criminal justice system. The therapy can also produce big cost savings. Although the price tag of MST treatment varies by state, the average is $8,000 per juvenile, according to Henggeler. By contrast, court-ordered placements in a reformatory or prison can run from $50,000 to $100,000 for a youth.

Henggeler acknowledged that families like the Bogles presented a very difficult challenge even for his innovative therapy. "The single most powerful predictor of antisocial activity is the adolescent's association with deviant peers, who are usually in school or the neighborhood," he said. The Bogles' own family is their deviant peer group. For a Bogle, Henggeler suggested, "the best alternative might be to move away."

A few months after Bobby was sentenced to MacLaren, Rooster took Tracey, who was still only eight years old, to visit Bobby there. No one recognized at the time, as some criminologists did later, that taking a child to visit his older brother or father in prison could be endangering the child, making him think that life in prison is normal, or even glamorous, not dangerous and frightening. That kind of response could undermine the whole basis of the criminal justice system, which is deterrence, the notion that going to prison should scare people out of committing crime. That is precisely what happened with Tracey that day. "I was very impressed how tough Bobby looked with all those other big teenage inmates," Tracey said. "It made him look heroic, and I wanted to grow up to be as bad as him."

Soon Tracey was thinking about the meaning of what was happening to his family. "Our father had raised us to be outlaws, to steal, and I began to realize that what you are raised with is very hard to escape," Tracey said later. "I began to think we lived under a family curse of crime, like it was something contagious."

Tracey managed to stay out of trouble until he was fifteen, when his older brother Glen came by their house one day in a Mazda RX-7 that he had just stolen. Glen proposed driving to visit their mother, who was then living in the Central Valley of California in a little town called Santa Nella. Later, Tracey wondered what impelled him to jump into the stolen car and make himself an accessory to automobile theft. All he could remember was that "it was not about stealing that particular car; it was just that stealing was what we did as a family, so it was just another day in our lives." The boys got arrested by the police in Santa Nella a few days later and were returned to Salem. Judge Norblad sent Tracey, as a first-time juvenile offender, to Hillcrest, the medium-security juvenile facility in Salem.

Things now suddenly sped up for Tracey, and he really *was* living under the family curse of crime. The next year, 1988, when he was sixteen, he and Bobby stole a big-rig tractor trailer in downtown Salem and crashed it into the wall of Anderson's Sporting Goods, a gun store. Whether they meant to crash right through the wall and steal some guns or whether they just drove badly depends on whose version you believe. But the crash was as far as they got, and Norblad sentenced Tracey to MacLaren. He sentenced Bobby, who was now an adult, to a short term in the Oregon State Correctional Institution, a medium-security facility.

Six months later, both boys were back out and living at home when they saw another big-rig tractor trailer in a truck parking lot in downtown Salem. It was loaded with $100,000 worth of liquid sugar, though the boys were unaware of that. They decided to drive the truck east on Interstate 84 all the way across Oregon and then through southern Washington to Moscow, Idaho, a distance of more than 350 miles. Their brother Michael was living there, in a residential neighborhood, and when they got close, Bobby saw some girls on the sidewalk and invited them to jump up in the cab with him and Tracey. "It was very crowded, with the girls jammed against the dashboard and the doors," Tracey said. A police car spotted the crowded truck driven by teenagers and followed it right to Michael Bogle's door. Bobby and Tracey were flown back to Portland to stand trial.

Tracey was still only sixteen, so he was sentenced to eighteen more months at MacLaren. Bobby got eighteen more months in the adult Oregon State Correctional Institution.

Tony, who was doing his time in the Oregon State Penitentiary in Salem, only a few miles away but a maximum-security facility, wrote Bobby a letter challenging him to do something crazy so the prison authorities would have no choice but to increase his security classification and send him to join Tony in the penitentiary. The brothers were in a perpetual competition to see who could be the baddest, or in their minds the greatest, outlaw. Bobby immediately started a fire and smashed some fire extinguishers and got his wish: Tony and Bobby were now together. Tracey was in MacLaren, on the glide path for adult prison himself.

The Oregon State Penitentiary loomed like a medieval fortress, a cluster of big, boxy yellow buildings with metal bars in their narrow windows set behind a twenty-five-foot-high gray concrete wall topped by towers with guards armed with rifles. Its design was classic American prison style, which dated to the prison built at Auburn, New York, in the 1820s. Inside the main building of the Oregon Penitentiary were five tiers, or layers of cells, stacked one atop another, with heavy steel doors that clanged open and then shut with a loud metallic sound, a somber note of finality that echoed through the whole building. The interior of the cellblock was derived from the design of the first warden at Auburn, William Brittin. There were walkways on either side of the honeycomb of cells, with the floors kept freshly washed and polished. Each cell was furnished simply with two steel bunks, one atop the other, plus a steel toilet and sink and several shelves with hooks for clothes. The tiers of cells were a prison within a prison: if a convict managed to break out of his cellblock, he still had to find a way to get over the high outer wall of the prison to escape.

The first American prisons in the 1820s, like the first insane asylums, were believed to signal a progressive reform to replace the medieval forms of punishment then in use in the United States as well as Europe. The most popular traditional sanctions included whippings, the stocks, heavy fines, banishment and the gallows for the most serious offenses. The goal of these penalties was not reha-

TOP, LEFT Louis Bogle as a baby sitting on the lap of his grandmother Narcissa Harding, in front of her log cabin in Daylight, Tennessee, about 1900

TOP, RIGHT Narcissa Harding (left) with her daughter Mattie Bogle, Louis's mother, circa 1890. Narcissa unsuccessfully petitioned the federal government for years to get her late husband's Civil War pension.

LEFT Sarah Hardin (right), the grandmother of Louis's future wife, Elvie Morris, in a photo said to be taken in 1915 in Sherry, Texas. The girl on the left is not identified. The free-spirited Hardin was a major influence on young Elvie.

A photo studio shot of Louis Bogle taken for his wedding to Elvie in 1921 in Paris, Texas

ABOVE Elvie Morris (right) with her mother, Florence Morris, 1919. Elvie's father had just died of influenza, and Florence used his small life insurance policy to buy new clothes for herself and her daughter after they moved from the rural crossroads hamlet of Sherry into the big town of Paris.

LEFT Louis and Elvie with their first two children—John, standing, and Dude. On the right is Elvie's mother. This photo was taken in 1925, shortly before Elvie had her mother committed to the North Texas State Asylum in Wichita Falls, Texas.

TOP, LEFT Circa early 1930s, the growing family of Louis and Elvie—John, the oldest, is in the back left; Charlie is in front of him; Dude is standing in front of his father; Babe is in front of him. Peggy is being held by her mother. Everyone is barefoot.

TOP, RIGHT Charlie Bogle in 1946, at age eighteen but looking much older. The dog is doing a trick Charlie had taught him in the carnival where his parents worked for years.

RIGHT John Wesley Hardin, a legendary nineteenth-century Texas outlaw, who killed many. Charlie, thinking him to be his mother's uncle, kept a photo of him in his trailer and identified with him.

ABOVE Mattie Bogle standing in front of the shack Louis had built for his family to live in, in Amarillo, circa 1960. The shack was made of old battery crates, stained with oil, that Louis salvaged from the junkyard where he worked.

LEFT Louis, in his junkyard uniform, with an aged Mattie

A mug shot of Dude Bogle on being admitted to a Kansas prison in 1950 for statutory rape. Dude had recently come back from serving in World War II in India and Burma in the Army Air Corps. He had risen no higher than the rank of buck private because of constant fights.

A mug shot of Rooster, the youngest child of Louis and Elvie, taken in 1960 when he was sentenced to the penitentiary in Huntsville, Texas, after joining with his older brothers in the burglary of an Amarillo grocery store

Rooster with his two wives, Kathy (left) and Linda, probably in the late 1960s when Rooster was living with both women

TOP, LEFT Tony Bogle, Rooster and Kathy's son, when he was seven years old, before a lifetime of being locked up in a succession of juvenile reformatories and adult prisons

TOP, RIGHT Tony in 2007 in an Arizona prison, where he is serving a life sentence for murder

**MARION COUNTY
CORRECTIONS
MUGSHOT PROFILE**

NAME: TRACEY ECKE   BOGLE

PHOTO#:
BOOKING#:   790299
IDENTIFICATION#:   8652169
BOOKING DATE (yyyymmdd):   20010523
CHARGE: SENTE
DATE OF BIRTH: 11/25/72
PLACE OF BIRTH: OREGON
SOCIAL SECURITY#:   543-86-2925
DRIVERS LICENSE#:
DRIVERS LICENSE STATE:

PHYSICAL DESCRIPTION

		SCARS/MARKS/TATTOOS
R/ *2	WHITE	
S:	MALE	
HEIGHT:	5'0"	
WEIGHT:	140	
HAIR LENGTH:	BELOW SHOULDER	
HAIR COLOR:	BROWN	
HAIR STYLE:	STRAIGHT	
SKIN TONE:	MEDIUM	ABDO:
EYE COLOR:	HAZEL	DESC:
EYE CHARACTERISTICS:	NORMAL	ARMS:
GLASSES:	NONE	DESC:
TEETH:	NORMAL	BACK:
FACE SHAPE:	OVAL	DESC:
FACIAL HAIR:	MUSTACHE W/ BEARD	BUTT:
COMPLEXION:	CLEAR	DESC:
BUILD:	MEDIUM	CHEST:
SPEECH:	NORMAL	DESC:
HEARING:	NORMAL	HANDS:
NARCOTICS OFFENDER:		DESC:
REGISTERED SEX OFFENDER:		HEAD:
GANG AFFILIATION:		DESC:
GANG DESCRIPTION:		LEGS:
		DESC:

CONFIDENTIAL FOR LAW ENFORCEMENT USE ONLY

8652169
Tracy/Bogle/ Book

PAULA BOGLE

Paula Bogle, Tony's wife, who was convicted for the same murder but received a lesser sentence

A document regarding Tracey Bogle produced by the Oregon Department of Corrections while he was serving a sixteen-year sentence for kidnapping, sodomy, assault and robbery, a crime he committed with his brother Bobby

Bobby Bogle on the right with his cellie at the Oregon State Penitentiary, Jeremy Vanwagner—his son. For the Bogles, crime was often a family affair.

Bobby Bogle on the left and Tracey Bogle on the right in the yard of the Oregon State Penitentiary, showing off their well-developed bodies and tattoos

Stepping Out Ministries in Salem is a Christian-based halfway house for sex offenders coming out of prison in Oregon. On the right is Tammie Bogle, its codirector. On the left is Tracey Bogle, her cousin, who was required to live there after his release from prison.

Tracey with the car he bought after his release from prison, though driving it was against the conditions of his parole. He did not have a driver's license or insurance.

Tracey Bogle with his mother, Kathy, after his release from prison. Kathy was about to go to jail for a year for Medicaid fraud.

Ashley Bogle, in a selfie she took at her college graduation, making her the first member of the Bogle family to graduate from college

bilitation but deterrence, to frighten the offender. The only jails at the time were small, meant to hold prisoners for very short periods pending trial, and they were expensive for a nation that had low taxes and an agricultural economy.

No one before the 1820s had thought building big prisons that would house offenders over long periods of time would accomplish anything more than waste a lot of the government's money. But in that decade, as befitting the new American nation with its democratic ideals, a fresh idea was put forward: criminals could be rehabilitated through newly designed prisons that kept inmates isolated from the vices of society—negligent parents, taverns, gambling halls and houses of prostitution. Given those supposed origins of crime, the reformers were convinced that malefactors could be rehabilitated by perfect isolation in this new form of jail. To realize this plan, Auburn's architects made their new inmates sleep alone in their cells at night and forbade them to talk with fellow convicts when at work, at meals and in their cellblocks. This plan, which came to be known as the silence system, left a profound impression on European visitors who came to study Auburn. In 1831, after an inspection, Alexis de Tocqueville wrote: "Everything passes in the most profound silence, and nothing is heard in the whole prison but the steps of those who march, or sounds proceeding from the workshops." After the prisoners were brought back to their cells at night, "the silence within these vast walls . . . is that of death. There were a thousand living beings, and yet it was a desert solitude." Given the reformers' aspirations that inmates could be rehabilitated, the prisons were called "penitentiaries" and the prison departments of state governments were called "departments of correction."

The early prisons were all built in the plentiful American countryside, away from the cities, where vices were believed to flourish. When the Oregon State Penitentiary was built, for example, Salem was a tiny town surrounded by farm fields and forests. Today the prison sits only a few blocks from the state's shining white marble capitol building topped by the gold-clad figure of an Oregon Trail pioneer wielding an ax.

The silence system eventually fell into disuse, though you could find remnants of it as late as the 1960s in some of the older prisons, like Wisconsin's Waupun Correctional Institution. Inmates there were still forbidden to talk in the hallways and workshops, and no banter was allowed in the large central dining room. Even today you can travel all across America, from Sing Sing in New York to Leavenworth in Kansas and on to the Oregon State Penitentiary, and all the older prisons look as if they had been built by the same man using the same set of building blocks.

Crime has long been known to run in families. Richard Louis Dugdale was a merchant and self-taught sociologist in New York City who became a member of the Prison Association of New York. In 1874 he was assigned to inspect thirteen county jails in upstate New York. Many of the inmates, he discovered, were related by blood or marriage, and Dugdale, to protect their confidentiality, gave these inmates a name, "the Jukes." They represented an amalgam of 42 families with 709 offenders. Dugdale's research in Ulster County led to a widely read and controversial book, *The Jukes: A Study in Crime, Pauperism, Disease, and Heredity.* Using local records and family trees that he created, along with extensive interviews, Dugdale attempted to determine whether it was nature or nurture that accounted for the large number of criminal offenders among the Jukes. Dugdale himself believed human behavior was a product of both heredity and the environment. A number of scholars, however, believed Dugdale was espousing support for eugenics, which was rapidly growing in popularity at the time, and his work was later tarnished by that.

Another relatively early investigation of crime in families was conducted by Thomas Ferguson, of 1,349 boys in Glasgow, Scotland, in the late 1940s. Ferguson matched a group of delinquent boys against a nondelinquent group from similar social and economic backgrounds and found that 12 percent of the boys who left school at the age of fourteen were convicted in court by the age of eighteen, mostly for theft and burglary. Much more interesting, Ferguson demonstrated that the percentage of boys who were convicted increased dramatically with the number of other members of their family who were convicted. Only 9 percent of the boys convicted had no other family member who had been convicted. If one other family member had been convicted, the percentage rose to 15; if two other family members had been convicted, the percentage was 30; if three or more other family members were convicted, the percentage was 44. The probability of conviction was especially high among boys who had a father or brother convicted.

Ferguson was also able to show that having a convicted family member predicted a boy's likelihood of becoming a delinquent regardless of other known risk factors for crime, such as poor grades in school, bad housing or an overcrowded household where supervision and discipline were difficult. Ferguson concluded that "the influence of another convicted member of the family is at least as great as that of any of the other adverse factors that have been studied." This is a remarkably accurate description of what happened in the Bogle family.

The first study of the intergenerational transmission of antisocial behavior in the United States, as mentioned earlier, was done by Sheldon and Eleanor Glueck, a husband-and-wife team of researchers at Harvard Law School. Using a sample of five hundred boys committed to juvenile reformatories in the Boston area in the 1940s and comparing them with another sample of five hundred Boston boys from similar households who were not committed, the Gluecks found that two-thirds of the boys sent by the court to a reformatory had a father who had been arrested. In addition, half of the boys committed to a reformatory had a grandfather who had been arrested, and 45 percent had a mother who had been arrested. The Gluecks' data is particularly striking because all the boys in their sample were white. This was at a time when most crime in the United States was still committed by whites. The Bogles were a carryover from this older tradition. Whatever was happening in their family had nothing to do with race, or with the myriad difficulties faced by African Americans because of the effects of discrimination in housing, education and the criminal justice system.

Perhaps the gold standard for the study of how crime runs in families, also mentioned earlier, was conducted using a group of 411 boys from South London, following them from the age of eight to forty-six. This study, as mentioned in the Prologue, carried out from 1961 to 2001, was done by a team led by David Farrington of the University of Cambridge, the leading criminologist in the United Kingdom, and is known as the Cambridge Study in Delinquent Development. It found that half of all the convictions of the boys were accounted for less than 6 percent of the families in the sample, and that two-thirds of all the convictions were accounted for by only 10 percent of the families. The study also found that having a father, a mother or an older brother or sister who had been convicted was a good predictor of a boy's later criminal activities. Having a parent who had been sent to prison was an even stronger predictor of a boy's later criminal life.

A number of other studies done in Philadelphia, Pittsburgh and Denver also reported similar results, that roughly 5 percent of the families of the boys in their samples accounted for half of all the crime, and about 10 percent of the families of the boys accounted for two-thirds of all crime. This would mean that some families, like the Bogles, have large numbers of offenders.

Trying to unravel what the impact is of growing up in a criminal family is a vital question since there are now 2.3 million people in prison or jail on any given day in the United States, a fourfold increase since the 1970s. More than 50 percent of these inmates are parents, and the number of children with a parent in prison reached 1.7 million a day in 2007, according to the Bureau of Justice Statistics. That is not counting the hundreds of thousands of children with a parent in jail or on probation or parole, all of which can be just as disruptive to a child's care, supervision, education and economic support. The number of children with a parent behind bars at some point in their lives is more than five million, according to an authoritative estimate by Patrick McCarthy, the president and chief executive officer of the Annie E. Casey Foundation, an organization dedicated to helping disadvantaged children. Some criminologists have called these children the invisible victims of our policy of mass incarceration, or its collateral damage.

What often gets overlooked in any discussion of these baleful figures is that, as the Bogles show, the more people we send to prison, the more new candidates we are creating among their children, who may later end up committing crimes and be put behind bars themselves. Mass incarceration thus becomes a vicious cycle.

Until very recently, there has been little public attention to the growing body of research showing that crime tends to run in families. One reason is that statistics on the effects of parental arrest and incarceration are difficult to come by, since no one in the criminal justice system is charged with keeping them. When the police make an arrest, they do not ask how many children the suspect has or how many members of his or her family have previously been incarcerated. In making an arrest, the police's interest is in apprehending the suspect—a public safety role, not a research role. Similarly, when a prosecutor prepares an indictment against a suspect, the suspect is not asked about how many children he or she has, whether any of them have been arrested or whether the suspect had other family members who have been to prison. The only point in the whole criminal justice process when an official might ask a defendant whether he or she had a parent who had been incarcerated is when a judge is preparing to sentence the defendant and the court's probation department prepares a presentence report to assist the judge in gauging the defendant's criminal background. Presentence reports can be lengthy, as they record all the defendant's previous crimes and prison sentences, along with any psychiatric evaluations. But these reports often contain little information on the criminal record of the defendant's family.

Once a convict reaches prison, his or her family background again seldom gets asked about by prison officials. They are in the business of keeping their inmates locked up, safely, and are not concerned with the number of children they have or how many members of their families have preceded them behind bars.

The research that does exist on parental incarceration has generated studies with widely divergent results. A number of reputable scholars or advocates for the children of incarcerated parents have published articles concluding that the children of prisoners are six times more likely than other children to be convicted or incarcerated. That is a stark finding and might explain something about the Bogles. The figure has come to be widely used in public discussions of parental incarceration. But in a recent book surveying ten other studies on the effects of parental incarceration on children, Joseph Murray, a researcher at Cambridge University, concluded more modestly that "taken together" these studies merely show that parental incarceration predicts some increased risk of antisocial behavior or mental health problems for children.

Obviously, it is tricky to disentangle the exact influences of incarceration on any given member of a family. In fact, it might just be the family itself that is the primary engine of dysfunction, though putting members of the family in prison may increase that dysfunction, and the more members who are incarcerated the greater the dysfunction, as Ferguson found in Glasgow.

Bobby wanted to look like a businessman when he finally got out of prison in June 1993. His release had been delayed because of multiple escapes and also because he violated a number of earlier paroles. Now Bobby had a plan to go legitimate and show his father, at last, that he could amount to something. During his time in prison, Bobby had run a protection racket for a number of gay and straight inmates who feared being raped, including fifty-year-old David Fijalka, who had himself been serving a sentence for rape. Fijalka owned a small auto-detailing shop in Salem in an old gas station downtown across the street from the hulking Oregon State Hospital. According to Bobby, and later court testimony, he extracted a promise from Fijalka that Fijalka would turn over half the ownership of the detailing business to Bobby in return for Bobby's protection while Fijalka was in prison. Bobby was so confident that he had a half ownership in the business that when he filled out the paperwork for his release from prison he listed the shop as his residence. Bobby also gave that address to his new parole officer, who checked with Dave Fijalka, who had been released before Bobby, and received a confirmation. Given all that, Bobby wanted to make a good impression when he went to Fijalka's house in Salem on July 1, only five days after being released. They were supposed to discuss plans for the new joint management of the detailing shop. Bobby's half sister, Debbie Bogle, had bought him a tan sport jacket, a button-down shirt, a new pair of trousers and good shoes for the occasion, and in a nice touch, she also lent Bobby her pager to make him appear very professional. Then she drove Bobby and their brother Tracey to Fijalka's house.

Fijalka had bad news for Bobby. He said that two of his employees in the auto-detailing shop, David Poole and Ray Rankins, ex-cons who had been in prison with Fijalka and Bobby, had pressured him into letting them take over the business. Fijalka suggested Bobby could get the business back either by "muscling" them or by killing them, according to later court testimony. Bobby and Tracey headed back to the shop a second time, now armed with a .38-caliber revolver they had stolen from the house of their half brother, Tim Bogle. They had fortified themselves with two forty-ounce bottles of beer, and Tracey, who had suffered from bouts of alcoholism ever since Rooster made him drink large quantities of beer and wine as a boy, got drunk and belligerent.

When they arrived at the detailing shop, Poole invited them in and poured them glasses of bourbon. Bobby and Tracey said they had come to take over the shop and that Poole and Rankins had to leave, immediately. Then "things got nutso, crazy," Poole said later in court testimony. "Bobby and Tracey had it in mind that they owned half the detailing shop with Dave Fijalka," Poole testified. But Fijalka had "squandered" his ownership, Poole said in court, without elaborating on whether Poole and Rankins had forced Fijalka into selling them the business or had just purchased it from him legitimately.

"Bobby and Tracey were talking nonsense, as far as I was concerned," Poole testified. "They were trying to make me understand that they owned the business. But to me it was crazy. They were firing me from a business that I owned. I couldn't get it through their heads that they had been conned."

Tracey took out the .38-caliber revolver and fired a round into a table next to where Poole was sitting.

To calm things down, Poole took out all his business records, including his license for the shop and the telephone bills, in his name. "With that, they finally realized that Dave Fijalka had blown his interest in the business," Poole later testified. The confrontation ended when Poole called Fijalka on the phone and he admitted he had somehow turned over the shop to Poole and Rankins. The Bogles, who had practiced conning people for a living, had just been conned.

Before they left, Bobby went up to Rankins and put his arm around him. "You're sure there's no way I can invest my money in your shop? Because this was really my chance," Bobby said, according to Rankins's court testimony. "This was a chance for me to show my daddy that we could really do something." Rankins said no, and Tracey and Bobby left.

Debbie, who picked them up later, testified that Bobby and Tracey had only wanted to run the auto-detailing shop as a way to become legitimate. "They didn't want any trouble," she testified. "The whole reason they wanted the business was so that they could straighten out."

At 11:30 p.m. on July 1, only five days after Bobby got out of prison, and with Tracey still on juvenile parole from the MacLaren School for Boys, the brothers barged into the house Fijalka shared with his girlfriend, Sandra Jackson. The brothers had been there earlier in the day without incident, but now Tracey had the .38-caliber revolver and was waving it around. "We're going to kill you," Tracey shouted to Dave and Sandra, she later testified. To make his point, Tracey fired a shot into the couple's stereo speaker, and Bobby pulled the living-room curtains closed.

"They were yelling for us to get down on the floor," Sandra testified, "and then Tracey hit Dave in the forehead with the gun and knocked him to the floor. Bobby went into the bedroom and found a set of handcuffs and proceeded to put them on me, with my hands cuffed behind my back. Then they took extension cords and tied Dave's hands up."

Next, Bobby went into the bedroom and found a shirt, which he ripped into pieces and stuffed in Dave and Sandra's mouths as gags. To complete their helplessness, Bobby pulled the telephone out of the wall and used the cord to hog-tie both victims from their necks to their feet. If they tried to move their legs, it would choke them.

Bobby and Tracey were pulling open every drawer in the house, "trashing the place," Sandra testified. "They wanted money." Since Sandra had just sold some of her furniture, she happened to have $600 in her pocketbook. The brothers took it along with some of Sandra's jewelry, a few rings and a necklace.

"They were acting wild and sweating like they were on drugs and just cussing and yelling," Sandra said.

Tracey was still holding his gun and repeatedly hit both Dave and Sandra in the head with its butt, opening a number of wounds that oozed blood. Bobby found a baseball bat and hit Dave in the head with it too, causing him to pass out. Sandra was trying to force herself to stay conscious.

Bobby then found a butcher knife in the kitchen and said to Sandra, "We're going to cut your face up."

"They wanted to kill us," Sandra later testified. "They just didn't want to give up."

Bobby found a small Kodak camera and stuck it in his pocket. "We're going to kill you and take pictures of you after you are dead."

At this point, Tracey walked into the bedroom and pushed Sandra, who was still hog-tied, down on the bed, with her head sticking over the edge. "Tracey looked at me, and he said, 'You're going to suck my dick, bitch.'"

"He had the gun cocked at my head, and he told me, 'If you bite, bitch, you're dead.'"

Tracey unzipped his pants and put his penis in her mouth, but he apparently was so drunk that he could not get an erection, Sandra testified. "After a while, he got distracted and went into the other room to see what Bobby was doing." A police swab later found no semen in her mouth.

When Tracey came back into the bedroom, Sandra pretended to be unconscious, so Tracey said, "She's out." The brothers decided then to leave, though not without discussing which brother would kill the couple, Sandra testified. "In the end, however, they decided they weren't going to kill us. They just figured that we were bound and gagged and we would just lay there and starve to death. Who's going to find us, you know?" Sandra said.

When the brothers went out the front door, taking with them the keys to Sandra's car, it was 1:30 a.m.

The Bogles had committed the kind of casual, senseless physical and sexual abuse that Bobby and Tracey had been exposed to since they were little children. Now they were reenacting it with other people as victims.

It took Dave Fijalka several hours to get himself loose and then free Sandra. Bobby had destroyed the telephone line, so they had to drive his car to a nearby Dairy Queen to call the police from a pay phone. Sandra described her car, which the brothers had stolen, and gave her license-plate number. From Salem, which sits right on Interstate 5, the Bogles could have fled north to Washington, east to Idaho, anywhere in Oregon or south to California. The Salem police department worked overnight, faxing prison photos of both Bobby and Tracey and information about the car—a red Volkswagen Rabbit—to police departments in four states.

At 3:30 p.m. that same day, a farmworker named Julio Morales in Willits, California, a town of five thousand in Mendocino County near the entrance to Redwood Country, called the California Highway Patrol to inquire whether a red Volkswagen Rabbit with Oregon license plates might be a stolen car. He was suspicious because a man he had never seen before had stopped him in Willits and given him the car and its keys after a chance encounter on the street. Morales noticed that the key ring contained several other keys that were not car keys and asked the man if he wanted them back. No, the man said, he didn't even know what they were for. The California Highway Patrol instantly confirmed that the license plates belonged to Sandra Jackson's stolen car and sent a tow truck to pick up the Volkswagen. The Bogles were making amateur mistakes. They would have been better off just abandoning the car on a lonely country road where it would have taken longer to find.

Two Salem police officers set off immediately for Willits, a ten-and-a-half-hour drive south of Salem on Highway 101, the coastal route that goes over some rugged mountainous terrain. In the meantime, Blaine Johnson, a Willits police officer, studied the faxed photos of Bobby and Tracey and, at seven o'clock that evening, distributed copies to other Willits officers who were patrolling Recreation Grove, the town park, where Fourth of July festivities were under way, with concession stands and fireworks. A few hours later, at one a.m. on July 3, a police officer spotted a man who looked like one of the Bogle brothers. Officer Johnson sped to the scene, along with other local policemen, and in minutes they had arrested Bobby. He was with a teenage boy who had the .38-caliber revolver in his waistband. The teenager said he was Scott Mayo and had been hitchhiking when Bobby picked him up near the Oregon border with California.

Before the officers even wondered where Tracey was, Bobby blurted out that Tracey was at the Pepperwood Motel, a few blocks away. Mayo conveniently had the room key in his pocket. It was almost as if Bobby wanted to be caught, or perhaps was convinced that the police could not make a case against him and Tracey.

Johnson and two other Willits officers went to the door of Tracey's room, with still others stationed out back just in case. They knocked, but Tracey was asleep, so they let themselves in and found Tracey on the bed. He surrendered without a fight. In the motel room the police found Sandra's stolen jewelry and the $600 in cash. They also found a long black raincoat that Bobby had worn during the attack in Salem. It had large splotches of blood on it, which later testing showed belonged to Fijalka. The police had all the evidence they needed. It had been just a little over twenty-four hours since Bobby and Tracey terrified Fijalka and Jackson at their home in Salem.

Bobby and Tracey were both indicted on eleven charges, including burglary, robbery, kidnapping, assault, automobile theft and being a felon in possession of a gun. Tracey was given an additional charge of sodomy, meaning deviate sexual intercourse under Oregon law. A conviction on the sodomy charge would make Tracey a sexual offender, according to Oregon law, and require him to register as a sex offender when he was eventually released from prison. The kidnapping charge carried the longest penalty, which might seem odd because Bobby and Tracey had never abducted Fijalka and Jackson and taken them out of their house. But it reflected Oregon law at the time.

At the opening of their trial in Salem that November, Tracey told his lawyer, Steven Krasik, to make a motion. "Mr. Bogle asks that we have only Christian jurors on the jury panel, though I've told him that can't be done under the Oregon constitution," Krasik told the judge, Jamese Rhoades. While in jail awaiting trial, Tracey had begun reading the Bible and had developed an interest in religion.

The brothers were enjoying their day in court. "Mr. Bogle also wants psychiatric evaluations of all the witnesses and drug tests of the victims to show they are drug dependent," Krasik said to Judge Rhoades.

"And Tracey wants Judge Rhoades to recuse herself since she was a former prosecutor," Krasik told the judge.

Finally, Krasik said, "Tracey feels there is a biblical proscription against females sitting in judgment on males, probably, I guess, First Timothy." He was referring to 1 Timothy 2:11, "But I suffer not a woman to teach, nor to usurp authority over man, but to be in silence." Tracey and Bobby were sitting in their seats at the defense table laughing loudly. Even being in court, with all these charges, their situation still didn't seem serious to them, perhaps a carryover from their childhood outings with their father and mother.

Judge Rhoades promptly denied all of Tracey's motions, without explanation.

The trial then moved smoothly and swiftly, from the prosecution's point of view. There were no defense witnesses of consequence, and the only argument was about the meaning of Oregon's law on kidnapping. Judge Rhoades quickly ruled that secretly confining someone in their own house constituted kidnapping.

At the end of the trial, after Bobby and Tracey were found guilty on all counts but before sentencing, Tim Bogle asked to make a statement to Judge Rhoades on behalf of his half brothers. "I told her that none of this would have happened if these two brothers didn't get together. In our family, it's always been about who is the baddest, who is the meanest. Tracey wanted to show he's worthy, that he is as bad as his older brother."

This was the terrible dynamic of the cycles of family crime.

Tracey was sentenced to sixteen years in prison, Bobby to thirty. Bobby got the longer sentence because he already had eight previous felony convictions as an adult and had been out of prison only five days when this crime took place. For Tracey, it was his first conviction as an adult. He was also now a certified sex offender.

[6]

Kathy

"Trailer Trash"

It was Mother's Day 2006, a bright, sunny day in Salem after the long rains that mark western Oregon's winters, but Kathy Bogle, now mother of eight grown children, was sad and lonely. None of her children could visit her, and she could not go see them. Her six sons were all in prison or jail. Her two daughters were living semi-clandestine lives, off the grid, doing drugs and hiding from bill collectors and the law.

Kathy could not visit her sons behind bars because she had become a felon. In 2002, her youngest child, Matthew Austin, had been arrested for burglary and drug possession but had fled. Kathy was hiding him in her house in Klamath Falls, a small rural city of twenty thousand people set in the mountains of southern Oregon. When the police found him there, she was charged and then convicted for hindering prosecution and custodial interference. Matthew was not a Bogle. His father was Dick Austin, a leader of the Gypsy Jokers Motorcycle Club in the Tri Cities area of southeastern Washington. Dick Austin had fourteen convictions over the previous decade for assault, domestic violence, drunk driving and speeding, according to his Washington State Department of Corrections file.

At her trial, Kathy received a sentence of probation, but she would be on probation for five years and, under Oregon law, had to pay her own supervision fee of thirty-five dollars a month. Kathy, however, regarded bills as mere annoyances and never paid them, so by the summer of 2006 she owed the Klamath County Probation Department $1,475. By then she had moved back to Salem, without receiving permission from her probation officer. A deputy sheriff from Klamath Falls made the five-hour drive north to collect the overdue bill. Kathy had no money, but she did have an old Bank of America checkbook from when she was still married to Rooster. She wrote out a check for the full amount to the deputy sheriff. Of course, the account had long been closed. It didn't take long for the sheriff's department to detect the fraud and file another criminal charge against Kathy. "Kathy was not a master criminal," said Perrin Damon, a spokeswoman at the time for the Oregon Department of Corrections.

Two probation officers from Salem were then called in to Kathy's small garden apartment in Salem to conduct a full investigation. They found marijuana and field-tested her for drugs. She was dirty for both marijuana and meth, Damon said. These were further violations of Kathy's probation.

But the authorities didn't really want to add to Kathy's sentence and cost the taxpayers more money. She was sixty years old, and her sentence was about to expire. "She is a chronic drug user, but she isn't going to do anyone else any harm," Damon reasoned. The probation department took away Kathy's rent-subsidized apartment, paid for by the county because she was partially disabled. This left Kathy to find a low-cost trailer in a trailer park in a run-down section of Salem next door to some other drug users. "This was not a good situation," Damon said. "I didn't like it. But honestly, what can you do? Kathy doesn't want to change. And we have bigger fish to fry." This is a dilemma the criminal justice system faces thousands of times a day, a troubling calculus of weighing whether to let chronic, low-level offenders essentially go free instead of locking them up. With each step Kathy took, she was sliding further down the socioeconomic pole, descending to depths from which it was hard to escape.

Kathy's appearance alone bore testimony to the toll of her way of life and its endless defeats and disappointments. She had ballooned to 170 pounds, according to the Marion County jail records. Her face had been transformed from that of a pretty little girl to an aged and angry woman, with puffy skin, a bulbous nose and green eyes almost hidden by the fatty folds of her cheeks. Her hair had turned gray and was unkempt. Her teeth were rotting from all the meth she had smoked. When I visited her that Mother's Day in 2006, she said, "I am recuperating from a long life."

She had unsuccessfully tried to visit her three sons who were in prison around Salem: Bobby and Tracey at the Oregon State Penitentiary and Matthew, the youngest, at Coffee Creek, a facility where newly admitted inmates were processed a few miles north on Interstate 5. She received more probation violations for trying to visit them.

Tony, the oldest son, was in prison in Arizona for life. Glen, who was on parole from prison in California, had tried to come visit his mother, but by leaving California without permission from his parole officer he violated his parole and was arrested in Salem and put in the Marion County jail. By coincidence, Michael, the other son, was there because when he last returned to Oregon he'd failed to register as a sex offender. By the end of Mother's Day, Kathy would be there as well, for all those probation violations. So Kathy got to spend Mother's Day night in the same building as her two sons Glen and Michael, though she just could not see or talk to them.

"This is an old story in the Bogle family," said Tim Bogle, Rooster's youngest son, by Linda. "Kathy is locked up, and every one of her sons is too."

Prison was a family affair for Kathy on her own side of the family as well, the Curtis family from Amarillo. Her older sister, Bert, got married to her first husband in the Walla Walla State Prison in Washington while he was incarcerated there, and she herself was later arrested and sent to prison in Nebraska for selling money orders that he had stolen. While in a women's prison in Nebraska, Bert was locked up with Caril Fugate, the fourteen-year-old girlfriend of Charles Starkweather, a teenager who achieved national notoriety for murdering eleven people in a killing spree in December 1957 and January 1958 in Nebraska and Wyoming. Kathy's younger sister, Lana, lived in Kaufman County, Texas, east of Dallas, where Clyde Barrow broke his girlfriend, Bonnie Parker, out of jail in 1932. Lana became a local celebrity too, in 1990, when she slashed her boyfriend with a butcher knife after they stopped at a gas station and she sent him in to buy them beer. "When he came out with the wrong kind, she reached into her pickup and grabbed her knife," said Deputy Kenneth Garvin, of the Kaufman County sheriff's office. "She had a real quick temper." Lana was convicted of aggravated assault and sentenced to four years in state prison. Both of Kathy's brothers also were sent to jail, in their cases for selling cocaine and meth.

But the member of Kathy's side of the family who got in the most trouble was a nephew, Corey Lee Wilson, the son of her sister, Lana. At the time Corey was born, according to Bert, his mother often left him alone in his crib, "throwing bottles of milk in there for him to feed himself." As a result, Corey became "attached to food, and later was so addicted to it as a way to comfort himself that he would pull himself up in his crib and eat a whole pumpkin pie, gorging himself," Bert recalled. In school, the only thing that interested Corey was football, because he was big and very heavy, but his grades were so poor the authorities declared him academically ineligible for school football. There were early signs of worse things to come, like one day in junior high school when Corey threatened to throw a girl student to the ground and rape her, Bert remembered.

In July 1990, when Corey was seventeen, he and a friend, Dan O'Rourke, burglarized a large brick house in the small community of Peeltown, kidnapping a forty-year-old woman named Sandra Jackson and driving her in her Buick across rural ranch roads to a corral in a pasture where they made her get out and kneel down. O'Rourke then put a gag in her mouth and tied her hands with cord before shooting her twice in the head with a .25-caliber handgun and shoving her body in the trunk of her car, according to later testimony in the trial of the two men for murder in 1991. They were turned in by Lana, who, as it happened, often acted as an informant for the local sheriff in exchange for not being arrested when she was caught selling drugs. O'Rourke received a life sentence for murder. Corey was given thirty years to life in prison just on the charge of burglary; he was released in 2015 after serving twenty-four years.

Bert had gone straight after her own stint in prison in Nebraska and often wondered why so many members of both the Bogle and Curtis families kept repeating the same mistakes and crimes. "When you get right down to it, they must like it," Bert said. "You have a choice. If you didn't like it, you wouldn't be doing it."

But there was another factor at work, Bert had come to realize over the years watching her own family and the Bogles. "It's the way we were raised. We imitated what we saw our families doing. So it was all we knew to do, and therefore it was the easy thing to do. We didn't have the skills or education to make other choices or get a job."

For Kathy, living this way had never had severe or painful consequences. But after years of hard drinking and heavy drug use, not to mention the physical and sexual abuse by Rooster, Kathy was having more and more trouble managing her everyday life. Each morning waking up was like living in a thick fog. She now had to wear false teeth because of the ravages of meth, and one day her son Michael stole her dentures. Her dog chewed up another pair. "Some days I just forget where they were," Kathy said. "I'd put them in my lap and get up, and unless I heard them fall, they'd just drop to the ground or the floor in the car and get lost." Kathy roared with laughter at these memories. She had been wearing false teeth for two years and had broken or lost so many pairs that she was now trying to glue some back together.

By 2008, with Kathy living in the small trailer, she had seemingly lost almost everything in her life. The probation department had already taken away her rent-subsidized apartment. Her trailer was too small for her furniture and clothes, so she had thrown many of her possessions away. Because of all the probation violations, she lost her Social Security payments as Rooster's former wife, her only legitimate source of income. "For Kathy there is no need to plan," said Linda, who stayed close to her, despite, or because of, all their years together with Rooster. "She has no real house, no furniture and no income, so everything is spur of the moment. She is living on the edge. And the funny thing is, it fits Kathy because she never grew up," Linda said. "She's real trailer trash."

It hardly seemed possible, but in August 2008 things got worse. Kathy's daughter with Rooster, Vickey, and granddaughter Robin, and great-granddaughter, Divinity, were arrested at Kathy's trailer home in Salem for possession of meth. Vickey, Robin and Divinity had been living out of Vickey's old Subaru and panhandling at rest stops on Interstate 5 between Salem and Eugene, fifty miles to the south at the bottom of the Willamette Valley. Vickey, who was forty years old, looked like Kathy had when she was younger—very short, very thin, her face still childlike. Vickey often wore a short blue denim jumper over a pink low-cut T-shirt with a Playboy Bunny symbol. She spoke in a little girl's voice, but in staccato fashion, like rapid bursts of machine-gun fire, so she seemed sweet and manic at the same time, perhaps a consequence of too much meth. Like most of the women in her family, Vickey had numerous arrests, but they were all for petty crime, like shoplifting at a Walmart, or drug possession or speeding. She never got more than a few days in jail.

But when Vickey and Robin were arrested in Kathy's trailer that August, it meant another probation violation for Kathy—who was not allowed to have drugs at her residence. She was taken to the Marion County Probation Department, where she started shouting at her probation agent, Linda Wilson. "They said they found drugs in my place, but they didn't find anything on me or in my place," Kathy was screaming. Instead, she said, it was really the trailer of her daughter's boyfriend, which made no sense to the probation agent. "It was all a dirty trick on me," Kathy shouted. "I'm not a drug addict. I'm a respectable woman."

Kathy's probation was revoked, and she was sentenced to spend eighteen days in jail. When she heard the verdict, Kathy said, "I say, you want to put me in jail, fine. It's rent-free." They were words that Kathy would regret.

Kathy's booking into the Klamath County jail was noted with concern by an unlikely person, a case manager for the Oregon Home Healthcare Provider organization, the state's Medicaid agency. The case manager immediately contacted the jail "to ensure that she was receiving proper medical assistance." Unbeknownst to most members of Kathy's family and people she dealt with regularly, Kathy had claimed for more than two years that she was completely disabled, suffering from arthritis, diabetes and cancer, and was unable "to drive, dress, bathe, cook and walk without assistance." Kathy had applied for Medicaid, and the Oregon Home Healthcare Provider program had been giving her $2,500 a month. When the solicitous case manager called the jail, she was surprised to learn that Kathy was housed in "general population," with the other inmates, able to walk, bathe and eat without assistance. The health-care worker therefore contacted the Oregon Department of Justice's Medicaid Fraud Unit, which opened an investigation and began videotaping Kathy's daily activities. Kathy was only the latest grifter in the extended Bogle family.

When she was released from the jail and returned to Salem, she was driven by Linda. The Medicaid Fraud Unit was following both women. Investigators filmed Kathy driving herself around Salem, going shopping at a local Safeway supermarket and picking up prescriptions at a pharmacy. They also filmed Kathy meeting Linda after Linda had picked up Kathy's monthly Medicaid vouchers from the Oregon Home Healthcare Provider's office. The vouchers were made out to Linda, who was splitting the money with Kathy.

In September 2008 both women were indicted by the Marion County Grand Jury, Kathy on twelve counts of making a false claim for health-care payments—that is, Medicaid fraud—and eight counts of theft. Both offenses were felonies. Kathy faced up to one hundred years in prison given her prior criminal record. Linda was charged with five counts of theft.

"It was an idea we both came up with," Linda said later. "We had a friend who was ill, and on Medicaid, and got help that Medicaid paid for, so it seemed like a natural thing to do." Linda did perform significant chores for Kathy, doing much of her shopping and often driving her around because she was both morbidly obese and enfeebled.

After being caught, Linda quickly pleaded guilty on October 16, 2008. She was ordered to perform 480 hours of community service and to be jointly responsible with Kathy for repaying the $60,000 in Medicaid funds they had stolen, and she was placed on five years of probation.

Kathy took the opposite approach. "I'm not guilty; I didn't do anything wrong," she told everyone she talked to, including her court-appointed lawyer, Brooke Holstedt, as well as the Oregon assistant attorney general who prosecuted Medicaid fraud, Rod Hopkinson, and finally Judge Norblad, who found yet another Bogle on his court docket. Linda thought Kathy was in denial or perhaps just running another scam. "She's scammed people her whole life," Linda said. "It's her default response to everything. She thinks she can just pretend her way out."

Kathy's attorney, the state prosecutor and Judge Norblad spent almost a year trying to talk Kathy into taking the least onerous punishment—admit her guilt and accept a plea bargain of one year in jail. If not, the judge and prosecutor told her, she would have to go on trial, with no real defense, and face a sentence of at least five years in state prison, and as much as one hundred years.

Kathy's behavior became increasingly erratic. Some days she failed to show up for court dates to discuss the plea bargain, risking a contempt-of-court citation. She repeatedly demanded that Norblad fire her attorney, whom she said was incompetent. The judge denied her requests and said her lawyer was doing a very good job, under the circumstances.

Finally, after months of chaos, Kathy's lawyer began driving to her house early in the morning to pick her up and personally bring her to court. In August 2009, Kathy signed a plea agreement. The next morning, though, Kathy called Norblad's office to say, "I'm not coming to court today. I'm not guilty. I'm going to change my plea. God has spoken to me." A few minutes later, Kathy was suddenly less sure of herself. "I feel like a pinball," she said. "I think I've lost my mind."

Linda thought the real problem was that Kathy was afraid of going to jail for a year because she would lose her access to marijuana. Kathy's landlady at the time, Jeannie Kelley, was a thoughtful psychologist who worked in a local hospice counseling the terminally ill and was sympathetic to Kathy, recognizing that she had serious emotional issues. "I think she has done so many drugs she has burned her brain," Kelley said. "She can no longer put things together."

On a Friday in late August, Kathy's lawyer called her to report that Judge Norblad had run out of patience and was going to issue a warrant compelling her to appear the next week to stand trial. Kelley said, "Maybe this is for the best. Kathy will be incarcerated and protected from herself, like someone with a mental illness. She is a danger to herself."

Besides, Kelley said, "Kathy has told me she likes prison because they have television and she says her whole world now is watching television."

Finally, on September 28, 2009, Kathy agreed to plead guilty, surprising both Judge Norblad and her own lawyer. When Kathy arrived at the boxy white marble courthouse in Salem's business district, a few blocks from the Willamette River, she was wearing a loose black velour blouse and even looser black velvet pants with a maroon pattern. Her hair was cut short on top and on the sides, but long in the back, like a hockey player's mullet. She had dyed her graying hair a dark red. Her mouth was turned down in a scowl, and the devastations of her life showed as anger in her eyes. When a camera crew for KATU, the Portland affiliate of ABC-TV, began to film her in the courtroom, she jammed a finger at the camera. "I am not guilty," she said. "You are very evil, very ugly. Get out of here."

Judge Norblad cut her off. "They have permission to be here. Your request is denied."

Norblad then explained the plea bargain for Kathy. "It is a gift," he said, considering what she had done and what her record was. Instead of the total of twenty counts of Medicaid fraud and theft, the judge was permitting her to plead guilty to only six counts. Hence the penalty would be only one year in county jail. The judge told Kathy that she would be jointly responsible with Linda to repay the $60,000 in Medicaid funds they had stolen.

Kathy mumbled her acceptance of these terms. But after Judge Norblad banged his gavel, she said to him and the prosecutor in a barely audible voice, "I'm not guilty. I didn't do nothing wrong."

At that point, the court officers moved to put their arms around Kathy to lead her to a van that was waiting to take her to the county jail. Kathy announced, "I have to go home to get my things and my dog." Watching from the front row of the spectator seats, Linda said, "Kathy is still in denial, as if nothing could touch her."

After Kathy was escorted out, Judge Norblad said, "The people in the Bogle family seem to be infectious; their ethical and moral code permeates the whole family like a contagion." Kathy, of course, was not a violent criminal who committed assaults, armed robbery or murder. But her brand of low-grade lawbreaking—drug possession, hiding a son from the sheriff, probation violations—still got herself and her family members locked up.

By his back-of-the-envelope calculation, Norblad said, Kathy Bogle alone had cost the taxpayers of Oregon "close to a quarter of a million dollars," and that was only in direct court, police, jail and Medicaid costs. It did not include the much greater cost for the damage caused by Kathy and Rooster's children and grandchildren.

Linda Bogle has worked at various jobs and has paid back $20,000 of the $60,000 that the two women took in fraudulent Medicaid payments. After Kathy was released, she absconded from parole, living at first in Montana with her daughters and then in Arizona with her sister. She has paid nothing back. The Oregon authorities have given up looking for her. A spokesman for the Oregon Department of Revenue, Derrick Gasperini, said it is virtually impossible to collect from people like Kathy who have no salary to garnish, no bank account to draw on and no property to attach. This kind of delinquency has become a major problem for many states, he said. In Oregon alone the amount of unpaid money from criminal fines and restitutions now amounts to $2 billion. Kathy had figured out how to make crime pay, the ultimate con.

[7]

Tracey

A Fateful Compulsion

A t precisely 8:00 a.m. on August 10, 2009, a solitary figure
emerged from the front gate of the sprawling Oregon State
Correctional Institution. The man looked small set against the
immensity of the yellow-painted prison complex, sheathed by
coils of gleaming razor wire. It was Tracey Bogle. He had just finished serving his full sixteen-year sentence for the attack on Dave
Fijalka and Sandra Jackson, and he was carrying a large plastic
trash bag that held all his worldly possessions: a well-thumbed
Bible, a few other books, his copious legal file and a change of
clothes. Tracey was wearing black slacks and a dark collared shirt
that had been donated to him by two volunteers from the Seventh Day Adventist Church. They had also given him $25, the only
money he had.

No members of Tracey's family were waiting to meet him.
His brothers were all in prison themselves. His two sisters were
leading vagabond lives, doing drugs and panhandling where they
could. His mother, Kathy, was about to go on trial and then go to

jail too. So Tracey had asked me—knowing that I was working on a book about the Bogle family—if I would pick him up. He needed a ride to the halfway house for newly released sex offenders where he would be required to live by state law, and he needed to be driven to meet his new parole officer and to a state office to get his allowance of food stamps so he could buy food. He also had to report to the Oregon State Police office to register as a sex offender.

At first I was reluctant. As a correspondent for *The New York Times* for thirty-six years, I had followed the paper's strict code of not becoming personally involved with a source to get a story. But Tracey had no one else to turn to, and I knew from reporting on criminal justice for the past fifteen years that the odds of a newly released inmate making a successful transition back to life outside prison were bleak. In fact, a comprehensive national survey of state prison inmates by the Bureau of Justice Statistics found that two-thirds of the 600,000 inmates released every year are rearrested within three years, and three-quarters of all inmates are rearrested within five years. Our prisons have become a giant, expensive recycling machine that feeds on itself. Repeated findings by criminologists about this high level of failure had led one leading sociologist, Robert Martinson, to conclude, "With few and isolated exceptions, the rehabilitation efforts that have been reported so far have had no appreciable effect on recidivism."

Martinson's conclusion was so damning that it soon became known as the "nothing works" doctrine in trying to rehabilitate inmates. Later research by other criminologists questioned Martinson's findings, but the "nothing works" notion helped lay the groundwork for America's great social experiment with mass incarceration in the 1970s, 1980s and 1990s as the way to solve our crime problem. So I thought that picking Tracey up on his release from prison and following him around for a week or two might give me an insight into why so few convicts were able to make a successful reentry into civilian life.

By this time I had observed the Bogles long enough to know that much of their criminal behavior was already baked in during their childhood upbringing, long before they spent years in various prisons. Nonetheless, Tracey had been in prison for sixteen years, and counting the earlier years he spent in juvenile institutions in Oregon, Washington, Idaho and Nevada, he had been locked up almost full-time since he was fifteen. He had, literally, come of age in prison, and not only his family members but most of his friends were inmates. Tracey was only one tiny digit in the explosion of our prison population. We now have 2.3 million people in prison and jail, and Americans spend an estimated $179 billion a year on prisons, police forces and our court system. That is more than the entire annual budget of any of the individual fifty states, including the largest and most expensive: California, New York, Texas and Florida.

Keeping that many convicts off the street certainly averts a large number of crimes. But is the experience of being confined in prison for long periods of time achieving anything else, causing any productive change in inmates' behavior? Or is there something in the convicts themselves so ingrained that prison cannot change them or make them less likely to commit more crime? I was looking for clues from Tracey.

Tracey had done what he was required to do under Oregon prison regulations to be rehabilitated. He had gone through mandated alcohol and drug treatment classes. He had passed his GED test, earning a high school equivalency degree though he had not gone beyond the seventh grade in school. He had taken the little vocational instruction that was offered, learning to be a janitor. He had also become, outwardly at least, a passionate and vocal Christian, reading the Bible every day and quoting scripture to other inmates when they kidded him about whether his newfound faith was real. Tracey had even applied to Chemeketa Community College in Salem, receiving what he said was a formal acceptance. On closer inspection it was only a form directing him to take reading and math placement tests when he got out before he could be admitted. This was the first of many stories Tracey passed off as true. Convicts live such constrained lives that they learn to manipulate rules and people as a way to get what they want. It is called being institutionalized.

Despite some seeming progress, there was one troubling issue about Tracey. During his incarceration from 1990 to 2006, he had exhibited symptoms of severe mental illness. His problems first showed up in 1996, when he started telling other inmates and his guards that he was hearing angry voices and seeing demons and angels. Sometimes, with his Bible in hand, Tracey announced to other inmates that he was an angel of God. Other times, if Tracey suspected a fellow inmate was staring at him, Tracey became paranoid and would beat the other man up. Although Tracey, like his brothers, was short, only five feet nine inches tall, he had bulked up from 170 pounds to 240 pounds through a relentless weight-lifting regimen and was a mean fighter. When Tracey assaulted another inmate, he was put in the hole, or solitary confinement. After several of these episodes, Tracey was sent to the mental health staff for diagnosis. But most of the counselors either dismissed Tracey as a faker or gave him a diagnosis of antisocial personality disorder. It was the default diagnosis for troublesome inmates, and it was a hard label to shed, because it was a mental condition rather than a mental illness, and there was no cure. In fact, it was not really a diagnosis at all but more of a checklist describing the behavior of inmates the staff did not like: they were manipulative, prone to violence and lacked any regard for others.

Then, in 1997, Tracey saw a new counselor in the Counseling and Treatment Services division of the Oregon Department of Corrections, Ann Heath, a licensed clinical social worker. She was a tall woman in her early sixties with short blond hair and blue eyes that seemed to perpetually smile. After meeting Tracey, she made a quick and important discovery: the other counselors had not spent much time actually listening to Tracey, because they didn't like him. "It was a rare commodity for Tracey to have any-one listen to him for forty-five minutes," Heath said, the length of time for a mental health appointment in prison. "It was rare for anyone to listen to him at any time in his life. He didn't really have a home. His father beat him and was drunk all the time. None of his teachers at school listened to him. No one at MacLaren," the reform school where he had been sent. But Heath did listen to him. "I think he liked me because I actually listened to him. I became a parent figure.

"Tracey was very delusional, and I thought he was really sick," Heath found. "He believed he was on a mission from God, and he could see and hear demons and monsters attacking him. Tracey was always bringing me a Bible and he was rewriting it. His mission was to change the world. I got the sense he had been very abused at home but didn't want to talk about it."

Heath wrote in a report dated January 15, 1997, that Tracey was suffering from paranoid schizophrenia. This was a serious diagnosis of a real mental illness and went much further than the other counselors had gone. "Tracey was clearly psychotic, and his delusions were very fixed," she recalled. "A lot of my work with him was to get him to take his meds," meaning Risperdal, an antipsychotic drug. "He didn't like the way it made him feel," Heath related, "so he tried not to take it. But when he took it, he was able to get along better with people and do his job as a janitor in the main hallway."

After four years of working with Tracey, Heath was pleased when the chief psychiatrist for the Oregon Department of Corrections, Dr. Marvin Fickle, examined Tracey and essentially corroborated her diagnosis by saying Tracey had a "psychotic disorder not otherwise specified." What this meant, Heath said, was that Dr. Fickle found that Tracey was psychotic but believed as a psychiatrist that he did not have enough evidence to conclude whether Tracey was schizophrenic, hearing voices and seeing things, or whether he was bipolar, suffering from alternating bouts of depression and mania, with high energy and rapid speech.

Looking back, Heath now thinks Tracey may have been bipolar, because he was very grandiose, believing he was an angel of God, and because he often talked very fast for long periods. In truth, she said, it can be difficult to distinguish between schizophrenia and bipolar disorder. Until the 1990s, Heath said, "American psychiatrists tended to say anyone with psychosis had schizophrenia."

Whatever the correct diagnosis, Heath's weekly sessions with Tracey and getting him to stay on his meds gradually eliminated his visions, and the voices subsided. It was a rare outcome, Heath said, because "usually these disorders last a lifetime. They don't just go away."

Heath did not know that Tracey's oldest brother, Tony, had been diagnosed with schizophrenia, or that his half brother, Tim, and half sister, Debbie, had both been diagnosed with bipolar disorder. If she had known all this, Heath said, she might have concluded that mental illness was being passed on in the Bogle family, because bipolar disorder has been found to be highly heritable.

When I picked up Tracey at the front gate of the Oregon State Correctional Institution on his release, he was smiling broadly. "I want to do good, but I get the jitters," he said to begin our conversation. "I don't remember what freedom feels like. It feels like I'm on Mars. I can't believe I'm not in prison."

Tracey had heard about all the things he now had to do and about all the restrictions he faced both because he was on parole and because he was a sex offender, even though Tracey still vehemently insisted that what he had done was not sodomy. The restrictions started with the place he had to live, until he proved he was capable of staying out of trouble. It was a halfway house approved by the Department of Corrections for newly released sex offenders called Stepping Out Ministries, and by coincidence it was run by one of Tracey's cousins, Tammie Bogle Silver. Her father, Babe Bogle, was one of Rooster's older brothers. It was a

Christian-based religious program with regular prayer services, a strict curfew and a no-alcohol policy. Unlike prison, which is the ultimate welfare state, where food, housing and medical care are free, Tracey would have to pay $300 a month for a bed, and the residents had to buy and cook their own meals.

On our drive from the prison to check in at his new housing, Tracey spotted a McDonald's in a strip mall and asked to stop so he could get his first Big Mac in sixteen years. Then Tracey saw a Domino's Pizza next door and changed his mind. In prison he had never had the luxury of choice. It was only as we came outside after lunch that Tracey saw there was a children's day-care center on the other side of the Domino's. Tracey had just violated one of the primary terms of his release as a sex offender: he was not allowed to be at a property next door to a school, children's day-care center, park or playground or any place where people under the age of eighteen regularly met. "I wasn't supposed to be there," Tracey said ruefully. "But how can I anticipate all the places I'm not supposed to go?"

When Tracey arrived at the quarters of Stepping Out Ministries, in a hulking former Catholic nuns' home, his cousin Tammie greeted him and assured him his first day out of prison would be the most difficult because the changes are so overwhelming. "Tomorrow when you wake up it will be real different," Tammie said. "You will not hear the doors slam or the guards yelling. But you will have to make your own breakfast."

Because Tracey would be on parole for three years, the next step for him was to meet his parole officer near the Marion County jail. The parole officer spelled out more rules for Tracey. Since Tracey had been drunk when he attacked Dave Fijalka and Sandra Jackson, he could not go to any bar, tavern or liquor store. He could not have any contact with his brother Bobby, with whom he had committed the crime. (Bobby was still incarcerated in the Oregon State Penitentiary.) Tracey was also not to drive a car alone. In addition, he would be subject to a curfew imposed by his parole officer, who could make Tracey wear an electronic ankle bracelet to monitor his movements if Tracey's conduct aroused his suspicion. And because he was a sex offender, Tracey was not supposed to use the Internet without prior approval by his parole officer, to avoid pornography.

After hearing all these terms, Tracey grew tense. "It seems they don't want me to do good," he said. "The parole board is attaching so many conditions that they will make me fail."

The next step was to go to the Oregon Department of Human Services to pick up Tracey's food stamps. They came in the form of an "Oregon Trail" debit card emblazoned with a picture of a covered wagon. It was loaded with $200 a month, the allotment for a newly released inmate. The state's assumption was that within the first month out Tracey would find a job and thereafter be able to pay for his own groceries, so after that first month his food stamps would be terminated.

The following day Tracey had to go to the Oregon State Police office in Salem to register as a sex offender. A female clerk took his photograph and advised Tracey that he would have to reregister every year within ten days of his birthday, and any time he moved, or he would be in violation of his parole. This condition would last for the rest of his life.

Tracey was becoming agitated with all these terms. He was clenching his jaw and fists, and his speech sped up. "Anyone who has sex with his wife is a sex offender," Tracey said to the female clerk, who ignored his outburst. "You are all hypocrites, labeling me as a sex offender. These were people I knew who stole a business from me. They were not innocent. You've got this all wrong. I am not a sexual predator. I shouldn't have to register. I am going to a judge to get my convictions reversed," Tracey said with confidence. He was thinking of Judge Norblad, the Bogle family's own judge, as they had come to see him.

Back at Stepping Out Ministries, Tracey told his day's story to another resident who had been in prison with Tracey and was also a sex offender. "You need to slow down, brother," the other resident said. "You don't want to dwell in the past and carry all that anger. Good luck with trying to fight being registered as a sex offender. You need to get on with the rest of your life."

On his third day out, Tammie told Tracey he needed to start looking for a job, and she gave him a list of possibilities. He could cook at a senior center; he could work in a woodworking shop; he could get a maintenance job; he could work as a porter in a property management company; or he could be a stocking clerk at one of the Plaid Pantry chain of convenience stores in Salem. "Your main job now is to get a job," Tammie said. "You need to start earning money to pay for your rent and your food. The important thing is to get on a set schedule."

This was not the message Tracey wanted to hear, and none of the job choices were glamorous or promised good pay or career opportunities, in Tracey's mind. At least in prison, Tracey said, housing and food were free and you didn't have to worry about finding a job. Tammie had told him that he needed to fill out four job applications that day. Tracey filled out only one, for a job at the convenience store.

That evening, after returning to Stepping Out, Tracey said he had a plan for where he wanted to live. He would buy twenty acres of land and build his dream house there, a house big enough to accommodate all his brothers and sisters, the whole Bogle clan. It would be built in what Tracey termed "Mexican colonial" style, with five bedrooms and a guest house. There would be fields planted with corn, a vegetable garden, an orchard with apple, pear and cherry trees, a pond stocked with goldfish and a stream with trout that ran down a hill. "The house and fields and fish would be a refuge for my entire family, who are vagabonds," Tracey said. He announced with confidence that he would design and build the house himself. "I am very good in construction."

Tracey's dream house was grandiose, reflecting the kind of grandiosity that Ann Heath had observed in Tracey while he was in prison. Tracey now took this grandiosity a step further. He said he had a lot of experience as a lawyer, working on appeals of his case while incarcerated. "I am now going to represent myself to get this sodomy conviction overturned and get the governor of Arizona to pardon my brother Tony." Tony was serving a life sentence for a murder he committed in Arizona, and there was no chance for a pardon.

If he didn't get his sodomy conviction overturned, Tracey said, he would get a gun and go after the judge who sentenced him.

"Someone needs to send these people a message," Tracey said, meaning the judges, district attorneys and lawyers who put him and his brothers in prison.

Another of the residents at Stepping Out overheard Tracey's comments and passed them on to Tammie, and she said, "That thing about getting a gun is a real red flag. The early signs from Tracey are bad."

Based on her experience with thousands of released inmates, and members of her own family, Tammie said that "Tracey is stunted emotionally. He seems like a child because he's stuck at the age he went in," fifteen, when he was first sent to MacLaren. "He will have trouble learning because he doesn't trust other people; convicts don't even trust themselves," Tammie said.

"Tracey's grandiosity in part is to compensate for his lack of self-confidence, like many convicts," Tammie explained. "He will need to stay here at Stepping Out for at least a year to catch up emotionally. He needs to avoid a relationship with a woman till then too. But the first thing a newly released inmate wants is a woman. Tracey is still reading his Bible a lot," she added. "But what is missing is the change of heart, his personal relationship with God. He is so full of anger that this is setting him up for failure."

On Tracey's fifth day out, he went to Chemeketa Community College in Salem to take his required placement tests, in reading, writing and math. When I picked him up after he finished the tests, Tracey was giddy. "They were very easy. I did really well. I passed them all." This was another flash of Tracey's grandiosity, or bloated self-confidence to compensate for his spotty education. In fact, he had flunked one of the tests and had to retake it.

"You should have seen the girls; they were really looking at me," Tracey said. "I think they wanted me." It was true that Tracey cut an unusual figure on campus. He was at least ten years older than most of the students, and he was wearing black shorts and a tight black T-shirt designed to highlight his muscular biceps and his manifold tattoos.

Tracey found out from college guidance counselors that he would be eligible for federal student loans under the Stafford and Perkins programs. Each loan paid up to $5,500 a year, a total of $11,000 annually. This was like learning you had just won the lottery to Tracey. "Can you believe it?" he said to me. "They will pay me to go to college." Tracey had found what he thought was his dream job. He could go to college and get paid a princely sum to do it. Tracey did not seem to realize that these were loans, not grants, and that legally he would be required to repay them.

Confident that he now had a real paying job, Tracey dipped into his savings from prison, $1,700 he had earned as a janitor over his sixteen years of incarceration. He had entrusted it to his legal-aid lawyer for safekeeping. Tracey bought a new watch, new gray pants for going to class, a green parka for the winter and his first cell phone. He also bought a car, for $900, a ten-year-old Dodge Neon that had been rebuilt by another ex-con Tracey knew, who had turned it into a drag-racing car. Tracey had neither a driver's license nor insurance, so he used his mother Kathy's expired license and her canceled insurance for the purchase. In buying the car, Tracey would be violating both his parole, which prohibited him from driving alone, and the rules of Stepping Out Ministries, which forbade its residents from having a car. Tracey was showing his old convict side: impulsive, manipulative and with a penchant for rule-breaking. When faced with a choice, Tracey seemed to have a compulsion to take the easy way out and make the wrong decision.

Watching Tracey's actions since his release, Tammie recognized something else. Inside prison Tracey had a well-established identity. In the outside world he had none. So he was moving quickly to build a new identity. He was a new man with a cell phone, car, good clothes and what he regarded as a well-paying job going to college. Tammie saw buying the car as another step toward failure. "He should be focusing everything on finding a real job and then going to college," she said.

On September 28, less than two months after getting out of prison, Tracey began classes at Chemeketa. There was one sign of coming trouble. Since Tracey's parole officer still believed Tracey was a danger, he had ordered him to start wearing a heavy electronic ankle bracelet, even when he was in class with all those attractive young women students. The ankle bracelet annoyed Tracey.

Tracey had soon obtained his first actual job, as a framer for a construction contractor who had volunteered as a pastor while Tracey was in prison. Tracey was framing doors in new houses for $10 an hour, forty hours a week. In Tracey's mind that worked out to earnings of $400 a week. When he got his first paycheck, though, it was only $100. The rest had been withheld for state and federal taxes, for Social Security and for Medicaid. "The government is robbing me," Tracey said. The everyday civilian world was an alien place for inmates accustomed to free housing, food and medical care and no taxes.

Tracey was becoming frustrated with the price of living at Stepping Out Ministries, even though it was only $300 a month and included some free food like cereal, milk and juice for breakfast. "I have to pay for everything now, housing, food, gas," Tracey said. Tracey also had to pay for a mandatory sexual-predator class. It all seemed unfair.

Tracey claimed he earned honors grades that first fall semester at Chemeketa, maintaining a B average. He took psychology, advanced writing and public speaking. Tracey wanted to give a talk in the latter class about Martin Luther, one of his religious heroes, but the instructor suggested he talk about being a convict. "The kids thought I was really cool and wanted to know more about me," Tracey reported with pride after his talk. In psychology there was discussion about how behavior gets learned in families, and Tracey wondered how that applied in his own family. "Is being a criminal something that you learn from your family as you grow up?" he mused. "Is it a kind of preconditioning? Or is it something genetic?"

On the whole, though, Tracey was concluding, "It's kind of boring out here." He was not allowed to buy liquor or go to a bar, because of the role alcohol had played in his crime. He couldn't go to the mall, because there were people there under eighteen and that would be a violation of his sex-offender regulations. Tracey began to think about doing some burglaries, just for the excitement, he said.

Then there was the grind of college, which was not as easy as Tracey had expected. "These kids have been going to school for years, and they know how to do it," he said. Things might be more interesting for him if he had a girlfriend, Tracey said. "But that department has been shut down and is out of business. I am a Christian."

Sometime after Christmas 2009, however, things changed for Tracey. By early February he had moved out of Stepping Out Ministries to a thirty-two-foot dilapidated travel trailer he had bought and had parked in the Salem neighborhood known as Felony Flats. In April, Tracey refused to take his regular mandated lie-detector test and was ordered to report to his parole officer every day.

The explanation for Tracey's change came quickly. He had met a woman during a church service at Stepping Out Ministries, Julie Phillips, and she was now pregnant. Tammie had kicked Tracey out of Stepping Out Ministries because there were minors participating in the church services, putting him in violation of his sex-offender restrictions. Things would become even more complicated when Tracey's new girlfriend gave birth because his sex offender restrictions meant he could not be around his own baby. Tracey's girlfriend was thirty-four years old, a college graduate with a business degree who worked for the Bank of America. And she was the daughter of a preacher, Tracey said.

"I got a girl pregnant, but I don't even like her," Tracey insisted. "I was just excited to have the chance to have a baby. I came very close to never being a father after a lifetime in prison. So this is a big thing for me.

"I don't think I have the capacity for a relationship," he continued. "Something inside me was broken because of all those years in prison. I was too isolated for too long from normal human relationships. I am a broken person.

"I realize now that life on the outside in some ways is harder than life in prison," Tracey said. He felt there were more conditions and demands on him, more restrictions, in the free world than in prison, where he was all too familiar with the strict rituals of incarceration. "All those years of people telling me what I can eat, when I have to eat, and when I have to go to bed, just wore me out," Tracey said. "I have some mental damage. I'm afraid I am a dead person. Julie is really nice, but I don't plan on getting married. I don't want the added responsibility."

A few weeks later Tracey moved his trailer out of Salem to a campground next to the Enchanted Forest amusement park that his brother Bobby had robbed as a kid. The rent was cheaper, Tracey explained, and he would have the freedom of being alone, something he never had in prison.

The prospect of more student loans kept Tracey going. He had long wanted to study veterinary medicine because he loved birds, and Oregon State University in Corvallis, a forty-five-minute drive from his trailer, offered a good veterinary program. Tracey applied, using his grades from Chemeketa, and was accepted for admission that fall.

"People say criminals don't have the brains to go to college," Tracey said. "But it's not true. I got honors grades at Chemeketa with a 3.0 grade-point average." He also was given a fresh round of Stafford and Perkins loans for a year at Oregon State, $10,000, Tracey claimed.

On the surface, things were going well. During the fall of 2010 Tracey was commuting from his trailer to Oregon State and his grades were good, Tracey said. "I've done something that no one in the family has ever done, gone to college. I was shocked. So it's very special to me. I've succeeded. This story has a happy ending. I wanted to break the family curse and I think I've done it."

Tracey had a baby by then, Isaiah, who was born that November. Tracey did not want him to have the Bogle name—that would be continuing the curse. The baby was given his mother's last name.

Under the surface, however, Tim Bogle, Tracey's half brother and closest friend, felt something was going wrong. When Tim visited Tracey's trailer he could tell Tracey was drinking again. This was a parole violation, but to Tim it was much more.

"It was drinking and getting drunk that led Tracey to commit the crime that got him arrested and sent to prison for sixteen years," Tim said. "Alcohol has always been a huge part of Tracey's life. He grew up with a drunk for a father who was drunk almost every day. Now, when I go over to his trailer, Tracey gets very argumentative with me, and when I tell him I see him getting addicted again, he tells me to mind my own business. This is Tracey's own choice, the drinking. It's as if he has a compulsion to make the wrong choice.

"Tracey is only going to college at all because it's his only way to get money, the student loans," Tim added. "He thinks it's free money." Tim began to suspect that Julie, Tracey's girlfriend, was doing the real studying and writing Tracey's papers for him.

Bobby, Tracey's older brother, also started worrying that Tracey was "getting drunk every day like Dad did." Bobby himself was still in prison, but called Tracey regularly to check in with him. "I think he's fixing to go back to prison," Bobby said. "All it takes is one fight or a cop pulling him over on the road when he's been drinking. Those are parole violations."

It finally happened on May 6, 2011. Tracey was drunk and burst into Tim's house in Salem wielding a Sawzall, a cordless electric saw with a five-inch blade that Tracey had earlier borrowed from Tim to work on a small cabin he was building next to his trailer. "Tracey was out of control, and I thought he was going to cut me," Tim said. "He blamed me for some trouble with his girlfriend, and he challenged me to go out to my garage and fight." Tim's wife, Chris, and his younger daughter, Britney, were standing there and were terrified about what might happen. "Tracey said he would whup my ass, and we started to fight, so I dialed 911.

"I hated to be the one who called the laws on Tracey, but he had been drinking and came at me with a weapon," Tim said. After the police arrived and questioned Tim and his wife and daughter, they went to Julie's house. The police witnessed Tracey threatening to rape her brother, and they also discovered his infant son, Isaiah.

"Of everyone in the family, Tracey was my best friend, and we were the same age," Tim said. "Our dad had taught us to fight, so Tracey's idea of solving things was fighting. And our dad taught Tracey to drink. So Tracey got drunk, and when he got mad all he could think of to do was fighting."

Tracey was booked into the Marion County jail in Salem on the evening of May 6, 2011. It was less than two years since he was released from prison after serving his sixteen-year sentence. Tracey was charged with burglary, for breaking into Tim's house, and with assault and assault with a deadly weapon. At his trial, on September 11 that year, Tracey got lucky—he was sentenced to just sixty days in jail, which he had already served, and five years of probation.

Tracey went back to living in his trailer, but he stopped going to Oregon State. Instead, he somehow managed to get a fresh set of federal student loans to enroll at Portland State University, a branch of the University of Oregon, fifty miles to the north in downtown Portland. According to Tim, Tracey also found a new girlfriend in Portland, who helped him with his homework at Portland State.

"Going to college is my job now," Tracey told Tim in March 2013. "I have to go to school to get paid." He was still at Portland State, somehow still getting new federal student loans and not paying interest on them and managing to get passing grades.

In April 2013, when his probation officer asked Tracey to come in for a routine urine-analysis drug test, Tracey refused. A few days later he refused again. It was the kind of reckless behavior that had gotten him into trouble so many times before, acting on a compulsion he could not stop. The police traced the location of his cell phone. He was in Portland at his new girlfriend's house. A team of police, along with several police dogs, went to her house and arrested him, taking him back to the Marion County jail in Salem. Tracey's probation for the burglary at Tim's house was revoked, and Tracey was quickly sentenced to six years in prison for the burglary with a dangerous weapon back in 2011. He was sent to the Snake River Correctional Institution in the high desert of eastern Oregon near the Idaho border. It was as far away from Tracey's home in Salem as you could go and still be in Oregon. He hadn't earned a college degree, and was unlikely to ever pay back all the federal student loans he had received, which totaled $20,000 or more. That would mean the end of any more federal loans.

Tracey's compulsion to make the wrong choice and to engage in lawbreaking behavior raises the question of where that pressure comes from. He himself suggested one explanation—that it was behavior he had learned as a child by imitating his parents and older brothers, social learning. But Tracey also wondered if there was something else at work in him. Perhaps it was genetic.

Some criminologists have long posited that criminals are born, not made, and pointed to some physical characteristics that can identify them. In the sixteenth century an Italian physician, Giambattista della Porta, founded a school of physiognomy that claimed criminals could be identified by facial features and expressions. Della Porta believed a thief, for example, had large lips and keen eyesight, and he argued that human character could be read from physiognomy. In the late nineteenth century another Italian physician, Cesare Lambroso, developed an elaborate school that believed criminals had evolved backward and are a lower form of life, closer to their apelike ancestors, and could be identified by their large jaws and powerful canine teeth. In Lambroso's view, criminals had a wide arm-span, which was greater than their height, another apelike feature. Lambroso worked out these characteristics by examining thousands of skeletons of well-known outlaws and living prisoners. Lambroso's influence lingered on into the twentieth century in the United States with the work of the physical anthropologist Ernest Hooten, who in 1939 published a large study comparing American prisoners with a noncriminal control group. He concluded, "In every population there are hereditary inferiors in mind and in body as well as physical and mental deficients." Hooten called for the segregation of these people of the "criminal stock," and he also advocated, as a proponent of eugenics, that they be sterilized.

These earlier studies have now been discredited as pseudoscience by advances in genetic research. Nazi experiments with eugenics in World War II also made most criminologists reject any genetic interpretations of criminal behavior. And America's history of racism has made virtually all our criminologists skeptical about research that attempts to find a genetic link to crime, preferring to look for its causes in society or the environment. In 1992, the University of Maryland was forced to call off a conference at the last minute titled "Genetic Factors in Crime" after complaints from the Congressional Black Caucus and the NAACP about the racial implications of attempting to link crime to genetics. Because blacks are convicted of crime disproportionately, the critics said, any effort to find genetic explanations for crime might be used to revive discredited theories that blacks are biologically inferior. The conference, which was sponsored by the National Institutes of Health, was canceled after the NIH withdrew its funds because of the criticism.

But in the past two decades, now that the human genome has been sequenced and scientists are studying the genetics of behaviors like alcoholism, some criminologists have cautiously returned to studying how genes might increase the risk of committing a crime and whether such a trait might be inherited. As Siddhartha Mukherjee put it in his best-selling book *The Gene: An Intimate History*, "It is like the return of the native—the emergence of the gene as a major driver for psychological impulses" after so many years of looking for causes outside the individual in society or the environment. Suddenly, using new, more sophisticated studies of identical twins, some raised together and some raised apart, scientists have been able to show that traits like impulsivity and novelty seeking—precursors for criminal behavior—have a genetic basis.

Researchers estimate that more than two hundred studies have now shown genes play a role in crime. But they emphasize that there is no "crime gene." Instead, they are careful to stress that genes play a role only as part of a complex interplay with the environment, which can either intensify or turn off violent impulses.

The most acclaimed findings have been by Terrie E. Moffitt, a professor of psychology and behavioral genetics at Duke University. In a seminal article published in *Science* in 2002, she found that a variant of the MAOA gene (monoamine oxidase A enzyme), which controls the amount of serotonin in the blood, can act as what she calls a clean-up gene on children exposed to maltreatment. Those children with a highly active version of the gene are less likely to become antisocial after exposure to abuse, while those with a lower active variant are more likely to become antisocial, Professor Moffitt said in an interview. Moffitt stressed that it is the social experience of childhood abuse that is the root cause of the behavior and that it is the variant of the gene that may cause the vulnerability to develop antisocial behavior. "It is a complex dance between the social experience and the gene," she said.

Moffitt found these results in a long-term study of a large group of children in New Zealand with her colleague and husband, Avshalom Caspi. Their findings have since been confirmed in a meta-analysis of twenty-seven studies by Amy Byrd of the Department of Psychiatry at the University of Pittsburgh. In a case like the Bogles, Moffitt suggested, the family environment and the genes could act as a one-two punch, reinforcing each other and leading to the buildup of so many family members' being antisocial and becoming criminals. In scientific terms, this is called a "gene-environment correlation," she said, where people at genetic risk end up in families with environmental risk because their families give them both their genes and their home life.

In addition, this coincidence of genes and environment can repeat cyclically all across the life course, Moffitt said.

> For example, if a small boy's mild genetic vulnerability leads him to be difficult to manage and unable to settle in the classroom, he will be reassigned to a classroom for disruptive children, come under their bad peer influence and act even more disruptively than before. If a teen's mild genetic vulnerability leads him to show off and drive recklessly, he may have a car accident and get a head injury that impairs his judgment and makes him more impulsive and more prone than before to get involved in crime. If an adult's genetic vulnerability leads him to frequent bars, he stands a good chance of meeting his girlfriend there, who also shares a lifestyle of

alcohol and drugs and encourages his involvement in more criminal activities to secure more drugs. If a young person with a mild genetic vulnerability to sensation seeking tries experimenting with petty rebellious crime and gets caught, processed through the courts and incarcerated in prison, his new criminal record might stop him from getting a good job, leaving him few opportunities to go straight.

Professor Moffitt also stresses that there is no single crime gene. "It is probably forty genes that make someone susceptible to alcohol," she said. "Or another fifty genes for sensation seeking. And more genes for the tendency to lose one's temper. And another group of genes for the tendency to have difficulty learning."

So far, however, behavioral genetics research has found little to explain why offenders like Tracey Bogle have so much trouble stopping their life of crime after being released from prison. For one thing, Professor Moffitt said, "We don't have a lot of studies of adult criminals, because most genetic research is focused on how children and teenagers become antisocial and then turn into adult criminals."

John Laub, the University of Maryland criminologist who analyzed the Gluecks' data on delinquents in Boston in the 1940s, believes Moffitt's research on the gene-environment interplay offers a possible explanation. When some people get both the gene and the bad environment, like growing up in the Bogle family, it is "a double insult," Laub said. It is this interaction that makes it very difficult for newly released inmates to stop committing crime. "It is just too hard and no fun."

Tracey had probably suffered from this "double insult."

8

Tony

A Murder in Tucson

It was February 1990 and Tony Bogle could not remember ever being so happy, even though he was locked up yet again, much as he had been since he was twelve years old, this time in the county jail in Kennewick, Washington. The local authorities had just allowed him to marry his longtime girlfriend, Paula Christian, in a ceremony performed inside the old jail.

Paula was a tall, voluptuous twenty-year-old with a sultry expression and bangs that swept low over her brow, almost tickling the bridge of her nose. She wore her dark hair long and had bright blue eyes that she accentuated with heavy blue eye shadow. Perhaps because she had been sexually abused as a girl by her grandfather, her uncle and a friend of her family in her hometown of Anaconda, Montana, an old copper-mining town, Paula had a strong need for affection and flirted easily with Tony when they first met, according to two of her closest girlfriends.

If the jail officials had looked more carefully at Tony's and Paula's psychological profiles, they might have had second thoughts about allowing them to marry. During the time they were dating, in fact, a psychologist for the Oregon Parole Board found that Tony suffered from antisocial personality disorder, a medical term for having a criminal personality. He was particularly likely to "decompensate under stress," the psychologist reported, or deteriorate into his criminal mode under pressure. Further, the psychologist said, Tony had a "psychological profile that was extremely alarming." And soon after they were married, with Tony in another Washington jail, a psychiatrist there found that Tony had a personality disorder with "schizotypal features," meaning that he exhibited severe social anxiety, paranoia and sometimes unconventional beliefs. Nevertheless, Tony was released from jail in Washington on August 30, 1991, and immediately absconded, leaving town without permission from his parole officer.

Tony and Paula had decided their best chance at a life together was to get far away, so they were hitchhiking to Tucson, Arizona, where his aunt Bert had been running a children's day-care center and had told them jobs were as plentiful as the Arizona sunshine. "We came to Arizona to start a new life," Paula later said. "Tony was going to get a job, and we were going to try to start a family."

As hitchhikers, they had no luggage. Tony had only the blue shirt and black pants and dark sneakers he was wearing. They had no cash, no driver's license and no credit cards. Tony had a counterfeit Arizona identification card and a fake birth certificate in the name of Kevin Austin, an alias he used. Their lack of possessions was a good snapshot of where they were in their haphazard lives. They had no property of any kind, no car, no job skills or résumés beyond Tony's long criminal rap sheet and no social capital like membership in a church or other community organization. Neither one had graduated from high school, though Tony had managed to finish eleventh grade while locked up at the MacLaren School for Boys.

On September 3, 1991, they arrived in Tucson, where the driver who had picked them up now dropped them off. Tony went straight to a 7-Eleven store to look at the classified ads in a local paper. Then he walked over to a pickup truck splattered with paint and asked the driver if he had any work available. The driver said yes, doing stucco for a home construction company. Tony accepted the offer. "It made me feel pretty good. I was finally going to make something of myself and show my father." His words were almost the same as those his brother Bobby had used describing how happy he would be to take over a car-detailing business in Salem. In their fraught, complex relationship with Rooster, sometimes pleasing him meant getting away with a crime, sometimes getting a legitimate job.

On their first few nights in Tucson, Tony and Paula stayed at a cheap motel using money Aunt Bert had given Tony to start his new life. They soon moved out to a small, one-bedroom apartment in a transient neighborhood rife with crime and drug trafficking. The apartment was in a courtyard of low pink duplexes with scruffy palm trees out front and a tiny, dirt-filled swimming pool in the middle. It was rented to a man named Joe Brennan, who insisted on being called "Chief" because he claimed he was descended from a famous Indian chief, though his father, in Louisiana, said that was just a story. Chief, who was forty-nine years old, was six feet tall but weighed only a gaunt ninety-eight pounds and suffered from both epilepsy and schizophrenia, according to his health records. Tony and Paula met Chief in a neighbor's apartment, and he promptly invited them to move into his unit, rent-free. He needed someone to look after him, he explained, because he was prone to seizures, and he also needed help with cooking. Chief would let Tony and Paula sleep in the bedroom, and he would sleep on the couch in the living room. The offer was a godsend to the couple because Tony had changed jobs and was now working for a landscaping company that installed drip irrigation pipes for people's lawns, but he would not be paid for several weeks.

From the beginning, Tony was suspicious that Chief was really after Paula. After all, she was very easy to look at, and Chief increased Tony's misgivings by announcing soon after they moved in that in keeping with Indian custom, they were now living in his teepee and therefore Paula was his squaw to do with whatever he wished. Chief could be "very unusual," Tony said later. "He would do powwow dances for me, and he was like, 'Don't argue with me,' because if you argued with him you'd be up all night."

Tony and Paula weren't the only people in the complex who thought Chief was eccentric. A neighbor, Robert Trimble, said that Chief was "like a hermit, kind of spacey, and you'd see him riding his bike in the middle of the street talking to himself, telling stories about what somebody taught him back in the eighteen hundreds about what happens on full moons." Chief also liked to shout at people and pick fights, Trimble said.

But it was Chief's continuing to ogle Paula and his attempts to touch her that had Tony most on guard. "What I diagnosed was this guy might hurt my wife, or me," Tony said. As a precaution, Tony began taking Paula to work with him, until his boss told him that was too disruptive.

On the morning of October 29, 1991, Tony was getting picked up by a truck for his landscaping job, and he cautioned Paula to stay in the bedroom and not come out, no matter what Chief wanted. Tony also said he was going to see his boss to finally get paid so they could move out of Chief's place. As the day wore on, Chief kept knocking on the door and shouting for Paula to come out, to prepare a meal for him and to be with him, Paula said later. About the time Tony would be coming home from work, Chief managed to break into the bedroom. "He got on top of me, trying to hold me down," Paula said. "He was telling me that I was going to be his squaw and that Tony didn't love me and that I didn't mean anything to my husband and that I was nothing but a no-good whore. This really frightened me. I had been raped before, and I had told Tony that if anybody ever tried to do that to me again that I would fight back. I would not let them hurt me no more.

"I was fighting Chief, trying to get him off of me," Paula said. "I finally did get him off of me and ran. And he followed me and he ripped my blouse. I ran into the living room. Then he grabbed me again and I seen a rock by the coffee table and I grabbed it." It was a rock Chief kept there to prop the door or the window open, Paula explained. "It was like his pet rock," about the size of a softball. "I grabbed the rock and I hit him in the head with it so he would leave me alone. It didn't stop him at first, and I kept on hitting him and he kept on coming towards me. I hit him a number of times. I don't know how many times I hit him. He fell and he got back up and he'd come back at me and I hit him again."

At that moment, Tony returned home "and he seen us struggling," Paula said. "He seen me hitting Chief with the rock. And then Tony came up behind him and grabbed him in, like, a choke hold, and pulled him away from me. I don't know if Chief was dead or if he was dying. But by the time Chief hit the floor, he was not conscious and he looked like he was dead. And he wasn't breathing. And I seen a knife in his hand."

Tony asked Paula to check Chief's pulse, since she had worked as a nurse's aide. "I kept on checking his pulse and he wasn't alive," Paula said. "I used my two fingers and I pressed on his forearm. I also checked on his neck. But I couldn't feel a pulse."

Chief was lying motionless on the floor for twenty or thirty minutes with a lot of blood coming out of his head, Paula said. The couple finally put him in the shower to see if he would wake up, in case he was just knocked out, Paula said. Eventually, the couple put a blanket down on the floor and put Chief on it. "And then we sat on the couch and thought about what we should do. If we should call the police or if we should bury him, 'cause we didn't know what to do," Paula said.

"Tony wanted to call the police, but I wouldn't let him. He was on the run for probation from Kennewick, Washington, for something," Paula said, and she was worried that he would automatically be put back in jail and they would be separated, maybe forever, given what had just happened, no matter whether Chief had tried to rape her.

"So we wrapped the body up in blankets and put him in the closet," Paula said. "It was kind of hard to think with him laying there in front of us.

"Tony then put some small plastic grocery bags over the Chief's head and tied them closed, to stop the blood from seeping onto the floor."

With Chief's body wrapped in blankets and safely out of their sight in the hall closet, Tony and Paula counted their money to see if they could afford to leave Tucson. They had less than $100 saved from Tony's two months of landscaping work. That was not enough to get to where they wanted to flee to—Reno, Nevada, where Kathy was staying. So Paula suggested they sell the home entertainment system Chief had rented, a combination of a television set, a stereo and a VCR.

Paula tried calling some people who had placed wanted ads in the newspaper, but there were no takers for the rented set. Eventually the couple went outside and began walking, stopping cars to ask if anyone wanted an entertainment center. A couple driving in a pickup truck bought it for $180 in cash.

"I went back in the house and I told Tony it was done and that we had enough, we could go," Paula said. "Tony didn't feel right about it, but I said, we can't depend on what's right or wrong right now. We got each other and if we call the police, they'll take us away from each other. And he said, Okay."

Tony also called his mother and sister Vickey in Reno, letting them know there had been a violent incident with Chief and they had to leave Tucson. Tony didn't realize this would leave an electronic copy of his mother's phone number on Chief's next phone bill that was sitting in his mailbox when the police were eventually called in to investigate a foul odor coming from Chief's apartment in the Arizona fall heat.

As Tony and Paula packed their meager possessions, they heard a helicopter overhead. "It was circling the apartment," Paula said. "We thought somebody had heard something and called the police, so we went out the window and we ran."

Tony and Paula then went to the Greyhound bus station and tried to get tickets on the late-night bus to Las Vegas, but it was full, so they went to a motel for the night and took the next day's bus to Las Vegas, as close to Reno as their money would allow. On the way they talked over what they would say to the police if they were arrested. "Tony told me to blame it all on him, that he didn't want me to go to prison or have to suffer anything for it," Paula said. "And I told him that I would, because I was afraid. And he is always very protective over me. So I agreed with him."

Tony had hoped his mother would drive down to Las Vegas from Reno to pick him up, but Kathy demurred, citing her poor health. In a lifetime of disappointments, this was just one more. So Tony and Paula hitchhiked north to Reno. They were staying with Kathy when the Tucson police found Chief's badly decomposed body on November 4, 1991.

A canvas of neighbors in the apartment complex quickly turned up the names of Paula and Tony Bogle, who had been staying with Chief, and at least one of the neighbors had learned about Tony's prison record from talks with him. When the phone bill arrived, it supplied the missing link about where Tony might have gone. A call to Kathy's number was answered by her daughter's boyfriend, who didn't like Tony, and he told the police where in Reno they could find him. Two Tucson homicide detectives were on the next plane to Reno, on November 13.

Paula was arrested a few hours after the detectives' arrival when they saw a woman matching her description walking down the street near Kathy's apartment. Tony, when he realized the police had found Paula, went to a rental-car agency that evening, broke in and stole a Lincoln Town Car, a safe containing $2,000 and a loaded twelve-gauge shotgun presumably for protection against a robbery. His plan was to use the shotgun and money to somehow break Paula out of jail. Soon the Reno police and the Nevada Highway Patrol were alerted that Tony was driving on a highway outside the city at speeds in excess of 110 miles per hour, and they set a trap for him by scattering metal spikes across the road to slash his tires. At nine o'clock on the evening of November 16, Tony too was under arrest.

At his core, Tony was a grifter, a con artist. It was his inheritance from Rooster, from his grandmother Elvie, stretching back in time to his great-grandmother Narcissa, who sought that Union Army pension for decades, and to his great-grandfather Carpenter Harding, who passed himself off as an unmarried Union Army veteran in rural Tennessee after the Civil War. Tony could not make the murder of Chief disappear. But he could not resist trying to scam the detectives who were investigating the case, and later the prosecutor and the judge. "Tony would not trust anybody unless he could con them," said the lawyer eventually appointed to defend him in the murder case, David Sherman. This was the impossible task Tony now set himself after he was arrested for the murder of Joe Brennan.

The effort began the day after his arrest, at ten o'clock on the morning of November 17, when he was interrogated by Detective Tony Miller, one of the officers who had flown in from Tucson. Tony Bogle said he was actually Kevin Dale Austin, the name on his fake birth certificate. He insisted he was surprised to be arrested because he did not know the police were looking for him. Apprised of Chief's death, Tony acknowledged he had stayed at the same apartment complex there but believed Chief had been killed by gunfire from a police helicopter that flew overhead on the night he fled the building. Detective Miller said that was not possible, so Tony had a second version ready. He claimed that Chet Hopper, another occupant of the building, who had given Tony his first job in Tucson, had beaten Chief to death using the porcelain lid on the toilet bowl, with the lid shattering into pieces on the bathroom floor as a result of repeated heavy blows. When Detective Miller rejected that version, Tony came up with yet another story—that Chet choked Chief to death with a chain.

After Detective Miller rebutted that story too, Tony tried to create a diversion. He said he had information about a murder he committed in Las Vegas while he was at the bus station there. A black man named "Leon" had given Tony a ride in his old red Oldsmobile, "a crap piece of car," Tony said. "Leon" had offered to sell Tony some drugs, they got in a fight over the price and Tony stabbed "Leon" to death, leaving his body in the desert outside the city. "There is a lot more to this story and it's not simple," Tony seemed to confide. "Murder is never simple," the detective responded.

Tony did have one consistent point. He said he wanted to make sure his wife, who he said was Paula Bogle, was safe, and he wanted to talk to her. "Then why is your name Austin?" the detective asked him.

"I got to see her one more time before everything goes down," Tony said, suggesting he knew something more and that he might now be willing to talk. "My life is over with.

"I was real proud of myself in Tucson because I found a job and would have kept it except for that nutcase, Chief," Tony went on. "For the first time in my life I was earning money to pay the rent and buy the groceries." By mentioning Chief, Tony had opened a line of inquiry for the detective, who had just been letting Tony talk and get comfortable.

"Yeah, we knew about that," the detective said. "We knew Chief had mental problems. We knew he was violent."

Actually, the Tucson police didn't yet know that, but it was good police work to keep Tony talking. "Are you willing to talk to us about it?" he asked Tony.

"Yeah, the whole story, but only if I can see Paula and tell her 'I love you,'" Tony replied.

"We've already talked with Paula," Miller said. "We believe her that she was not involved in Chief's death, that she was in the bedroom when you and Chief began to argue in the living room, and afterward, when she came out of the bedroom, you had already put Chief in the closet."

"That's right," Tony said. "My wife, man, did not murder anybody. Even in her mind, she didn't even know what was going on." Tony was carefully sticking to the script he and Paula had agreed on during the long bus ride from Tucson to Las Vegas, that he would take all the blame.

"I don't want my wife, man, to go down for something that she hasn't done," Tony repeated fifteen minutes later, under further questioning.

Finally, after eleven hours of interrogation, with frequent breaks for coffee from a vending machine, Tony broke and said he alone "killed Chief, but it wasn't premeditated.

"I didn't plan it that way," Tony added. "It just turned into a big old stink, that's all. About him and my wife."

"And how did you kill the Chief?" Miller asked.

"With a rock, that was on the coffee table," Tony said. "Chief was crazy, and weird. He even talked to that rock. He'd stare at the TV for hours looking for lines on the screen, and he'd say, 'This right here, if I leave it this way, it'll bring in the Playboy channel.'"

"Well, you've gotten a lot off your chest tonight, haven't you?" Detective Miller said, as if reassuring Tony.

"The reason why it's driving me crazy is because I know what it's gonna do to me, how it's gonna affect my marriage," Tony said with resignation. "It's all over with."

"Do you have any feelings for the people that died?" Miller asked him as they were preparing to wrap up the questioning.

"Well, I got feelings for me now because it's gonna be me that's gonna die," Tony replied, expecting he would get the death penalty. "The gods come for me now."

After a pause, Tony added a final thought that closed the interview. "I got a lot of brothers. I can't believe I'm actually leaving them forever. That's my punishment from God."

.   .   .

After Tony confessed, on November 17, 1991, clearing Paula of any role in the murder, they were both flown back to Tucson. Tony was indicted for first-degree murder, a potential death-penalty crime in Arizona, but Paula was indicted only for theft of the home entertainment center, a charge that could at most send her to prison for a few years.

Locked up in the Pima County jail in Tucson awaiting his murder trial, Tony stewed about the unfairness of his predicament and obsessed about how Paula would soon be free to have sex with other men. Jealousy was a powerful force in his life, perhaps exacerbated by the paranoia that was part of his diagnosed episodes of schizophrenia. On December 15, Tony asked a guard to get in touch with Detective Miller. "My wife and I gave some false statements from the beginning," Tony told the guard. "I was clearing my wife of any involvement in the murder and confessing to doing the whole dang thing by myself," Tony said in a tape-recorded conversation. "But she hit this man in the head with a rock, you know, and it knocked him silly. And then she hit him again and it knocked him really silly and then she gave it one real good one. And then I came home and grabbed him around the neck and it killed him.

"I cannot just let my wife get outta jail and leave me," Tony said to the guard, "leave me to do the whole sentence by myself, or maybe leave me to the chair. They are blaming the whole thing on me."

The guard contacted Miller, who showed up early the next morning to talk to Tony and began by asking whether Tony had informed his then court-appointed attorney, James Cochran, about meeting with the detective. No, Tony replied. He knew his lawyer would advise against talking to the police, but he had something important he needed to say.

"Back in Reno all I wanted to do was to protect my wife," Tony said. "But I don't want to go down and do twenty-five years or get the gas chamber either, and there is a whole lot of people telling me the truth now is better for me than a lie."

"What is the truth?" Miller asked.

"The truth is that Paula was involved with the murder," Tony blurted out. "She hit him. Hit him in the head. She was hitting him in the head with a rock. She knocked him silly. And then she gave him one real good one."

How many times did Paula hit Chief with the rock? Detective Miller asked.

"I don't know," Tony answered. "I saw Chief had a knife, and he was real good with knives, like an Indian, so I grabbed him around the neck, because I was scared of him with that knife. And this is the truth. I know I'm gonna do time. I know that I've lost my freedom. But I'm not going to go to the electric chair."

"When you stopped was he dead?" the detective asked.

"He was. I murdered him," Tony said.

"This is the third story that you've told me," Miller said.

No, Tony replied. "The fourth, fifth, sixth, whatever. Chief was a genius, but he was nuts. He was crazy and he wanted my wife. He kept saying, 'Under Indian law, she's under my roof and I get to have some of her.' I kept warning him about that and we got into fights about it, and that's what made this all happen."

"I still don't understand why you did it. I hope this version might be the truth," said Miller.

The following day the detective went to see Paula in the women's part of the county jail. He explained he had talked with Tony the previous day and that Tony was changing his story to now implicate Paula in Chief's murder. He advised her again of her legal right not to speak to him and asked if she was still willing to talk. Yes, Paula said.

"Yeah, I might as well," Paula said. "I don't think anything is gonna hurt anything. Chief tried to rape me."

He was trying to rape her on the day of the killing, Paula related, but he had tried it before too. It was getting close to evening time, Paula said, with Tony due to come home from work, and Chief began by trying to fondle her. He was "grabbing my breast and my butt," Paula said. "I told him to leave me alone. And then he said I was a whore and that I deserve what I am going to get and he approached me and tried to rape me. He ripped my shirt open, and I struggled and then I seen the rock and I hit him with it and got him away from me. I had hit him three or four times when Tony came in the door and grabbed Chief around the neck and started choking him."

Paula said she shook Tony and asked him to stop, but he didn't hear her for a minute. When he did let go, Chief fell to the floor. She could see an open knife in Chief's hand. When she checked his pulse, there was none.

If Paula had accepted a suggestion by Tony at this point to call the police, that might have been the one thing to save him from a long prison sentence or the death penalty, said David Sherman, the public defender who was ultimately assigned to defend Tony. "Tony had a triable case, that he was acting in self-defense," Sherman said. In addition, it was never medically clear which of the two of them inflicted the mortal wound, Paula by hitting Chief in the head with the rock or Tony by putting him in a choke hold to pull him off her. But they didn't call the police.

All these statements and the trail of evidence were a bonanza for the prosecution in the killing of Chief. They also posed some tricky legal and ethical challenges. Tony and Paula had both initially claimed they were innocent. Then they both confessed. Ultimately, they said they did the killing together. Before bringing either of them to trial, the prosecutor would have to decide who really had killed Chief and what was a fair interpretation of the evidence.

The prosecutor assigned to the case, Kenneth Peasley, a deputy

Pima County attorney, was the most feared prosecutor in Tucson, if not in all of Arizona. "He was a cop's prosecutor," said Tony Miller. "The cops loved him. He didn't plea bargain. He hung the bad guys up by their toes. He told us he didn't care how we investigated a case, just get the results."

Peasley had a prodigious memory for the details of a case and did his cross-examinations and closings from memory, without notes, Miller said. Peasley was a slight figure with slicked-back gray hair and a gray beard, and when he was doing a closing argument all the other lawyers in the courthouse would come in to listen. He spoke in a deep, fast growl, like one of the fighter jets taking off from Davis-Monthan Air Force Base on the south side of Tucson. He often got right up in the face of a defendant as a way of indicating how deeply he was convinced of the man's guilt, and would stick his finger close to the defendant's eye in an intimidating gesture.

Peasley had an extraordinary record of success in convicting defendants. He bragged that from 1978, when he began as a prosecutor in Tucson, until the time he tried Tony and Paula, he sent more men to death row in Arizona than any other prosecutor— about one-tenth of all prisoners on death row in the state. Peasley tried 250 felony cases during that time, including 140 homicides.

In early 1992, Peasley decided to start by trying Paula, but only for the theft of the home entertainment center. On April 2, 1992, she was quickly convicted of the theft and sentenced to five years in state prison. At her sentencing Paula surprised the judge and the prosecutor by announcing that she was more responsible for Chief's death than her husband was.

"It's not fair that my husband is taking full responsibility for the homicide," Paula told Judge Gilbert Veliz of Pima County Superior Court. "I was involved in it. In fact, I probably killed him, not my husband."

Nevertheless, before imposing his sentence, Judge Veliz said he would ignore her murder confession because she was not charged with that crime.

I asked Peasley how he decided whom to prosecute for Chief's murder. One of his strongest recollections of the case, Peasley said, was how bizarre Tony had been. Tony first told the police that he alone had killed Chief, but then after being brought back to Tucson, he wrote Peasley letters addressed to "The Avenging Angel."

"Tony became consistent that he wanted me to prosecute her," Peasley said. "It was pretty unusual. He wanted to make sure his wife went to prison, not out there having sex with other men. Jealousy seemed to be a big part of the story."

But beyond that, Peasley said, "I didn't really need to figure out who did it. I was persuaded that Tony did it. He had the long criminal record. And I always wanted to get the really bad guy." Peasley was not following the established rules of the criminal justice system, a breathtaking leap for a prosecutor.

Peasley had Tony alone indicted for first-degree murder in the killing of Chief, and the trial began in Tucson in late March 1993, a year and a half after the crime. Tony made it clear that defending him was not going to be easy. The first three attorneys assigned by the Pima County Superior Court to represent him all petitioned Judge Veliz for permission to withdraw. The last of these three lawyers, James Cochran, wrote that since Tony's arrest in Reno in October 1991, he "has related various versions of the incident to nearly everyone who was willing to listen," and had also, contrary to Cochran's advice, "engaged in a letter-writing campaign directed to the police, the prosecutor" and other legal authorities. "An analysis of the statements made by the Defendant to date show that the Defendant has consistently been unable to tell the same story twice," Cochran wrote. Separately, Richard Bozich, a private investigator assigned by Judge Veliz to help with Tony's defense, reported that his behavior was so bizarre that it made working to help him impossible. "During an interview, the defendant would look at the wall or ceiling and speak to it as though it was me or another person," Bozich said. In addition, he reported, Tony "does not appear to grasp the seriousness of the crime for which he is charged," and that he "would appear calm and collected one moment and then become enraged the next and start yelling."

Ultimately, the task of defending Tony fell to David Sherman, a smart, experienced and even-tempered public defender. Sherman said he quickly came to realize Tony had been so damaged by his family upbringing that "his orientation to reality was off, skewed, even delusional, and that he had his own way of seeing the world that he would stick with even when it was transparently absurd and wouldn't help his case." Tony's emotional state even showed up in the handwritten letters he sent to Sherman, Judge Veliz and the prosecutor. The script might start off large and then turn small, even tiny to the point of being miniature and illegible, or go from printing to cursive and then run right off the edge of the page. Tony often continued his letters by writing all over both the outside and the inside of the envelopes in which they were enclosed, so it was difficult to decipher what he meant.

What comes through in several letters Tony later wrote to me from prison in Arizona is a kind of dangerous insanity mixed with painful memories of his youth. In one letter, Tony said that "Paula got pregnant at age fourteen and gave birth at age fifteen. Her lover, Mario, was an illegal immigrant from South America who was crazy about having sex with under-age girls. Jack King (Paula's stepdad), asked me to kill Mario."

Tony then jumped, with no transition, to recalling how his father used to drive him by the Oregon State Correctional Institution when he was a teenager. "He would point right at it and say, 'You'll soon be there, son.' My dad never saw me doing great in the future, he saw me going to prison.

"It was easy for him to predict since his hands shaped my future and made me a pirate," Tony wrote. "He didn't need a crystal ball to make that prediction. His own failures made him aware that I would be the byproduct of his own handiwork. Like a lazy farmer knows his crops will only be third grade produce. The die was cast even before I was born. Dad knew his offspring won't be senators and boy-scout leaders and police officers."

Reading Tony's letters and spending hours talking with him before his murder trial, Sherman observed that Tony had a real "dichotomy in his personality. He could be articulate and insightful about his case one minute, then crazy the next." One day when they were working on his defense, Tony told Sherman, "Don't worry. I won't spend much time in prison even if we lose."

"I asked him what he was talking about," Sherman related. "He said, 'My brothers will break me out.'"

"I said, 'What, do you think they will fly in to rescue you in a helicopter?'"

"And Tony said, 'I like that idea. But no. They will kidnap a bunch of schoolkids and threaten to execute one every hour till I am released.'"

Sherman was stunned but assumed Tony was joking.

Sherman now also realized he could not present a conventional defense. So in his opening statement to the jury, after saying that Tony was "legally justified" in killing Chief because Chief was in the process of trying to rape Paula, Sherman startled the jury. "Now, let me tell you what this case is not about. This case is not about whether Tony Bogle is a liar, because if that's what the case was about, I could make it real easy right now and tell you, he's a liar.

"Let me tell you what else this case is not about," Sherman continued. "This case is not about what kind of character Tony Bogle has, because I'll make that one easy right now too. He is a very strange character. And you're going to hear evidence about his strangeness. He has a history of mental problems. He's had a history of living on the margins of society, of being in trouble with the law, of having a bad upbringing. He is not somebody who has been involved in the mainstream of society. Everyone in this case—the defendant, the man who is dead, Tony's wife, Paula, some of the other witnesses—all of them are not exactly working on all cylinders.

"Now, let me tell you what this case *is* about," Sherman said to the jury. "Your decision in this case will come down to one question: What happened in that room that night? It's true that Joe Brennan died in that room. And it was a horrible thing. But why did he die? How did he die? Where is the evidence of what happened in that room, the physical evidence, the witnesses, the statements?"

Framing the argument this way, Sherman thought, was the one chance he had of getting Tony off, of using all the conflicting, contradictory admissions by Paula and Tony in his favor and taking advantage of what Sherman knew would be inconclusive physical evidence by the medical examiner about who actually delivered the fatal blow to Chief. Sherman had Paula testify that Chief was trying to rape her and that she grabbed a rock and hit him multiple times in the head before Tony came home and put Chief in a choke hold.

In fact, the medical examiner, Dr. Ann Hartsough, testified that "the cause of death was blunt force trauma with asphyxia." Chief had been hit four or five times in the head, not hard enough to cause fractures to his skull, but enough to cause bleeding from his scalp," Dr. Hartsough said. He had also suffered from something that reduced the flow of oxygen to his brain, which could have been "caused by an arm being placed around his neck." The blows to the head were not "in and of themselves fatal," the doctor said. Nor was there serious damage to Chief's neck, she testified. In her opinion, it was not just the blows to the head or just the choking of Chief's neck that killed him, but the combination.

Until this point in the trial, Sherman thought he had a chance of getting Tony acquitted on the first-degree murder charge. To achieve that, Sherman believed he had to keep Tony from taking the stand and testifying. Tony was simply too unpredictable, too crazy and too prone to telling outrageously false stories to survive a cross-examination by Kenneth Peasley. "I begged him not to testify; I said we had a chance to get a few jurors and hang the case up," Sherman recalled. "But Tony said, 'No. I am going to testify. I will persuade them.' He believed he could con them. He was just like his father."

Peasley made no attempt at small talk when his turn came to cross-examine Tony, no effort to soften him up. He went right to the murder. "When you went in the apartment, sir, and grabbed Chief around the throat, did you apply as much pressure as you possibly could?" the prosecutor asked. "Did you squeeze him as hard as you possibly could, sir?"

"I—I—I grabbed him," Tony mumbled in response, thrown off balance.

"My question was, Did you squeeze him around the neck as hard as you could, sir?" Peasley added.

"Yes, I grabbed the Chief around the neck as hard as I could and—"

"And you kept squeezing him around the neck, didn't you?" Peasley asked.

Tony struggled to reply. "Yes, I did, sir, but—"

"And you were angry when you were doing it, weren't you, sir?" Peasley asked.

"No, I was not angry," Tony said.

"And you took Chief down to the floor?"

"Yes, I did," Tony said, trying to find a break in the line of questioning.

"Okay. And on the floor, did you continue squeezing him as hard as you could around the neck, sir?" Peasley pressed his advantage.

"I don't remember how long I held the Chief," Tony said, looking over at his own lawyer, sheepishly, as if acknowledging he had made a mistake in taking the stand. The transcript of Peasley's cross-examination continues for forty-two pages, more than enough to make Tony look very bad.

When it came time for closing arguments, on the fifth day of the trial, Sherman tried to repair the damage Tony had done to his own defense. "We may never know what really happened," Sherman told the jury. "But your job is just to determine whether the State has met its burden of proof." He said Peasley was "an expert lawyer and a very convincing man, the way he puts little facts together. But think about it. Where is the investigation in this case? Where is the evidence? If you leave out Tony's initial statement to the police in Reno that he killed Chief, where is the evidence? Paula confessed to hitting the Chief with the rock too. And then there's the autopsy. Dr. Hartsough testified that the blows to the head did not cause fractures, that they were consistent with a woman like Paula Bogle striking them, not a man in a violent rage. Why weren't there skull fractures?"

Even Judge Veliz was struck by the contradictory nature of the evidence. Before asking the jury for its verdict, the judge said that what set this case apart, what made it difficult to decide, was that "there have been many lies and many different stories."

The jury quickly found Tony guilty of first-degree murder.

David Sherman now had a new task—to try to present sufficient mitigating evidence to keep Tony from receiving the death penalty. He brought Tony's aunt Bert in to testify about how Rooster had raised Tony. She had gone out with Rooster in Amarillo, before Kathy did, and she had lived in Salem for a period of time after the Bogles moved there, so she had known Tony since birth. She had also run her own children's day-care center in Tucson for the past fifteen years, giving her a measure of expertise in the formation of character. As for Rooster, Bert called him "the most evil human being that's ever been born."

Rooster had brought another woman into the house where Kathy and the children lived, meaning Linda, Bert testified, and he forced the children from the age of seven or eight to watch him have sex with both their mother and Linda. Rooster also beat both women "to a bloody pulp," Bert said, and he whipped his children for any infraction of his strict and capricious rules. One of these was that Rooster demanded the boys have sex with older women from the age of about eleven or twelve, she added. Rooster also forbade his children to play with other boys and girls. "They had no friends. It was clannish," Bert said. The children were so terrified of their father that they were all bed wetters, which subjected them to more beatings. "You just don't do that to little children," said Bert. As a result, "when Tony laughs he really wants to cry," Bert said, "but he believes he has to hide his feelings. So nobody knows the pain he is feeling." It was a terrifying if honest synopsis of Tony's childhood.

Sherman introduced a memorandum prepared by a court-appointed psychiatrist, Dr. Martin Levy, who interviewed Tony and read all the psychological and psychiatric reports on him going back to his stays in the Oregon State Hospital as a boy. "This man had an unusually disturbing childhood, marked by victimization which was well beyond his control," Dr. Levy concluded. "It appears that Mr. Bogle never had a chance to be a normal person and has spent most of his life institutionalized."

This fit with Sherman's own conclusions after spending months with Tony. "If you were going to go out and create the perfect criminal, this is how you do it," he told me in an interview. "It's the Bogle blueprint. You take young children and mentally and psychologically torture them. Take away all their dignity as a human being. So they have no sense of empathy for others. Then they become perfect psychopaths."

Together, Bert's personal observations, Dr. Levy's psychiatric evaluation and Sherman's interviews with Tony come as close as anyone had yet gotten to understanding the role the Bogle family played in causing one of its members to become a criminal, in this case a murderer. Sherman was frustrated that the criminal justice system, as currently set up, did not allow for a deeper dive into more information on Tony and his family. He was sure that if police forces could share more information with probation and parole officers, or if hospitals, including mental hospitals, could share more information with the police and prison authorities about dangerous offenders, people like Tony would be detected earlier and separated from other family members, like Rooster, who exerted such a malevolent influence over his children, and be given more help to divert them from a life of crime. In other fields, this kind of data mining is now an everyday event, penetrating every level of society, with companies such as Amazon, Google and Facebook able to harvest huge amounts of information useful in selling products and keeping people in instant touch with their friends. But there was no way for Sherman or anyone outside the Bogle family to know, for example, that both of Rooster's grandmothers had died in state mental hospitals, and that three of Tony's siblings had been diagnosed with bipolar disorder or schizophrenia. Nor was anyone aware that sixty members of the extended Bogle clan had been sentenced to prison, jail or probation and parole.

Sherman's wish for more information-sharing in the criminal justice system reminded me of a highly innovative program for youthful offenders in Jacksonville, Florida. There, the local state attorney, or prosecutor, Harry Shorstein, developed a program of meetings in his office for agencies that would not normally share records, including representatives from the police, the school board, the state children's protective service organization and the local hospital. Once a week, under the leadership of a psychologist Shorstein had hired, the different parties would meet to discuss information they each had on three young people, from age six to fifteen, who had committed a crime or had serious behavior problems at school.

One case involved a seven-year-old boy named Freddie who had hit a young girl in the head with a brick. Normally, Freddie would have been taken before a juvenile court judge a few times and then shuffled through the overburdened juvenile justice system, and whatever had made him so violent so young would simmer until the next in perhaps a lifetime of violent outbursts. But with Freddie's arrest in Jacksonville on charges of aggravated assault, the group sitting in Shorstein's office looked through his records to try to understand what made him do it. They discovered that he had been born addicted to drugs and with congenital syphilis, to a mother who was a cocaine addict. His mother and father, who were not married, had both been reported for abusing Freddie. His difficulty learning and trouble staying still had already required him to repeat kindergarten. With such a troubled background, the group decided, Freddie was likely to continue being delinquent. So the prosecutor's office decided that instead of trying him in juvenile court and sending him to a reformatory, they would persuade Freddie's mother to sign a civil contract placing the boy under its supervision for a year, with a requirement that Freddie attend school under the guidance of a mentor. The mentor would make sure Freddie got up on time every morning and had breakfast. The mentor would take him to school and would be there again in the afternoon to bring Freddie home and help him with his homework. Jacksonville was a good place to find volunteers to serve as mentors because it had big Navy and Air Force bases and a large population of retired career military families. Making use of unpaid volunteers made the program inexpensive, something important in a conservative city whose voters wanted to keep taxes low. In exchange for participating in the program successfully, Freddie would have his juvenile record expunged. He was never arrested again. Unfortunately, the Florida legislature has since stopped funding the program as a cost-saving measure.

In the end, in Tony Bogle's trial, Sherman did not have to introduce Bert's mitigating evidence or Dr. Levy's report. Judge Veliz decided that Tony's actions were not heinous enough to merit the death penalty. The judge still sentenced Tony to twenty-six years to life in prison. Today he remains in prison in Arizona.

But the case was not over. Kenneth Peasley was furious that Paula had changed her testimony in Tony's trial to say that she had hit Chief repeatedly with the rock. During Tony's trial, Peasley had Paula secretly indicted by a grand jury for the murder too. In February 1994 Paula was back on trial in Tucson for murder. Peasley now argued that Tony was *not* solely responsible for Chief's death. "The truth is they worked together" and were equally responsible, Peasley told the new jury. The jurors found Paula more sympathetic than Tony and convicted her of *second*-degree murder. She has since been released from prison.

Looking back on the case, Sherman said, "I found it to be ethically troubling." After all, Peasley had first argued that Tony alone murdered Chief, and the jury convicted him for that, beyond a reasonable doubt. "That establishes a fact," Sherman said. "You can't then come back and try someone else for the same crime."

Unknown to Sherman at the time, Peasley was about to have his own legal career ruined by his tendency to decide for himself who was innocent and who was guilty. In a 1992 triple murder in Tucson, Peasley introduced testimony by one of the homicide detectives—who also worked on Tony Bogle's case—that Peasley knew to be false. The Arizona Bar Association conducted an investigation, and in 2004 Peasley was disbarred. That earned him the distinction of being the first American prosecutor to be disbarred for intentionally presenting false evidence in a death-penalty case.

When I asked Tony which version of Chief's killing was true, he grinned. "Flip a coin," he said. "Take your pick."

[III]

BREAKING
THE FAMILY
CURSE

Death and life are in the power of the tongue.

—Proverbs 18:21

9

Tammie

Walking with Jesus

On the wall of her modest trailer home next to a grove of hazel-nut trees in the western Willamette Valley, Tammie Bogle kept a fading black-and-white photo of herself at the age of five, back in the early 1960s, with her father, mother and one of her brothers, Louis. Tammie was a towhead at the time, with a round face and a warm smile full of freckles. The photo is a rare souvenir of a happy time before her own branch of the Bogle clan was consumed by alcohol, drugs, violence and too much time locked up behind bars. Twenty-one members of her immediate family, starting with her father, an older brother of Rooster's known as Babe, have been sentenced to jail or prison. Tammie's brother, known as young Louis, himself was incarcerated forty times, by his own count, before eventually being injected by his drug dealer with a hot shot of liquid Drano, instead of what he thought was meth. The injection left him in a coma, and when he unexpectedly regained consciousness, he was a quadriplegic; he was bedridden for the last eighteen years of his life. "Too mean to die," he liked to joke. The weekend before he passed away, Tammie went to visit him and heard Louis talking with someone. "I asked him who it was, and he said, 'Tammie, I've been talking to an angel. I'll see you with God.'"

A deep religious faith, in fact, was what kept Tammie from succumbing to the perils and pitfalls of the kind that destroyed so many of her relatives. Religion for Tammie was not only her personal salvation, but also a shield against the temptations and the contagions that consumed the Bogles and made the family itself a cause of crime.

Inside her trailer, painted beige with red trim, there were photos of Tammie's three children. One, Jason, went to prison for eight years but then became director of a Christian-based halfway house for inmates leaving prison. The other two, Shannon and Amy, married former prisoners and now work as counselors—one in a drug rehab program and the other as the head of a preschool program. On the trailer's narrow walls there are also pictures of Tammie's fourteen grandchildren, along with photos of some of the three hundred foster children the local courts have entrusted to her over the years. As a young girl, Tammie picked up her interest in religion from her mother, Lola, herself a devout Southern Baptist who was part Native American from Oklahoma, where missionaries drilled Christianity into her on the reservation. Faith was a refuge for Tammie from the time when her father would preach on Sunday mornings and then get drunk on the way home from church and beat his wife until her face was bloodied. Tammie would then direct her brother Louis, who was a fast runner, to take off across a farm field to distract her father and make him give chase. "Those beatings used to really hurt me too," Tammie said.

The natural world outside the trailer was also a haven for Tammie, a place where she found God. Tammie had gardens planted with wisteria, honeysuckle and clematis. In one section sat an old bathtub filled with butterfly bushes in bright lavender, yellow, pink and purple. Early each morning Tammie walked through a grove of young fir trees being grown for sale at Christmas, and she prayed in the soft dawn light coming through the green branches. There were rabbits, pheasants, skunks and foxes moving among the trees.

"I am walking with Jesus out here," Tammie liked to say. "It is as close to heaven as I can get. I am talking to Jesus, praying to him, listening to the birds. It is a healing place for me. Some of my grandkids say they have seen angels out here."

Tammie had a small sculpture of a bronze angel in a fountain sitting on an old wooden whiskey barrel someone gave her. "When I hear the fountain and the water, I think about the Lord's peace."

For her, Tammie said, "Jesus is as real to me as anyone in our family. The factor in our family that differentiates people is the ones who choose God, to keep them out of crime. I look at the Lord as my spiritual daddy because I didn't have a real strong relationship with my dad."

From all her years of watching her fellow Bogle family members, and raising so many foster children, Tammie developed her own philosophy of what makes children into criminals. "Throughout our family, the boys always said, 'I am such a screwup; I am going to turn out like my dad,'" Tammie said. "They believed they were cursed and could not change their destiny. We called it the Bogle curse."

Tammie found a passage in the Bible, Proverbs 18:21, which seemed to fit her family precisely: "Death and life are in the power of the tongue."

"So when someone in the family said, 'You are going to turn out just like your dad,' it was as if the power of death was spoken over us," Tammie said. "This created a link among our family members."

It was another way of stating the social learning theory of becoming a criminal.

Tammie was born in Amarillo two years before the Bogles moved up to Oregon. Her father, Babe, had been a young ironworker trying to connect some bolts on a forty-foot-high oil-refining tower owned by Phillips Petroleum in June 1960 in Borger, Texas, when he slipped and fell face-first into a pit of carbon black. Both his arms and wrists and both legs were broken, along with his back, and carbon black penetrated the bones of his face. A doctor who examined him wrote, "This patient will, in my opinion, be totally disabled for at least a year, and I doubt if he will ever be able to return to heavy labor." Babe was placed on a morphine drip to relieve his acute pain, and that led him to alcohol. As predicted, he could never find full-time employment after that, so the family lived off his $300 a month in Social Security disability payments, along with whatever he could earn as what Tammie called a "shade-tree mechanic," someone who "could fix anything with an engine, a car, a motorcycle or a truck, if you pulled it under a tree."

Over time, Babe's drinking got worse, and when he was drunk he'd beat his wife until her lips were split and her glasses were broken, Tammie said. "One time he got so drunk, he passed out and we tied him up and wanted to set him on fire," Tammie recalled. "We begged our mother to let us burn him, but she said no.

"This happened so often and was so widespread in our family that we thought of it as normal family stuff, with the men violent or criminal or drunk and the women codependent," Tammie said.

When she turned sixteen and was of legal age to marry, to get away from the troubles plaguing her family she decided to marry a young man she had met, Durrell Burden, whose own family were migrant farmworkers. As her father led her down the aisle of the local Baptist church, he had a sudden clarity of vision and said to Tammie, "Take off and run."

"My dad really meant it," Tammie said years later. "It was not a joke. He knew what that family was like and that I would just be repeating the same mistakes as the Bogles. It wasn't a good omen."

In fact, Tammie moved in with her husband's family, and they were just like her own, except now it was Tammie's new husband getting drunk most nights and she was the one taking the beatings. He was eventually sent to jail for being drunk and disorderly. By then Tammie was pregnant, and soon she was worried that her husband, when released, would beat her in the stomach and might injure their baby in the womb. After their son, Jason, was born, her husband became uncontrollably suspicious that the baby wasn't his child and so increased the beatings, leaving Tammie unable to walk some days. When Jason was three months old, her husband beat Tammie and the baby she was holding in her arms, sending them crashing to the concrete floor.

"It was okay to beat me because I was worthless anyway," Tammie recalled. "But it was not okay to beat my baby. So that was it. I called my mom and said come get me. I never went back to him." She had just turned seventeen.

Tammie soon met and married her second husband, Curt James, who earlier had been sent to jail for attempted murder. He was originally from Missouri, and said he was a direct descendant of Jesse James. Even though he was on parole when they met, Tammie thought the marriage would work because they had been introduced by a friend in her church and James seemed to be doing really well at the time. "I thought it would be great," Tammie recalled. "But he soon went back to doing drugs and started beating me, and even threatened to kill me if I told anyone about the beatings." Tammie eventually had two daughters by James, Shannon and Amy, before she divorced him.

Tammie's choices for husbands were what criminologists call "assortative mating," selecting partners with similar characteristics, in this case men from families with criminal backgrounds, or a history of incarceration, drunkenness and violence much like that of her father and other Bogle relatives. This tendency, criminologists have found, is another explanation for the transmission of crime across generations. A Danish criminologist, drawing on

Danish national statistics, has shown that "women who experienced parental contact with the criminal justice system when they were girls could transmit delinquency across generations through their choice of a partner." This kind of assortative mating "makes women just as likely as men to transmit delinquency across generations," concluded the criminologist, Lars Hojsgaard Andersen. In a way, this tendency to pick marriage partners with similar lifestyles and outlooks is like what political scientists and demographers have found in American politics in recent elections. Democrats and liberals are more likely to move to the northeast or the Pacific Coast, to Blue states, while Republicans and conservatives are more likely to cluster in the South or the Midwest, in Red states. Pollsters have come up with a name for it—the Big Sort.

In Tammie's case, a few years after she divorced Curt James, she found herself in a small church outside Salem, where she met a tall, lean, muscular man about her age, thirty-five, with short sandy hair, long sideburns and a gunfighter mustache that drooped around the corners of his mouth. His eyes were a piercing blue and looked sad, until he smiled at Tammie. She had her own three children with her, plus the three children of her brother Louis and two of her foster children. Tammie was on her way to see Louis, and the man smiling at her volunteered to watch all the kids for her. His name was Steve Silver, and, as it turned out, he had grown up in foster care because his own father was in prison. Steve had also been sentenced to the MacLaren School for Boys as a teenager and later to the Oregon State Penitentiary, so he had "grown up in the system," was how Tammie sized up the situation. Improbably, Steve had also become an ordained minister, and when he looked at Tammie and all the children and thought about Louis's predicament, he quickly asked if he could go pray over Louis. During their drive to visit Louis, Tammie explained that she did foster care, and Steve asked her if she would have any trouble helping him with his own new work doing prison ministry, helping counsel convicts in prison with their spiritual needs and finding housing and jobs for men coming out of prison. "I just laughed at that and thought, You don't have a clue, buddy." So she told him, "The people in prison are my family. I'm used to going to prison to visit my family. It would be nice to help people in prison who are not my relatives. So, yes, I'm all for that."

They started dating, and Tammie soon discovered that Steve was very good with her foster children. "My kids could never figure out how he always knew what they were up to. They couldn't con him."

Steve was in the process of putting together some friends from a church where he served as a minister to invest in a decrepit 1920s Roman Catholic nursing facility in a run-down neighborhood of Salem called St. Bernards. He planned to turn the sprawling building into a transition facility, or halfway house, for inmates coming out of the Oregon State Penitentiary and the Oregon State Correctional Institution. They were two of the prisons where the Bogles had been incarcerated: Rooster's sons, Tony, Bobby, Tracey, Glen and Michael, as well as Steve himself and Tammie's brothers Louis and Mark and her son, Jason. This would have been a huge challenge for a well-endowed and experienced charity, but Steve wanted to try the impossible. He told the Oregon State Department of Corrections he would take only inmates who had been convicted as sex offenders, the most troublesome to work with, given the nature of their crimes and the stringent legal restrictions they would now have to live under. As an indication of how difficult the task would be, there were no other places to live for newly released sex offenders in the Salem area. Many of these men would be homeless when they got out, which usually led to them getting into more trouble.

The rambling wooden two-story frame building was repainted a pleasant blue-gray and the interior cleaned and carpeted, all by the thirty-five residents Steve had initially accepted. In 1995, Steve renamed it Stepping Out Ministries, to signify the momentous action the newly released convicts were undertaking. Steve also directed the residents in building a weight room and a computer room. Steve and Tammie insisted that the home be Christian-based, with required nightly devotional Bible lessons. Given the constitutional separation of church and state, this meant that the government of Oregon could provide no funding, leaving the home's finances dependent on the generosity of Steve's investors and payments of $300 a month that each of the residents were supposed to make when they found work, which was a requirement for living there.

Steve was always careful not to say he belonged to any one denomination. "We are in the broad, Charismatic, Pentecostal tradition" was how he liked to describe his brand of Protestantism. "I see myself following in the path of the apostles, trying to do the Lord's work, and my task is to work with these former offenders. I had to get over the corporate idea of being head of some large church."

None of this came easily to Steve. He knew since childhood that there was a fine line between good and evil. It was not until Steve was in his thirties that he learned the man his mother told him was his father was really his stepfather and that his father had been in prison when he was born. His stepfather began sexually abusing Steve at the age of six, and later sold Steve to some friends for a bottle of whiskey. When Steve was fourteen, and full of anger, he ran away and began his own crime spree: robberies, burglaries, assaults, stolen cars and kidnappings. He ended up in prison for a total of five years. As he was being released, a guard said to him, "You'll be back." To which Steve replied, "You'll have to kill me first." Fearing he would be sent back to prison gradually led Steve to religion. "In a sense I lived up to my word," Steve said. "I died, and now I'm a new man in Christ." To keep himself from slipping, Steve decided to go back into prison to bring the lessons he had learned to other inmates. This led him to the idea of a prison ministry, and to Tammie.

. . .

Tammie already knew, from her own family, that she might be able to help save some relatives from alcohol, drugs and crime, but it was an ongoing struggle and some, she learned, she could not save.

There was her favorite brother, Louis, whose drug habit ended up leaving him paralyzed. There was her younger sister, Flory Bogle Black, who was sexually molested by their father when she was eleven and he was drunk. Soon after that Flory became a drug addict, starting with marijuana, and moving on to acid, cocaine, heroin and meth. "I would do what I could get," Flory said. "When I didn't have the money I'd hook up with someone who did, and I'd lose all my morals." Flory had her first child at fourteen and was married at fifteen.

"You can't get out of all that alone," Flory recalled, "and Tammie would pray for me, but I hated that for a long time." One day, high on drugs, she grabbed a knife from her husband at the time and stabbed a girl who was her best friend. Flory was charged with assault and was sent to jail for the first of many times.

While Flory was incarcerated, Tammie took custody of her three children. Both of Flory's husbands were sentenced to prison, as was her son, Robert Wayne Cooper Jr., who was convicted of drug possession and stealing a car. Gary Black, her first husband, eventually died from a drug overdose.

"Flory has been to jail so many times even she doesn't remember how many," Tammie said. One time Flory went to Tammie's house to say she had received a summons to appear in court for yet another arrest. "But she said she couldn't remember when the date was because she ate the ticket," Tammie said, laughing at the memory, even though it was more sad and pathetic than funny.

For a period of time, Flory worked in a center for mentally-ill seniors, but lost her license because of all the drugs and crime. Now, years later, Flory is finally off alcohol and drugs and she is going to church on Sundays, but she is homeless and lives in a small campsite with other homeless people on the banks of the Willamette River outside Salem. "Even if I had a house, this is what God wants me to do," Flory told Tammie. "He wants me to help these people." It is not much of a life, but Tammie thinks her sister is finally at peace.

There was also Tammie's other brother, Mark Bogle, and his wife, Lori. They both have served multiple prison sentences for identity theft and manufacture of methamphetamine, living for a period of time in a cabin in a state park where they printed fake identification cards and bank checks using a computer. Mark and Lori also lost their son, Joshua, who was taken away by the state government under an Oregon law that says a couple cannot maintain custody of a child if they are both incarcerated for more than twelve consecutive months. Joshua was given up for adoption to another family by the state.

As time passed and more and more of Tammie's family members were incarcerated, she often tried to estimate what all the drug and alcohol addiction and crime in her family cost to society. She had become convinced that the only way to stop the costs from increasing was to find a way to keep her Bogle relatives, when they got out of prison, from moving back in with their families, much like Judge Norblad had concluded.

"And not just for my family members," Tammie said, "for other inmates getting out also. That's why we established Stepping Out, as a different place for the men to go." Otherwise, Tammie said, "they are continuing the vicious cycle."

Their biggest success at Stepping Out was an inmate who initially refused to leave prison when he was released because "he was afraid of going home and cooking meth again," Tammie said. "Then, when we opened Stepping Out, he came here and he stayed with us for eight years. He even got married, and now he is helping run another prison ministry facility."

There is one widely respected academic study of the costs imposed on American society by a typical career criminal, starting at birth. It was derived by Professors Mark A. Cohen of the Owen Graduate School of Management at Vanderbilt University and Alex R. Piquero of the John Jay College of Criminal Justice in New York. Their estimate considers not only the obvious costs such as the number of offenses a persistent offender commits over a lifetime, plus the average expense of a year in prison and the costs of maintaining police forces and court systems, but it also takes into account the social costs of pain and suffering caused by crime. The study concludes that a typical career criminal, like a member of the Bogle family, with six or more arrests, is likely to impose between $4.2 million and $7.2 million in costs on the United States. Considering that at least sixty Bogles have been sent to jail or prison, many for multiple years and multiple sentences, the study suggests that the total cost they have imposed on American society ranges between $252 million and $432 million. Whatever one's politics, liberal or conservative or in between, that is a staggeringly high price.

In 2012, after Steve and Tammie had been running the big, rambling Stepping Out Ministries house for seventeen years, with three thousand former convicts having lived there before finding their own housing, they were stunned to discover they were being sued by the woman they had themselves appointed to be president of their board of directors. Her name was Sue Willard, and she worked as a paralegal for a lawyer in Portland. Willard charged Steve and Tammie with buying personal items like new cars with the ministry's funds and charging other expenses including a hot tub and their cable-television bill on a ministry credit card. Willard's accusations at first seemed frivolous, since Steve rode a secondhand Honda motorcycle and Tammie still drove the same battered van, and they didn't have a hot tub. Believers in the biblical practice of tithing, Tammie and Steve had been giving 10 percent of their income to other churches around the Willamette Valley. The minutes of meetings of their board show that this tithing had been approved, but Willard contended it was embezzlement totaling as much as $39,000. With help from the lawyer she worked for, Willard went to court and got a no-trespassing order blocking both Steve and Tammie from setting foot in Stepping Out ever again. Steve and Tammie had no money to hire an attorney to defend themselves.

"Steve and I were in shock," Tammie told me. "Here was this ministry we had founded—it was our whole life—and now we were being ordered to stay away. We had prayed with these men. It was crazy. I couldn't believe it. All we wanted to do was help these men. For two weeks all I could do was cry."

At Thanksgiving, which had been an important holiday at Stepping Out, when the residents, friends of theirs and volunteers got together to cook turkeys and hams and all the stuffing and cranberry sauce, Steve decided to take a chance and dropped in to wish everyone a happy holiday. Willard had taken the precaution of alerting the police, so an officer was on duty inside the building. Willard wanted the officer to arrest Steve for trespassing, but he was a friend of Steve's and recognized the preposterousness of the situation, so he just asked Steve to leave the building.

Afterward, Steve and Tammie conducted their own investigation among the other directors and grew to suspect that Willard had fallen under the influence of a resident of the facility who had hoped to gain control of Stepping Out and siphon off its funds for himself. Whatever the case, Willard's overthrow succeeded. Willard and the remaining directors later sold the building to the bigger and older Union Gospel Mission in Salem, and Stepping Out ceased to exist as a separate entity. Steve and Tammie lost their life's work.

The county and state ultimately declined to press legal charges against them for fraud or embezzlement. Tammie now volunteers part-time at a free clinic in a Baptist church and helps take care of an elderly neighbor with dementia next to their trailer in the farm fields where she can still walk with Jesus in the mornings.

"It may be better this way," Tammie said. "We now realize that by doing ministry full-time, you can lose your own identity."

10

Ashley

The First to College

Ashley was born into a marriage that remains illegal to this day. As is the Bogle tradition, the wedding of her underage parents, Tim Bogle and Chris Kanne, was a scam, a con job dreamed up by Tim's father, Rooster, to fool the authorities.

The union of her parents could not have been more unlikely. Tim was loud and disruptive, like many members of his family. Chris was quiet and shy to the point that she could be in a room full of people for hours and no one would notice her presence.

There was also the awkward fact that Tim had already been arrested and locked up, like his father and his six brothers. Chris's father was a former police detective who had become a prison guard and rose to be captain of the guard at the Oregon State Correctional Institution. As Tim would later say, "He practically raised my brothers. I was his worst nightmare come to life, and it took him seven years to speak to me." When Captain Kanne finally did speak to Tim, he told him, "Do you know what I was going to

do to you? I was going to arrange to put you in the middle of a murder scene and send you to prison." Tim gave his father-in-law an
incredulous look. "You couldn't have done that," Tim blurted out.
Without hesitation, Captain Kanne shot back, "Oh, yes, I could."

Chris introduced a strain of stability into Tim's life, and together
they produced a daughter, Ashley, who would be one of the very
few Bogles to finish high school; then she became the first Bogle in
150 years to graduate from college.

Tim and Chris met in the summer of 1988 at a ramshackle dance
club for teenagers called Streets in a run-down section of Salem.
It had a bar that served only nonalcoholic beverages, a dimly lit
dance floor and a disc jockey who played light rock tunes. Tim
kept eyeing a pretty brown-haired girl sitting at a table with her
friends until he got the nerve to go over and get her name and
phone number.

Tim, fifteen, already had a girlfriend, but given the chaos in
his home life, he was determined to get married and start his own
family, away from his father. "I didn't want to be ruled by my father
anymore," Tim later recalled thinking. He had just told his half
brother and closest friend, Tracey, "The next girl I meet I'm going
to marry." Tim said it was a serious decision, not a whim.

It was a tricky situation for Tim, even without knowing who
Chris's father was, because he was already on juvenile probation
for stealing two bicycles and had to report to a juvenile facility
in Salem to chop wood every weekday and go to a special school
for four hours each evening. On his free nights, Tim began dating
Chris, keeping her out late, until her parents grew suspicious and
learned Tim's last name. Captain Kanne was furious. He already
knew Tim's brothers Tony and Bobby too well, from having them
in his prison, and sometimes having to send them to solitary confinement for fights or attempted escapes. So he went to court and

got a restraining order prohibiting contact between Tim and his daughter.

Tim eventually persuaded Chris to go with him to a little town near San Jose, California, where Rooster's first wife, Kathy, had a small house. Tim was driving an old car, which broke down along the way, so they had to hitchhike. When they arrived, they found the house was badly burned, because Kathy had accidentally set the house on fire while cooking. They decided to stay there anyway, until Kathy arrived unexpectedly and told them, in a surprise fit of morality, that she would not allow Tim to sleep with Chris in her house. Kathy also handed Tim $10 in food stamps, saying, "You're a man now. Survive like a man."

To try to keep Chris's father from sending out an alarm, Tim told Chris to call her grandmother in Salem, who was a nurse. When Chris reached her and said she was safe, her grandmother responded, "There are all these charges against Tim now: kidnapping, a probation violation for leaving the county without permission, and violating the no-contact order." When Tim took the phone, Chris's grandmother added, "The police are after you now. They will catch you. And when they do you'll be gone forever." To which Tim responded, with more bravado than good sense, "Tell them I wish them luck."

Tim and Chris decided to hitchhike back to Oregon's central coast, where Tim's older half sister, Vickey, had a house. Vickey's husband at the time liked young girls, which worried Tim, and the husband mixed up a drink full of alcohol that he called "jungle juice" and pretty soon they were all drunk. Vickey eventually called the police, who arrived in several cruisers. Tim hid under a bridge, but when the police found Chris and Vickey and questioned them, Tim decided he had to act, and he walked over to a detective's car, trying to divert attention from Chris. "When the detective saw me, he asked who I was, and he found the charges against me and figured the whole thing out pretty quick," Tim recounted. "I got myself caught."

Tim was put in a local jail. Chris's father drove down from Salem to bring her home. Then Tim was extradited back to Salem and sentenced to three more months in the Marion County Juvenile Detention Center for another probation violation, leaving Oregon without permission. He was lucky not to be charged with kidnapping.

After Tim finished his short sentence, Rooster asked him, "Do you want to marry that girl, son?" When Tim said yes, Rooster quickly responded, "Then I'm going to get you married."

"Dad knew this was the only way to get me off the track I was on, because his rule was, you marry someone, you have to take care of her," Tim recalled. "He wanted me on the family track, not the crime track." This was another side of Rooster, the conventional father, which had been missing for years.

Rooster worked for a month on an elaborate, secret plan to pull off a marriage between Tim, who had just turned sixteen and was still on probation, and Chris, who was fifteen, in a state where the legal age of marriage was eighteen. They began by making phone calls to find out what was required to get married. They would need to create false birth certificates. They would have to create disguises to make themselves look older as well as find a minister willing to marry them. Finally, they would have to figure out how they could get a marriage license signed by both parties, in the county courthouse, and have a wedding with witnesses, when by court order Tim and Chris could not be together.

They went to work to forge new birth certificates. Tim made about fifteen photocopies of both his and Chris's original Oregon birth certificates. Then, using an X-Acto knife, they cut-and-pasted numbers and letters taken from other copies to create new ages for Tim and Chris, making him appear to be eighteen and Chris to be twenty-two. "When we were finished, it looked real," Tim said.

Next, Rooster instructed Tim to go to a magic store that sold fake mustaches made out of real hair so he could glue a mustache on when he went before a judge to get the normal three-day wait-ing period waived, and later when he appeared before a clerk in the marriage-license section of the county courthouse. They also borrowed a dark suit for Tim to wear over his thin frame.

Then they persuaded a woman in her early thirties from the neighborhood where Tim lived to stand in for Chris. Tim pasted on his fake mustache and dressed in his borrowed suit and set out with the older woman for the Marion County Courthouse. The judge didn't notice the obvious discrepancy in their ages when he agreed to waive the three-day waiting period. "He just asked, 'So you want to get married?,' and I said, 'Yes, sir,'" Tim recalled. When the judge signed the license, he smiled and said, "Good luck." The other woman signed Chris's name on the marriage-license application.

Tim hustled over to the local Burger King where Chris was working. He explained that his father had already arranged for a minister from the Baptist church near where the Bogles lived, the Reverend Art Cooper, to perform the wedding ceremony. The minister married the couple on March 4, 1989, according to the marriage certificate later filed with the Marion County clerk.

When they came out of the church, Rooster said to the newly-weds, "You've got to consummate your marriage or it's not final. I've got a motel room for you." Later that evening Rooster drove Chris home to her family, as if nothing had happened, Tim said.

The scam worked, but only for exactly one day. "There was one thing we didn't think of," Tim recalled. "When you get married, it comes out in the newspaper," in this case the Salem *Statesman Journal*.

"The next morning I got a call from my probation officer," Tim said. "He asked, 'So you got married?' I said, 'What makes you think that?' He said, 'It's right here in the paper, Mr. Bogle. This time you've really got yourself in trouble.'"

Tim and Chris were both arrested. Tim was charged with

"Unsworn falsification" in Marion County juvenile court, meaning, "Said child did unlawfully and knowingly make a false written statement to a public servant, to-wit, an employee of the Marion County Clerk's Office in connection with an application for a benefit, to-wit, a marriage license."

Tim and Chris were taken to juvenile court on March 22, 1989, where both were sentenced to fines of $100 and three days in juvenile lockup. Judge Connie Hass, who was presiding, told Tim, "Congratulations, you have made history in this juvenile department. In all the years I've been a judge, I've never seen anyone attempt such a thing, much less succeed."

Captain Kanne wanted Judge Hass to order the marriage annulled. After all, both Tim and Chris were under eighteen, he pointed out. But because Tim was already on juvenile probation before the sham marriage, he was a ward of the state and therefore Judge Hass had authority over him. Hass did not realize that it was not Chris who signed her name on the marriage application, which would have automatically made the marriage null and void. So after hearing arguments, the judge ordered Tim and Chris to undergo six months of marriage counseling, during which time they could not live together. After that period, Hass said, she would rule on whether the marriage could continue.

In the meantime, she also ordered Tim to remain in school or hold a full-time job. Before the scam was discovered, Tim had planned to hide out at his uncle Dude's house in Montana until he and Chris both turned eighteen and could legally be married. Tim didn't really want to go back to school, so Rooster came up with another scheme. "You need a job, a trade, to support your new wife," Rooster told Tim. Rooster said he could get Tim into the ironworkers union so he could work as a welder, but that meant another set of lies, because to join the ironworkers' union Tim again had to be eighteen and also had to be able to pass a series of welding tests. Tim was vaguely familiar with welding from spending time around his father on some jobs, but Rooster insisted to the union instructor that Tim was ready to take his ironworker's apprentice test immediately.

"Okay," the instructor said, as Tim remembered it. "We'll find out about that right now. We'll give him a test."

"Oh, no," Tim thought.

The instructor gave Tim a welding hood. "In some way, shape or form, I don't know how, I got it half right," Tim said. The instructor was clearly skeptical, but said Tim had done well enough to qualify to enter an advanced welding class, and could join the union. But for that he needed a valid identification card showing he was at least eighteen. Rooster helped Tim create a forged Washington State driver's license that gave his age as nineteen.

"This was Dad's one shot for one of his boys out of seven to take up his trade and maybe make something of himself, to take the work road instead of the jail road," Tim said, "so I really wanted to succeed." By this time, the six months of marriage counseling was finished, and Judge Hass determined that Tim and Chris could stay married. The judge never discovered the deception about Chris's signature on the marriage-license application.

Chris now was able to move in with Tim, who was getting regular welding jobs. He eventually worked on some major projects, helping in the construction of Safeco Field, in Seattle, where the Mariners play baseball, and what is now the Moda Center in Portland, where the Trail Blazers play basketball.

Ashley was born during this time, in February 1992. Tim was acutely conscious that this was the moment to change at least one Bogle's destiny. "When Ashley was born, my dad and I were sitting in the hospital, and I told him, 'This is where the chain breaks. Ashley will be raised differently,'" Tim recalled. Indeed, for Ashley, life was almost normal from the beginning. Tim was busy during the week, working on welding jobs. Chris was a kind, devoted mother, first to Ashley, and later to another daughter, Britney, and then a son, Little Tim, as he was called in the family. Chris was quiet, calm and unflappable, qualities she may have inherited from her father, who also spoke little. Tim and Chris were determined to set a good example for the children. There were regular mealtimes and bedtimes, with a rule against sleepovers outside their own house. There was benevolent, nonviolent discipline and well-monitored supervision of their activities, and none of the beatings or open displays of sex that Rooster had made his children endure. "It was a turning point in my life," Tim said.

What was happening was what John Laub and Ralph Sampson had discovered in their long-term follow up study of the five hundred boys from Boston originally studied by Sheldon and Eleanor Glueck in the 1940s. The boys, who started out as delinquents, could be weaned from their criminal ways in adulthood by strong social and emotional ties—a close, lasting marriage, a steady job, deep religious faith, or military service. These bonds created informal social controls that turned them away from trouble. For Chris, there was also the fact that her father was a former police detective turned senior prison guard and that her grandmother was a nurse, providing another layer of stability.

Although Tim and Chris did not keep any books in their house, or enroll Ashley in preschool enrichment programs, she proved to be an excellent student from the start, bringing home straight A's. "I always loved going to school; the schoolwork was easy for me," Ashley recalled.

Chris's mother-in-law, Linda Bogle, noticed that Ashley was intensely motivated and didn't want to fail any class, so she always got her homework done on time, whatever the distractions. "I think that determination came from inside her," Linda said. "She always had it."

Ashley's motivation also showed up in the way she handled the household chores she was assigned, doing the family's laundry and keeping her room clean. When she was only three or four years old, her favorite television show was *Barney and Friends,* the children's series on PBS, and her favorite character was Barney, the purple dinosaur. One day, in a minor act of rebellion, Ashley started throwing some of the clothes she had just washed, dried and folded onto the floor, until Tim saw what was happening and said, "You're in trouble now." What Tim always remembered, years later, was that when he said that, Ashley immediately started putting the clothes back into their basket neatly and chided herself, singing a Barney song:

> Clean up, clean up, everybody, everywhere.
> Clean up, clean up, everybody do your share.

Keeping up her success, in a family filled with relatives who became drug addicts or criminals, was sometimes difficult for Ashley. "I didn't want to stand out and make my family think I felt special," Ashley said.

It was also hard for Ashley that her father moved the family often, at least once a year. At first this was to follow construction sites for Tim's work, and later, after Rooster died from cancer in 1998, it was because Tim became very depressed and was eventually diagnosed with bipolar disorder. He had to quit his job and was on medication, and the family moved from town to town around the Willamette Valley in search of cheaper housing because they had to live on Tim's Social Security disability payments plus a small pension from the ironworkers' union. This meant a new school each year for Ashley until she reached high school and they settled in Salem. "I was very shy, and it was difficult for me to have to make new friends all the time," she recalled. "Some days I would be terrified of going to another new school with new classmates, and I would beg my mom and dad to let me stay home," Ashley said. "And some days I would be so terrified it made me physically sick." Eventually, a school psychologist determined that Ashley suffered from a panic disorder, and she was put on medication. To help her get through these anxieties, some days Chris would go to school with her; other days it was Linda.

But the A's kept on coming. By the summer after her junior year at North Salem High School, Ashley had a perfect 4.0 grade-point average. Ashley was interested in attending a college with a nursing school. Western Oregon University, a branch of the University of Oregon in Monmouth, had a nursing school and was only seventeen miles southwest of Salem. Given Ashley's grades, they offered her a scholarship.

That summer Ashley also received a letter from the National Youth Leadership Forum on Medicine, which said she had been selected to attend a program the year after she graduated from high school studying at Harvard Medical School or the UCLA's School of Medicine, where she would be given the chance to work with doctors in a hospital or laboratory. "Fewer than one percent of all high-achieving high school students are presented with this opportunity, and many alumni of the program report that it is a life-changing experience," said the letter, written by Dr. Shashin Doshi, who was the director of the program.

Tim, Chris and Ashley hardly knew what to make of the invitation. With the failed exception of Tracey, no one in the entire Bogle clan had ever been to college. They weren't even familiar with the College Board or the SAT or all the other complexities of applying to college. I purchased one of the standard guides to studying for the SAT and gave it to Ashley. But as best I could determine, no one in the family ever read it. The invitation from the National Youth Leadership Forum on Medicine went unanswered. It was all too overwhelming and foreign for Ashley and her parents.

Ashley herself, at seventeen, was still tiny, not quite five feet tall and perhaps eighty-five pounds, with a small button nose and long brown hair, which she kept pulled up in a top knot. Her skin was very pale, porcelain in hue, which added to her doll-like appearance.

There was always a fine line that her father had to walk in making Ashley part of the Bogle family and not placing her on a pedestal while also protecting her against the Bogle contagion that had ruined so many members of the family. Tim talked to her openly about his brother Tracey and the crimes that had sent him to prison, and he even took Ashley to visit Tracey in prison a few times. Similar visits to see family members in prison had proved disastrous for other Bogles, for Tracey and Bobby, for example, who felt the attraction of being a tough outlaw like their father and brothers. Ashley, though, was her own person. "The whole Bogle stigma didn't apply to me," Ashley said. "I don't think about it, honestly. I just figure that everybody in the family has the opportunity to make their own choices. If they make bad choices, that's up to them. I chose not to make bad choices." Ashley had discovered a mechanism to detach, to protect herself from the family contagion.

In Ashley's senior year of high school, however, she hit a few bumps. She unexpectedly found some of her classes to be harder, and her GPA dropped to 3.73. That was still high enough to allow her to graduate with honors, finishing thirty-third in a class of 350 students, according to her final high school transcript, a huge accomplishment for anyone in the Bogle family.

Ashley now also had a steady boyfriend, and she was spending more time with him. She was growing nervous about leaving home to go to nursing school, even if it was close by. The size of the school—4,800 students—concerned her, and it felt like a big financial commitment, though with her scholarship and student grants and loans it would be far less than the regular in-state tuition of $8,000. There was also her father's first brush with the "laws," using his term, since before Ashley was born. Tim had been caught speeding at ninety miles per hour, with Britney and son Tim Jr. in the car. His mother said he was distracted by his kids' arguing over the music on the car radio. Nonetheless, he was still sentenced for negligent driving and reckless endangerment and given thirty days in the Marion County jail.

Ultimately, Ashley decided that going away to college would be overwhelming. She took a semester off, then, in January 2011, enrolled in Chemeketa Community College, near where her family lived in Salem. Instead of studying nursing, her major would be health-management services. When she graduated she would be a medical technologist working in a hospital or a doctor's office.

Normally, earning an associate's degree from this program would take a student two years, meaning Ashley would graduate in December 2012. But there were more bumps. To earn enough money to pay what her scholarship, government grants and student loans didn't cover, she began working part-time in a Chipotle fast-food restaurant at the big mall near the Chemeketa campus. She soon discovered she was pregnant. She and her longtime boyfriend had broken up, so in October 2014 she became a single mom with a daughter named Aubrey.

Meanwhile, more members of her family were getting in trouble. Her younger sister, Britney, with whom she had been very close, got pregnant and had a child, and also developed a drug habit and was arrested and put in jail for drug possession and child neglect.

For a period of time, to save money, Ashley moved in with Tim's older sister, Debbie, who also lived in Salem. Debbie was another of the handful of Bogles who had managed to graduate from high school, and then, at the command of Rooster, she had enlisted in the Air Force at the age of seventeen, in 1987. After basic training, Debbie was sent to a U.S. Air Force base in England as a member of the Air Force Security Forces, the equivalent of being in the Army Military Police. Debbie, though, was soon diagnosed with bipolar disorder, just as Tim would be a few years later, and she was transferred back to the United States and discharged from the Air Force.

At home in Salem, and emotionally unstable, Debbie became addicted to meth and let a gang of other drug users move in with her. They were growing marijuana plants in her closet. She gave birth to two young boys. When the police raided her house one day, they found the marijuana plants and charged Debbie with the manufacture of a controlled substance and with child endangerment. Because she had no previous criminal record, she was kept in jail for only one night and then sentenced to probation.

This was the beginning of a prolonged period of chaos for Debbie. When she stayed on her meds, she was lucid and highly intelligent. When she went off her meds, which happened often, she could be psychotic—depressed and angry one moment, then suddenly full of enormous energy the next, like a tornado.

As her two sons, Jorden and Kaleb, grew older, they were in and out of prison themselves. Jorden was first sent to prison at sixteen for the new crime of sexting. He had sex with a sixteen-year-old girl who came to visit him when he was staying at a mutual friend's apartment, and then another boy used Jorden's cell phone to take a video of them on the bed and sent the video to their friends at high school. The video went viral. More recently, Jorden was sent to prison for a second time for four years for the attempted strangulation of his new wife. Kaleb was sentenced to prison for six years for taking part in beating and robbing a man at a Salem convenience store. He had just turned eighteen when he was convicted.

A psychiatrist in Salem who has treated Debbie for the Veterans Administration, Dr. Satyanarayana Chandragiri, asked her if she or other members of her family had ever had genetic tests to see if anything could be learned about their propensity for developing mental illness and committing crime. Dr. Chandragiri, originally from Bangalore, India, said he had seen mental illness and criminality co-occurring in families in both India and the United States over three and four generations. "As a result of practicing psychiatry in two countries for more than twenty years," he said, "I have come to the conclusion that the old, binary way of looking at people as criminals or noncriminals is too simple. I have come to think of it as something more than that. There is something genetic, moderating or aggravating, that is going on," he said. Doctors now must take epigenetics, the interplay of the environment and genes, into consideration in dealing with mental illness and other diseases, he said. "So why not with crime?" Dr. Chandragiri asked. It was much the same idea as the research done by Professor Terrie Moffitt at Duke University. None of the Bogles, though, have ever been tested for any genetic markers, and virtually all such testing is illegal inside America's prisons. This is partly the result of revulsion against the terrible genetic experiments performed by the Nazis on concentration-camp inmates, and partly a fear that genetic tests on American prisoners could be misused to stigmatize African Americans.

Despite all the chaos in her family, Ashley managed to persevere in her studies, but it took her four years to earn her associate's degree, twice as long as she had projected, though she did it with honors. A photograph taken at her graduation, with Ashley dressed in her academic black gown and mortarboard hat, shows her with a broad smile, as if she was profoundly relieved at her accomplishment in graduating. "She is still pretty shy, and she was very happy that it was all over," her father observed.

Ashley has gotten a job as a medical-records technician at Santiam Hospital in Stayton, Oregon, a small town a few miles southeast of Salem. She is doing coding of patients' medical records. Eventually, when she has saved some money, she wants to go back to college to earn a full bachelor's degree.

In the meantime, she has found a duplex apartment for herself and her now three-year-old daughter. Ashley has entered mainstream America in a rapidly growing profession. Her daily commute from her apartment to the hospital takes her directly by the big Oregon State Correctional Institution, where her grandfather long was captain of the guard and many members of her extended family served prison sentences, including at present her cousin Jorden. But Ashley does not dwell on this curious coincidence. She has broken the Bogle family curse, free to live without crime, violence or prison.

Epilogue

Bobby Bogle had never read a book about criminology. He knew even less about the research showing that 5 percent of families account for half of all crime, and that 10 percent of families account for two-thirds of all crime. But he had learned, instinctively, from his own family, that crime often runs in families. After all, Bobby has been locked up in a series of juvenile reformatories and adult prisons since he was twelve years old, and his eight brothers and sisters have all been incarcerated themselves. Altogether, with a little figuring, Bobby could count at least sixty members of his own extended family who have been sentenced to jail or prison or placed on probation or parole—in other words, put under the supervision of the criminal justice system. Like other members of the Bogle clan, Bobby had come to believe they lived under a curse of crime, where crime was an incurable virus that had infected them. "My brothers always end up here eventually," Bobby said during an interview in the Oregon State Penitentiary.

"They always show up. It's an honorable thing to do for your family, as a criminal. It's normal."

But even Bobby was not prepared for the day when he met Jeremy Vanwagner, a youthful-looking inmate with big, protruding ears like many members of his family. They were out in the penitentiary's exercise yard and they got to talking. "This new guy says he is from a town called Angola, Indiana, and suddenly a wave of excitement came over me. It made me want to jump," Bobby later told me. "It sounded very familiar to me because when I was fourteen in 1977 I met a woman named Ginger who worked with my mother in a nursing home, and we followed her back to her hometown, Angola, Indiana," Bobby said.

Ginger was a year older than Bobby and she was very open sexually, and pretty soon they were sleeping together. Bobby noticed that "she had a large birthmark on her butt." He also remembered that he contracted gonorrhea from Ginger and that his mother took him to a local hospital for treatment.

Now, out in the prison yard, Bobby asked Jeremy when he was born, and Jeremy answered that it was 1978, which fit the timing Bobby was calculating in his head. Jeremy could be his son. Bobby then asked Jeremy what his mother's name was. Jeremy said she was named Ginger.

With that, Bobby grew more cautious. In prison you never wanted to reveal too much. It could open you up to a fight, or create enemies or some gang grudge. But Bobby also felt something he had never felt before—that he might have a son, an experience all those years of incarceration had denied him. So, without explaining anything, Bobby invited Jeremy to be his cellmate, since his previous cellie had recently been released.

Once they were sharing the five-by-seven-foot cell, with two steel bunks stacked one on top of the other, Bobby mentioned that he had known a Ginger from Angola, Indiana, and that she had a birthmark on her rear end.

"I was amazed," Jeremy said during a prison interview. "I had no idea who my father was. My mother just said my father was a gangster and a gypsy, and now here was Bobby, who had a gypsy tattoo and said his family were gypsies." Bobby even knew about his mother's birthmark. "This whole thing just landed in my lap," Jeremy said. "I was not upset about my father being in prison. I was glad to finally find out who my father was."

Jeremy's mother had been an alcoholic who beat him when she was drunk when he was young, Jeremy told Bobby. And she had boyfriends who hit him in the head with a baseball bat and a golf club, and he had the scars to prove it. Jeremy said that, as a result of this physical abuse, he had run away from home and got into drugs and stealing cars and was eventually caught and sent to prison.

Bobby and Jeremy found themselves talking for hours about what the story of their lives and its intersection meant. Jeremy later said, "It really helped me to find my father. He helped me to see there is such a thing as a true family. I had missed a lot of important things in my life."

For Bobby, ending up in the same prison cell as his son produced some unfamiliar introspection. It had long been an accepted fact of his life that his father and uncles and his older brother, Tony, had passed on a criminal life to him. They were living exemplars, right in his father's house, of how crime can run in a family. But how, exactly, Bobby now wondered, did that criminal proclivity get passed on to Jeremy, a son he had never met. "I became afraid that there was something genetically wrong with me and our family. That we were doomed," Bobby told me.

After three years of being a cellmate with his father, Jeremy was scheduled to be released in 2012. Bobby knew his own earliest possible release date would not be until 2023, and even that depended on a decision by the parole board, which would not be favorably inclined, given Bobby's record. So Bobby set himself an unusual task. "I told Jeremy, you are ruining me, man," Bobby said. "I lived a life without love from my family, so I had to be hard, without emotions, to survive in prison. I was a very messed-up human being. Now you've showed me a different way from outlaw culture."

Bobby said he had a big request to ask of Jeremy. "When you get out, don't mess up. Stop the crime. I don't want to see you back here."

That was five years ago, and Jeremy has not gone back to prison. That was another way to break the cycle: create a strong family bond.

A Family Guide

Following is a brief guide listing the sixty members of the extended Bogle family with criminal records. I have included only the family members I could identify who were arrested by the police or were sentenced by a court to prison, jail or a juvenile reformatory, or placed on probation or parole. Because many family members were convicted multiple times and some sentences were much longer than others, the list is not intended to be exhaustive. In the interest of brevity, the list gives only the person's name, his or her family relationship and the most serious crime or crimes he or she committed, along with the corresponding punishment.

The First Ancestors

LOUIS BOGLE—Making moonshine liquor, sentenced to prison, with the sentence suspended, 1923

ELVIE BOGLE—Arrested as an accessory to burglary, 1959, and later released

The Children of Louis and Elvie Bogle

JOHN BOGLE—Reformatory, for stealing a truck

LLOYD "DUDE" BOGLE—Prison, for burglary

CHARLIE BOGLE—Prison, for burglary

ELVIE "BABE" BOGLE—Jail, for drunk driving and beating his wife

ROOSTER BOGLE—Prison, for burglary

The Family of Rooster Bogle

FAMILY OF ROOSTER AND HIS FIRST WIFE, KATHY CURTIS:
KATHY—Jail, for Medicaid fraud and drug possession

Their children:
MELODY BOGLE—Jail and probation, for drug possession and drunk driving
TONY BOGLE—Prison, for murder
PAULA BOGLE, TONY'S WIFE—Prison, for murder
BOBBY BOGLE—Prison, for kidnapping, assault and robbery
JEREMY VANWAGNER, BOBBY'S SON—Prison, for auto theft and drug possession
MICHAEL BOGLE—Jail, for statutory rape and failing to register as a sex offender; prison, for a series of burglaries and auto thefts
GLEN BOGLE—Prison in Washington and California, for auto theft, selling drugs, burglary and parole violations
VICKEY BOGLE—Jail, for drug possession and trespassing
SONNY RUTLEGE, VICKEY'S HUSBAND—Prison, no record on the charge
ROBIN FOWLER, VICKEY'S DAUGHTER—Jail and probation, for assaulting a police officer and drug possession
TRACEY BOGLE—Prison, for kidnapping, sodomy and assault

FAMILY OF ROOSTER AND HIS SECOND WIFE, LINDA WHITE:
LINDA—Probation, for Medicaid fraud
TOMMY WHITE, LINDA'S BROTHER—Prison, for stealing a money-order machine

TIM BOGLE—Jail, for negligent driving and reckless endangerment

BRITNEY BOGLE, TIM'S DAUGHTER—Jail, for drug possession

DEBBIE BOGLE—Jail, for child endangerment and manufacturing drugs

JESSE JAMES, DEBBIE'S HUSBAND—Jail, for child endangerment and drug possession

JORDEN BOGLE JAMES, DEBBIE'S SON—Prison, for sexting and attempted strangulation of his wife

KALEB BOGLE JAMES, DEBBIE'S SON—Prison, for assault and robbery in a convenience store

Family of Kathy Curtis Bogle

BERTHA WILSON, KATHY'S SISTER—Prison, for selling stolen money orders

LANA REE LUNA, KATHY'S SISTER—Prison, for stabbing her boyfriend

COREY LEE WILSON, LANA'S SON—Prison, for burglary in conjunction with a murder

DICK AUSTIN, KATHY'S SECOND HUSBAND—Jail, for assault and domestic violence

MATTHEW AUSTIN, KATHY AND DICK AUSTIN'S SON— Prison, for burglary and drug possession

JIM BOB CURTIS, KATHY'S BROTHER—Jail and probation, for drug possession

CARL ED CURTIS, KATHY'S BROTHER—Prison, for drug possession

Family of John Bogle

JERRY MICHAEL BOGLE, JOHN'S SON—Jail, for automobile theft; also used a homemade bomb to rob a pharmacy

of morphine and then died of a drug overdose in his
car as the police chased him and fired at his car

JERRIE LYNN BOGLE JONES, JOHN'S GRANDDAUGHTER—Jail,
for prostitution, robbery and forgery

JERRY PAUL BAKER, JOHN'S GRANDSON—Jail, for possession
of heroin and burglary before he hanged himself

Family of Lloyd "Dude" Bogle

RICK BOGLE, DUDE'S SON—Federal prison in Montana, for
selling cocaine

RICKY BOGLE JR., DUDE'S GRANDSON—Prison, for drug
possession, assault and drunk driving; died from an
MRSA infection after a drug overdose

LLOYD BOGLE JR., DUDE'S SON—Probation, for drug
possession

DARRELL BOGLE, DUDE'S SON—Prison in Montana, for
drug possession and escape

Family of Charlie Bogle

NAN BOGLE, CHARLIE'S DAUGHTER—Prison, for drug
possession

JERRY PAUL MACKEY, CHARLIE'S GRANDSON—Prison, for
drug possession

Family of Elvie "Babe" Bogle

TAMMIE BOGLE SILVER, BABE'S DAUGHTER—Never
arrested; ran halfway house for ex-convicts

DURRELL BURDEN, TAMMIE'S FIRST HUSBAND—Jail, for
drunk driving and disorderly conduct

CURT JAMES, TAMMIE'S SECOND HUSBAND—Jail, for
attempted murder

STEVE SILVER, TAMMIE'S THIRD HUSBAND—Prison, for
robbery, kidnapping and assault; the son of a man sent
to prison; after Steve's release, he went straight and ran
a halfway house for ex-convicts with Tammie

JASON BOGLE, TAMMIE'S SON—Prison, for drug possession
and armed robbery

SHANNON BOGLE JAMES, TAMMIE'S DAUGHTER—Probation,
for theft, prostitution and trespassing

DARREN WADE, FATHER OF SHANNON'S OLDEST CHILD—
Prison, for drug use

LOUIS BOGLE, TAMMIE'S BROTHER—Prison, for drug
possession, automobile theft and escape from jail

DEBORAH BARNES, LOUIS'S LONGTIME GIRLFRIEND—Prison,
for drug possession

TOMMY BOGLE, LOUIS'S SON—Jail, for drug possession

ALICIA BOGLE BARNES, LOUIS'S DAUGHTER—Prison, for
drug possession

MARK BOGLE, TAMMIE'S BROTHER—Prison, for
manufacture of meth and for identity theft

LORI BOGLE, MARK'S WIFE—Prison, for manufacture of
meth and for identity theft

FLORY BOGLE BLACK, TAMMIE'S SISTER—Prison, for drug
possession and stabbing a friend

GARY BLACK, FLORY'S FIRST HUSBAND—Jail, for drunk
driving

ROBERT WAYNE COOPER, FLORY'S SECOND HUSBAND—
Prison, for drug possession

ROBERT WAYNE COOPER JR., FLORY'S SON—Prison, for auto
theft and drug possession

Acknowledgments

This book owes a primary debt to three people without whose support it would not have been possible. Foremost and always to my wife, Elizabeth Mehren, herself an accomplished journalist and author and more recently professor of journalism at Boston University, who provided advice, good cheer and extraordinary patience, especially when our son, Sam Butterfield, passed away unexpectedly midway through the writing. Second, to my editor at Knopf, Jon Segal, who persevered in supporting the book long after most editors would have canceled the project. His suggestions on how to make a difficult subject more readable were always on target. And third, but certainly not least, I am deeply grateful to Linda Bogle, Rooster's second wife, who opened a door to the Bogle family when many other members were skeptical, or even hostile, not seeing any benefit to making their story public.

In the end, most Bogle family members agreed to participate in interviews and even share letters, photographs and school and medical records. Of particular help were Rooster's brother Charlie, and Rooster's sons Tony, Bobby, Tracey and Tim, as well as his niece Tammie and her husband, Steve Silver. In turn, Tim's daughter Ashley, who became the first Bogle to graduate from college, was an inspiration. Kathy Bogle, Rooster's first wife, also was a good source of information when she was willing to talk. In addition, Kathy's older sister, Bertha Wilson, who served time in prison herself, was a reliable informant about their side of the family. To all of them, and all the many other Bogles who talked with me, too numerous to name here, I express my deep thanks.

I must also acknowledge the critical role played by Steve Ickes, who first identified the Bogles as a family with a significant number of members in prison. At the time, Steve was an assistant director of the Oregon Department of Corrections and I was a correspondent for *The New York Times* covering criminal justice. Steve generously helped arrange for me to interview some of these Bogle family members in the Oregon prisons where they were incarcerated. Later Steve moved to Arizona, where he became deputy director of the Arizona Department of Corrections and made it possible for me to interview Tony Bogle, who was serving a life sentence in prison in Tucson for a murder he committed there. Similarly, I want to thank a former spokesman for the Oregon Department of Corrections, Perrin Damon, for helping track down some of the Bogles' criminal records.

For the origins of the Bogle family in Tennessee I thank the late Mae Smotherman of Brentwood, a suburb of Nashville, who as the daughter of Louis Bogle's older sister, Lula, grew up in the same log cabin in Daylight, Tennessee, as Louis. Similarly, I am grateful for the research on the Bogles done by Cassandra Czarneski of Arkansas, also a descendant of Lula. James Dillon Jr., a historian in McMinnville, Tennessee, generously showed me around Daylight and shared his knowledge of the hamlet where Louis Bogle lived until he moved to Texas.

For Elvie Bogle's formative years in the tiny crossroads village of Sherry, in northeast Texas, I am indebted to a local historian and genealogical researcher, Johnie Lee, who tracked down old land-ownership and tax records, as well as school reports and criminal files. I was also aided by the memories of a longtime resident of Sherry, Pat Westfall, who knew Elvie when she was a young girl. Two descendants of Elvie's grandmother's family, Betty Morris Dodd of Texas and Diane Norton of Snowmass, Colorado, shared their memories and research with me, helping put pieces of the family jigsaw puzzle together.

For the Bogles' time in Amarillo, I thank their longtime neighbor Margaritte Garcia, who still recalled Louis and Elvie and their boys with remarkable clarity. For details of Rooster's fight with Jimmy Wilson, I am indebted to Jimmy Wilson himself and to Rooster's second, Pat Dunavin. For information on the family's burglary of the grocery store in Amarillo, I thank Tom Scivally, the store's then owner, and Detective E. N. Smith, who solved the case and arrested most of the family.

On the murder of Sandra Jackson of Peeltown, Texas, by Corey Lee Wilson, a nephew of Kathy Bogle's, I am grateful to Kenneth Garvin, a sheriff's deputy who helped solve the crime, and to Mark Calabria, Corey's defense attorney, as well as to Corey himself for agreeing to several extended interviews in prison.

In Tucson, where Tony Bogle and his then wife, Paula Bogle, were convicted of the murder of the man referred to as Chief, I wish to express appreciation to David Sherman, who was assigned the task of defending Tony; to Barbara LaWall, for many years the Pima County Attorney; to John Leavitt, then a deputy police chief in Tucson; and to Kenneth Peasley, the assistant county attorney who prosecuted Tony and Paula. I also owe a significant debt to Linda Beck, a clerk in the Pima County Courthouse, who fully transcribed both trials, a text that ran to about three thousand pages.

For expert academic advice on criminology, I am particularly grateful to John Laub, a distinguished university professor in the Department of Criminology and Criminal Justice at the University of Maryland, and to Terrie Moffitt, the Knut Schmidt-Nielsen Professor of Psychology and Neuroscience at Duke University. For help understanding the patterns of marriage and divorce in the rural nineteenth-century South, I want to thank Nancy Cott, a professor of history at Harvard University. And for information on the predominance of Southerners among the early settlers of Oregon, I thank Scott Daniels, an Oregon historian.

I must also offer tribute to my literary agent, Carol Mann, who was both patient and firm in guiding this whole enterprise. Finally,

I need to say a special thanks to Judge Albin Norblad of Marion County Circuit Court in Salem, who opened the door to his courtroom and to his private chambers so I could hear parts of the trials of multiple members of the Bogle family and benefit from his wisdom. When Judge Norblad died, in 2014, he was Oregon's longest sitting judge.

A Note on Sources

The bulk of the primary sources for this book come from interviews I conducted over a ten-year period with members of the Bogle family. Some of these interviews were done inside prisons in Oregon, Arizona and Texas; other interviews were conducted in their homes, mostly around Salem, Oregon, but some as far away as Helena, Montana; Tucson, Arizona; Paris and Amarillo, Texas; and Nashville and McMinnville, Tennessee. In the interest of space, I have cited specific sources for my information in the notes that follow rather than attempt to list all of them here.

But some particular items deserve mention. Foremost among these are the two murder trial transcripts of Tony and Paula Bogle from Arizona, which run to about three thousand pages, and the joint-trial transcript of Bobby and Tracey Bogle from Salem, Oregon, which is almost one thousand pages. I have also benefited from hundreds of letters sent to me by Tony, Bobby and Tracey Bogle while they were in prison, answering questions I asked them. For the earliest history of the Bogle family, the lengthy reports by the Bureau of Pensions of the Department of the Interior on Narcissa Harding's claim for a Union Army pension, which run from 1880 to 1914, contain wonderfully rich details and depositions by neighbors and members of what would become the Bogle family. State prison records from Washington State on Charlie Bogle, from Kansas on Dude, and from Texas on Rooster as well as his sister-in-law Lana Luna and her son, Corey Lee Wilson, all provided invaluable information. Texas state death certificates confirmed that the mothers of both Louis Bogle and his wife, Elvie

Bogle, died at the North Texas State Mental Hospital. The tax and school records of Paris, Texas, show how impoverished Louis and Elvie Bogle were in the 1920s and 1930s as they began to raise their growing family, having to move every year when they couldn't pay the rent and having so little income they did not have to pay taxes.

As indicated in the notes, I have benefited greatly from the work of many criminologists and other experts. Two books were especially valuable and need mention. They are both by John H. Laub and Robert J. Sampson: *Crime in the Making: Pathways and Turning Points Through Life* and *Shared Beginnings, Divergent Lives: Delinquent Boys to Age 70*. These volumes described the two criminologists' rediscovery and analysis of a classic set of data on five hundred delinquent boys from Boston in the mid-twentieth century by Sheldon and Eleanor Glueck. Taken together they showed how crime could be passed on in families. I am also indebted to the rich work by David P. Farrington, of the University of Cambridge, in particular his study of 411 boys from London whom he and a team of researchers followed from age eight to forty-six and found that a mere 6 percent of their families accounted for half of all crime and that 10 percent of the families accounted for two-thirds of all crime.

All the dialogue and thoughts attributed to people in the book are real, based on either interviews or letters from Bogle family members or from courtroom transcripts. Each time a person is speaking, I have tried to indicate the source in a note, unless it is repetitious in the same chapter.

Notes

Prologue: *It Takes a Family to Raise a Criminal*

3 Bobby could remember only one: Interview with Bobby Bogle.

5 One night Rooster led them: Interviews with Bobby and Tracey Bogle.

5 "What you are raised with": Interview with Tracey Bogle.

6 One of the happiest moments: Interviews with Tracey and Bobby Bogle.

6 stealing big-rig trucks: Ibid.

8 as little as 5 percent of families: See David Farrington et al., "The Concentration of Offenders in Families, and Family Criminality in the Prediction of Boys' Delinquency," *Journal of Adolescence* 24, no. 5 (2001): 579–96.

8 The Gluecks found that two-thirds of the boys: Sheldon and Eleanor Glueck, *Unravelling Juvenile Delinquency* (New York: The Commonwealth Fund, 1950), pp. 98–101. For a later, brilliant analysis of the Gluecks' data, see the two books by John L. Laub and Robert J. Sampson: *Crime in the Making: Pathways and Turning Points Through Life* (Cambridge, MA: Harvard University Press, 1993) and *Shared Beginnings, Divergent Lives: Delinquent Boys to Age 70* (Cambridge, MA: Harvard University Press, 2003).

9 Michael Harrington: See Michael Harrington, *The Other America: Poverty in the United States* (New York: Scribner, 1962), pp. 96–101.

10 a quadrupling of the U.S. prison population: *The New York Times*, April 11, 2006.

10 John Laub: Interview with John Laub, professor of criminology at the University of Maryland, and see his book *Crime in the Making*, pp. 97–116.

10 "Once you get in it": Interview with Tracey Bogle.

11 "Look carefully": Interview with Tony Bogle.

12 "The past was kept back from us": Interview with Tracey Bogle.

12 blue dots on their left cheeks were a mark: Truman Capote, *In Cold Blood* (New York: Random House, 1965), p. 35.

1 Louis and Elvie: *The Carnival*

17 In June 1920: This account of where Louis Bogle was born and why he moved to Paris, Texas, is based on several sources, including the version he himself passed on to his children, as well as an interview with a nephew of Louis, Lloyd Harding, who was born in Paris just after Louis arrived there, and also separate interviews with Murray Harding, a cousin of Louis's, and Mae Smotherman, a niece. The dates are confirmed by the censuses of 1910, 1920 and 1930 and by Louis's later Social Security file.

18 In every decade: For a good account of this large-scale migration from the Old South to Texas after the Civil War, see Randolph B. Campbell, *Gone to Texas: A History of the Lone Star State* (New York: Oxford University Press), p. 325.

18 Louis Bogle was infatuated: For a detailed account of what life was like in Paris, Texas, at the time, see the two memoirs by William A. Owens: *This Stubborn Soil: A Frontier Boyhood* (New York: Nick Lyons Books, 1966) and *A Season of Weathering: The Autobiography of a Texas Country Boy Making His Way Toward an Education in the Hard Times of the Twenties* (New York: Charles Scribner's Sons, 1973).

19 Ervin and Herman Arthur: Skipper Steely, *1920 Lynching Stunned, Sobered City's Leaders and Paris' Reputation Suffers* (Paris, TX: Privately published, 2001), and Walter L. Buenger, *The Path to a Modern South: Northeast Texas Between Reconstruction and the Great Depression* (Austin: University of Texas Press, 2001), pp. 167–69.

20 Louis's uncle and his son, Charlie Harding: Interview with Lloyd Harding.

20 Louis's favorite place: Interviews with Lloyd Harding and Skipper Steely, a local historian in Paris, Texas.

21 Elvie Morris: Her date of birth is listed in the census of 1910 for Red River County, Texas. Her father's status as a poor, landless sharecropper can be seen in the tax records of Red River County for the years from 1895 to 1918. Details about her early life and the death of her father in the big influenza epidemic of 1918 come from an interview with a then neighbor of Elvie's family in the hamlet of Sherry, Pat Westfall.

21 This embellishing: The details about Narcissa Harding, Louis's grandmother, and her marriage to Carpenter Harding, a former Union Army soldier, are contained in the extensive file compiled by the Bureau of Pensions of the Department of the Interior when Narcissa repeatedly applied, unsuccessfully, for Carpenter's Union Army pension from 1890 to 1914. Narcissa can also be found in the censuses of 1850, 1860, 1870, 1880, 1900 and 1910.

22 Union Army pensions were like a golden ticket: For a full explanation of the importance of Union Army pensions in late-nineteenth-century America, see Theda Skocpol, *Protecting Soldiers and Mothers: The Political Origins of Social*

Policy in the United States (Cambridge, MA: Harvard University Press, 1992), pp. 1–62.

24 Louis and Elvie had grown up: Owens, *This Stubborn Soil,* pp. 21–25.

24 Louis offered to show Elvie how to drive: Interview with Tony Bogle, her oldest son.

24 Once a week it was his duty: On the Sherry postmaster fetching the mail once a week, interview with Pat Westfall, a longtime resident of Sherry who had known Elvie when she was young.

25 By now, Louis and Elvie were in love: Marriage of Louis and Elvie on April 2, 1921, found in the Lamar County, Texas, courthouse records.

25 hit song made popular by Bing Crosby: Printed text of funeral service for Elvie, 1987, courtesy of Linda Bogle.

25 northeast Texas had just fallen into a sharp economic recession: Buenger, *The Path to a Modern South,* pp. 143–49.

26 Harding decided to move back to Tennessee: Interview with Lloyd Harding, a nephew of Louis Bogle's, who was born in Paris in 1920 and lived in the house with Louis Bogle. The Lamar County deed book shows that Louis Harding, the uncle of Louis Bogle, sold his home in Paris for $200 in 1921.

26 Their first child: John Bogle was born on December 8, 1921, according to the Texas Birth Index for the period from 1905 to 1997.

26 Her earliest memories as a child: Interview with Pat Westfall.

26 Elvie's father, James Morris: His appearance is taken from the description on James Morris's World War I draft-registration card. His status as a sharecropper is also taken from that draft card and from an interview with Pat Westfall. That Morris owned no land and paid very little in taxes comes from the Red River County tax records.

27 her mother, Florence: Biographical details on Florence are from the census of 1880 for Pope County, Arkansas.

27 whom she had married in 1894: Florence's marriage to Jim Morris in 1894 is recorded in the Red River County marriage records.

27 Florence deserted her husband: See the census of 1910, which records that Florence was then living in a boardinghouse in Wichita Falls, Texas, and said she was not married and had no children. On Jim Morris divorcing Florence on the grounds of desertion, see the divorce records from the Red River County district court from May 1910.

28 "Florence was a loose woman": Interview with Betty Morris Dodd, a daughter of Jim Morris's older brother, Charles Morris, who lived next door to Florence and Jim Morris in Sherry. Dodd said her mother was the source of her information on Florence.

28 Sarah Morris Hardin: For biographical information on Sarah Morris Hardin, I am indebted to a descendant of her large family, Diane Norton, of Little

Rock, Arkansas, and Snowmass, Colorado, who has compiled a comprehensive genealogical history of the family.

29 Recent historical research: Nancy F. Cott, *Public Vows: A History of Marriage and the Nation* (Cambridge, MA: Harvard University Press, 2002), pp. 29–33. Also, an interview with Cott, who is a professor of history at Harvard.

29 In Arkansas: For the size of Sarah Hardin's family, see the census of 1880 for Jackson County, Arkansas.

29 an ending like something out of a Jane Austen novel: For the judge's ruling that Sarah's marriage was not legal, see James Hardin's 1891 probate file in the records of Independence County, Arkansas. Also, Diane Norton has an 1897 letter from one of James Hardin's children describing the court case.

30 Sarah loved to dance: Interview with Betty Morris Dodd, her granddaughter.

30 There were trained lions and elephants: Description of the carnival is from the *Paris Morning News,* October 14, 1921. For a description of the early motordrome that Elvie rode in, I am indebted to Lowell Stapf, a longtime operator of carnivals in Texas who was based in Amarillo.

31 As it happened: Description of Elvie's job driving a motorcycle in the carnival motordrome is from interviews with her son Charlie Bogle and her daughter-in-law Linda Bogle.

31 a young woman who was found murdered: *The Clarksville Times,* July 28, 1919.

32 People in Clarksville had a saying: Interview with Mary Hansler, a retired Red River County clerk who grew up in Sherry. Hansler is also the source of the view that working in a carnival was not proper and was unwomanly.

32 that she herself was a gypsy: Interview with her son Charlie Bogle.

32 Elvie and Louis began drinking heavily: Interview with Linda Bogle.

33 In private, her aunt began to call Elvie "trash": Interview with Betty Morris Dodd.

33 "surely one of the greatest incentives": Campbell, *Gone to Texas,* p. 366.

33 Elvie used her driving skills: Interview with Charlie Bogle.

33 Louis was less fortunate: For the arrest, trial and conviction of Louis for selling moonshine, see the Lamar County District Court clerk's minute book 5, for 1925.

34 "There seems to be an unmistakable drift": *The Deport Times,* May 18, 1923, Deport being a small town near Paris.

34 On July 20, 1925, Louis was arrested: Lamar County District Court clerk's minute book 6 and 7 for 1925.

35 committed to the new Texas state mental hospital: Interview with Charlie Bogle. Also, the Texas Department of State Health Services death certificate for Florence.

35 Dr. Liza Gold: Interview with Dr. Liza Gold.

36 Louis's mother, Mattie: Interviews with Charlie and Linda Bogle.

2 Charlie and Dude: *Growing Up Criminal*

37 Elvie gave birth: John Bogle's date of birth is from the Texas Birth Index for the years 1903–1997. The description of the houses the growing Bogle family lived in at the time is from interviews with Dude and Charlie Bogle.

38 Other children soon followed: Dude's date of birth is from the Texas Birth Index for the years 1903–1997. That is also the source for Charlie Bogle's date of birth.

38 Elvie cooked the same food: Information about the meals Elvie Bogle cooked is from interviews with Dude and Charlie Bogle. Dude recounted his love of fishing in an interview. And both Dude and Charlie talked about their father's racial views in interviews. The lack of money in the family for Christmas presents is from an interview with Charlie. Also, the photos of the boys without shoes were provided by Charlie.

39 Not long after Charlie was born: The Bogle family's lack of knowledge about the Depression is from interviews with Dude and Charlie Bogle.

39 In 1914, the Texas legislature: The passage of a Texas state compulsory school attendance law is from Walter L. Buenger, *The Path to a Modern South: Northeast Texas Between Reconstruction and the Great Depression* (Austin: University of Texas Press, 2001), p. 111. The fact that Louis and Elvie registered their children for school, as required by the law, but then did not send them to school because of the parents' work in the carnival is from interviews with Dude and Charlie Bogle. The Paris school records also showed that the children were officially registered, and listed a different address for the family in Paris each year from 1931 to 1941.

40 Louis said he was a veteran: On Louis's claim to be a veteran of World War I, see the listing for Louis Bogle in the 1930 census for Lamar County. On the fact that Louis never actually served in the war, see his draft certificate from Tennessee.

40 Despite their lack of education: That Louis and Elvie continued working in carnivals into the mid-1930s is from interviews with Dude and Charlie Bogle, who also provided details about their mother's prowess in riding her motorcycle in the motordrome.

41 Elvie and Louis continued to augment their tiny pay: Information about Louis continuing to brew moonshine and Elvie selling it is from interviews with Dude and Charlie Bogle.

41 "It was the Depression": Interview with Charlie Bogle.

41 As William Humphrey wrote: William Humphrey, *Farther Off from Heaven* (New York: Dell Publishing Co., 1976), p. 176.

41 Elvie and Louis particularly admired: Interviews with Dude and Charlie Bogle. Dude and Charlie also remembered Pretty Boy Floyd stopping at

their house in Paris. In addition, Charlie proudly recalled Floyd giving his mother money to buy shoes for the boys.

42 The caption under the picture: The old black-and-white photo Charlie kept on the wall of his trailer home in Salem that he thought was of his uncle, the nineteenth-century gunman John Wesley Hardin, was still there at Charlie's death in 2016. And Charlie delighted in telling the story of how his supposed uncle had shot a man dead because he was snoring in a hotel room next to him in Abilene during a cattle drive. For more on the real John Wesley Hardin, see Randolph B. Campbell, *Gone to Texas: A History of the Lone Star State* (New York: Oxford University Press), p. 305.

43 Charlie loved to hear: That Charlie and Dude began to identify with legendary Texas outlaws from the stories their parents told is from interviews with Charlie and Dude.

43 In fact, imitation forms the basis: For the origin of social learning theory and its role in criminology, see Freda Adler, *Criminology* (Boston: McGraw-Hill, 1991), p. 61.

44 The discipline "criminology": For the origin of the field of criminology and the role of Raffaele Garofalo, see Adler, *Criminology,* p. 6.

44 the "father of modern criminology": Ibid., p. 50.

44 "In East Texas in those days": Interview with Charlie Bogle.

45 Dude went fishing: Interview with Dude Bogle. On Dude being sentenced to ten days in the Lamar County jail, see the Lamar County Criminal Minutes Index for April 15, 1939.

45 Charlie had begun stealing money: Interview with Charlie Bogle. On Charlie's arrest for stealing the milkman's money, also see the Lamar County Criminal Minutes Index for February 3, 1941, and April 9, 1942. On the farmer's wife getting into bed with Charlie, that is also from an interview with Charlie.

46 "To me, they were heathen": Interview with Mae Smotherman, whose mother, Lula, was Louis Bogle's sister. Also from an interview with Cassandra Czarnezki, a granddaughter of Lula's, who has done research to compile a history of her extended family.

46 charged with stealing a truck: Interviews with Dude and Charlie Bogle, and the Lamar County Criminal Minutes Index for November 10, 1938.

47 Gatesville State School for Boys: There is a powerful, haunting account of what life was like for boys sentenced to Gatesville in Robert Perkinson, *Texas Tough: The Rise of America's Prison Empire* (New York: Henry Holt and Company, 2010), pp. 34–35, 253–56, 362. Also see John Neal Phillips, *Running with Bonnie and Clyde: The Ten Fast Years of Ralph Fults* (Norman: University of Oklahoma Press, 1996), pp. 13–20.

48 twenty-five lashes with the heavy strap: Interviews with John's brothers Dude and Charlie Bogle.

49 He would carry his shoeshine box: Interview with Charlie Bogle.

49 "I was taking after my daddy and mommy": Ibid.

49 "I knew about gals": Ibid.

50 About this time, in 1942: Ibid.

50 His brother and closest friend: Interview with Dude Bogle.

50 "I loved to fight": Ibid. The photos of Dude in Burma during World War II were in his trailer home in Helena, Montana.

51 After Charlie and Dude were gone: Interview with Charlie Bogle.

51 The family may have been poor: Interviews with Charlie and Linda Bogle.

52 He was arrested in Topeka: Interview with Dude Bogle, and Dude's arrest record from the years 1946–1949, which is contained in his Oregon State Police file.

52 Charlie had picked up his own: Charlie's arrest record in the late 1940s is from an interview with him and also from his Washington State prison records.

52 "I was the only one that went in": From Charlie's confession, which is included in his Washington State prison file.

53 He was taken to the state prison at Monroe: Charlie's conviction and prison sentence are from an interview with him and his Washington State prison file.

53 "I had to take the rap": Interview with Charlie Bogle.

53 "The Bogles live in a very small shack-type house": Mabel Ray's report on the Bogles' living conditions in Amarillo is contained in Charlie's Washington State prison file and is dated September 16, 1948.

54 Elvie also advised Ray: From Ray's report on Charlie contained in his Washington State prison file.

54 Dude found one consolation: Interview with Dude Bogle.

55 "They didn't show me anything": Interview with Charlie Bogle.

3 A Burglary by the Whole Family

56 "There is nothing between us": Quoted by E. N. Smith, a longtime detective in Amarillo who rose to be the city's police chief.

58 "without a bad bone in his body": Interview with Margaritte Garcia.

58 "She never worked a day": Ibid.

58 One day Mrs. Garcia saw: Ibid.

59 "This is the first actual house": Ibid.

59 "the pick of the litter": Ibid.

59 Officially, Rooster was born without a name: From Rooster's Texas birth certificate, courtesy of Linda Bogle. On Rooster's growing suspicions about the reason he was born without an official name, interviews with Rooster's two wives, Kathy and Linda Bogle. On Elvie going back and getting Rooster an

official name, the Texas Department of Health, Bureau of Vital Statistics, certificate of birth, dated November 22, 1956, courtesy of Linda Bogle.

59 he was always called Rooster: Interview with Kathy Bogle, Rooster's first wife.

59 "They call me Rooster": Interview with Jimmy Wilson, a classmate and rival of Rooster's.

60 his second-grade report card: Courtesy of Linda Bogle.

60 "He wanted to be a Bogle": Interview with Charlie Bogle.

60 Mrs. Garcia's two boys: Interview with Margaritte Garcia.

61 Phillip Garcia: Interview with Phillip Garcia.

61 Dennis Lindvay: Interview with Dennis Lindvay.

61 When it came time to elect: Ibid.

61 Rooster had been getting into trouble: Interviews with Rooster's two wives, Kathy and Linda Bogle, and an interview with his classmate Jimmy Wilson.

62 Rooster had become well known to the police: Interview with E. N. Smith.

62 a teenager kicked him in the head: Interview with Kathy Bogle, who was Rooster's girlfriend at the time.

62 "Rooster was always in trouble": Interview with Margaritte Garcia.

62 "only pretended to discipline Rooster": Interview with Linda Bogle.

63 To compound the problem: Interview with Margaritte Garcia. On Elvie Bogle being furious when Louis whipped Rooster, interview with Linda Bogle.

64 "the largest predictor of delinquency": John L. Laub and Robert J. Sampson, *Crime in the Making: Pathways and Turning Points Through Life* (Cambridge, MA: Harvard University Press, 1993), p. 95.

64 "our research suggests": Ibid., p. 97.

65 They were attracted by: Interview with Kathy Bogle, who lived near Rooster at the time.

65 He often practiced his kicking: Ibid.

65 One night Rooster snuck her out: Ibid.

65 At the time, Rooster had another girlfriend: Interviews with Jimmy Wilson and Kathy Bogle.

66 "He slammed her up against the wall": Interview with Jimmy Wilson.

66 Wilson challenged Rooster: This account of the fight is from interviews with Jimmy Wilson and Pat Dunavin.

66 He remained unconscious: Information about Rooster's severe injuries, his hospitalization and the surgery he underwent are from news stories about the fight in the *Amarillo News* and the *Amarillo Globe* from September 6, 1957, to October 7, 1957.

67 He suffered from epilepsy: Rooster's physical and mental condition after he was released from the hospital are from his Texas Department of Corrections file dated April 24, 1961.

67 His personality changed too: Interview with Kathy Bogle.

67 One group of people who have suffered: For findings about the connection between brain damage and changes in behavior, see Drew Barzman and John Kennedy, "Does Traumatic Brain Injury Cause Violence?," *Current Psychiatry* 1, no. 4 (April 2002): 49–55. Also see Alan Schwarz, "Research Traces Link Between Combat Blasts and PTSD," *The New York Times,* January 9, 2016.

67 Dude wanted to try out: The planning of the burglary is from interviews with Dude and Charlie Bogle.

68 Tom Scivally was happy: Interview with Tom Scivally.

68 Dude invited Charlie: Interview with Charlie Bogle.

68 Dude instead enlisted two other men: The account of the burglary is from interviews with Dude and Charlie Bogle; an interview with E. N. Smith, the lead Amarillo police detective on the case; an interview with the store's owner, Tom Scivally; and news stories in the *Amarillo Globe Times* and the *Amarillo Daily News* from December 8, 1958, to April 3, 1959.

69 "I'm coming with you": Interview with Charlie Bogle.

70 The five men then drove back: Ibid.

70 "The boys weren't smart enough": Interview with Russell Towery, the son of A. B. Towery.

70 The cash portion: Interview with E. N. Smith.

70 "She was hard as nails": Ibid.

71 "Ma Barker": Interview with Russell Towery.

71 They shipped him back to Amarillo: On Rooster being arrested in New Orleans and then sentenced to five years in prison in Texas, from Rooster's Texas Department of Corrections file. Also, interviews with Charlie and Linda Bogle.

72 A report by a psychologist: The report by the psychologist and the separate report by a psychiatrist are both contained in Rooster's Texas Department of Corrections file.

72 Dr. M. D. Hanson: Dr. Hanson's findings about Rooster and his letter to Elvie Bogle are contained in Rooster's Texas Department of Corrections file.

72 Charlie was not so fortunate: Charlie's bad experience at Eastham is from interviews with him.

73 Clyde Barrow, the outlaw: For a good account of Eastham when Clyde Barrow was sent there, see Jeff Guinn, *Go Down Together: The True Untold Story of Bonnie and Clyde* (New York: Simon and Schuster, 2009), pp. 67–88.

73 "I changed": Interview with Charlie Bogle.

4 Rooster and His Boys: *On to Oregon*

77 "If there was any kind of break-in": Interview with Charlie Bogle.

78 "But I can't even drive": Ibid.

78 "The word came expressly": William G. Robbins, *Oregon: This Storied Land* (Portland: Oregon Historical Society Press, 2005), p. 41.

79 It might make a good new home: Interview with Charlie Bogle.

80 An early emigrant: Harold Peters, ed., *Seven Months to Oregon: Diaries, Letters and Reminiscent Accounts* (Tooele, Utah: The Patricia Press, 2008).

80 "his mother seems to be over protective": Roy Crumley's progress report on Rooster, June 26, 1966, in Rooster's Texas Department of Corrections parole file.

81 Kathy's family was even poorer: On Kathy's marriage to Rooster, interview with Kathy Bogle.

81 "Doubtful that subject will ever hold": Report on Rooster is by his parole officer, Roy Crumley, in Rooster's Texas Department of Corrections parole file.

82 "They looked like a bunch of hillbillies": Interview with Margaritte Garcia.

82 "at which point he slipped": Report by Rooster's Oregon parole officer, Leonard McHargue, contained in Rooster's Texas Department of Corrections parole file, January 8, 1962. That Rooster got an insurance settlement of $928 for his supposed accident, also from McHargue parole report, on September 7, 1962.

82 "Lie down and say you're pregnant": Interview with Kathy Bogle. The "accident" was also reported by McHargue in his September 7, 1962, parole report.

82 "subject states that most of his free time": McHargue parole report, dated October 2, 1962, in Rooster's Texas Department of Corrections parole file.

83 "Subject has no prospects for employment": Ibid.

83 "Too lazy to work for welfare": McHargue parole report dated April 3, 1963.

84 he was arrested for having sex: On Rooster's arrest for having sex with a fourteen-year-old girl, see the sentencing document in the case, "The state of Oregon vs Dale Vincent Bogle," with a sentencing date of January 13, 1965, found in the Marion County Circuit Court. On the nature of the crime, interview with Linda Bogle, who learned about it from Rooster.

84 It was around Christmas: Rooster's meeting with Linda White and their growing relationship are from a series of interviews with Linda.

87 "It was just a big con job": Interview with Linda Bogle.

87 "It was horrible": Ibid.

87 Yet she kept seeing Rooster: Ibid.

88 "When he was drinking": Ibid.

88 "How does that feel": Ibid.

88 Tim recalled that there were days: Interview with Tim Bogle.

88 "Are you ever going to smoke again?": Interviews with Tim, Tracey and Bobby Bogle.

88 Rooster had each of his boys learn to box: Ibid.

89 "Rooster thought presents and toys": Interview with Tracey Bogle.

89 He made himself sound like: Interviews with Tim, Tracey and Bobby Bogle.

89 "Those talks really impressed me": Interview with Tony Bogle.

89 As the children got older: Interviews with Tim, Tracey, Bobby and Tony Bogle.

89 Rooster needed the cash: Interview with Linda Bogle.

90 Eventually, Rooster learned enough: Interviews with Linda and Tim Bogle.

90 Rooster took a special: Interviews with Linda, Tony, Bobby and Glen Bogle.

91 Bobby had drilled a small hole: Interview with Bobby Bogle.

91 "We really didn't have a childhood": Interview with Tracey Bogle.

91 The boys did not have toys: Interviews with Tony, Bobby, Michael, Glen, Tracey and Tim Bogle.

92 Perhaps because Tony was the eldest: Interviews with Tony, Bobby, Tracey and Tim Bogle.

92 he ordered Tony to stand sideways: Interview with Tony Bogle.

92 Kathy was lax: Interviews with Tony, Bobby, Tracey, Tim and Linda Bogle.

92 "My mother wasn't very responsible": Interview with Tracey Bogle.

92 To make matters worse: Interview with Linda Bogle.

93 Not surprisingly, Tony, as the eldest: Interview with Tony Bogle.

93 "My boy did nothing wrong": Ibid.

93 Four of his fingers were cut off: Interviews with Tony, Bobby and Glen Bogle.

93 Tony had also begun to set: Interview with Tony Bogle.

94 Tony's cousin, Tammie Bogle: Interview with Tammie Bogle.

94 "My mother and my other mother": Interview with Tony Bogle.

94 Judge Albin Norblad: Interview with Judge Albin Norblad.

95 "With a family like that": Ibid.

96 a natural experiment: David Kirk, "Residential Change as a Turning Point in the Life Course of Crime," *Criminology* 50, no. 2 (2012): 329–53. Also, two interviews with Kirk on his research findings.

98 "Sons follow their fathers": "Breaking Up the Family as a Way to Break Up the Mob," *The New York Times,* February 10, 2017.

99 This was because of a quirk of history: The best estimate of the strongly Southern background of the early Oregon Trail pioneers is in John D. Unruh Jr., *The Plains Across: The Overland Emigrants and the Trans-Mississippi West, 1840–60* (Urbana: University of Illinois Press, 1993), pp. 403–5.

99 Pro-slavery politicians dominated: For a good account of how close Oregon came to seceding from the Union when Abraham Lincoln was elected, see Tom Marsh, *To the Promised Land: A History of Government and Politics in Oregon* (Corvallis: Oregon State University Press), pp. 37–44.

99 many other mental hospitals: For a masterful account of the new asylums in the United States in the 1800s, see David J. Rothman, *The Discovery of the Asy-*

lum: Social Order and Disorder in the New Republic (Boston: Little, Brown, 1971), pp. 130–44.

100 The Oregon State Insane Asylum: For a detailed history of the Oregon State Hospital, see Diane L. Goeres-Gardner, *Inside the Oregon State Hospital: A History of Tragedy and Triumph* (Charleston, OR: The History Press, 2013).

101 Tony Bogle found himself a patient there: Interview with Tony Bogle.

101 Tony was assigned to what was called the Forty Ward: For Tony's time at the Oregon State Hospital, I have drawn from my interviews with him and also from his presentence report, prepared by the Adult Probation Department of Pima County, Arizona, as part of his trial there for murder in 1993. The presentence report has the great benefit of being able to draw on all of Tony's criminal and mental-health records, including his file from the Oregon State Hospital and the MacLaren School for Boys in Oregon.

102 Tony had a history of setting fires to kill animals: For Tony setting animals on fire and stealing from mailboxes, see his Pima County, Arizona, presentence report in 1993.

103 In the divorce: On Rooster getting a divorce from Kathy and then marrying Linda, interviews with Kathy Bogle and Linda Bogle.

103 "I can't keep him": Interview with Tony Bogle.

104 MacLaren, as everyone called it: For an excellent and devastating description of MacLaren, see Mikal Gilmore, *Shot in the Heart* (New York: Doubleday, 1994), pp. 144–61. Mikal Gilmore was the younger brother of Gary Gilmore, the murderer made famous by Norman Mailer in his Pulitzer Prize–winning best seller *The Executioner's Song*.

104 "When I arrived at MacLaren": Interview with Tony Bogle.

105 Tony was discharged: Ibid.

105 It was there in April 1982: Tony's account of the sodomy charge against him at MacLaren is from ibid.

105 "He tossed the book at me": Ibid.

5 Bobby and Tracey: *The Family Curse*

107 Kathy would go out to bars: Interview with Tracey Bogle.

107 Tracey in a swimming pool: Ibid.

108 "One day my mother dropped me off": Ibid.

108 After Rooster saw that his checks: Interviews with Tracey and Linda Bogle.

108 "When we saw him get off the plane": Interview with Linda Bogle.

109 "Out came this stripper": Interview with Bobby Bogle.

110 One of these innovative programs: Interview with Scott Henggeler.

112 A few months after Bobby was sentenced: Interview with Tracey Bogle.

112 "Our father had raised us": Ibid.

112 "it was not about stealing": Ibid.

113 Norblad sentenced Tracey to MacLaren: Ibid.

113 They decided to drive the truck: Interviews with Tracey and Bobby Bogle.

113 Tony, who was doing his time: Interviews with Tony and Bobby Bogle.

114 classic American prison style: For a history of the development of prisons in America, see David J. Rothman, *The Discovery of the Asylum: Social Order and Disorder in the New Republic* (Boston: Little, Brown, 1971), pp. 79–100. Also see Rothman, "Perfecting the Prison: United States, 1789–1865," in Norval Morris and David J. Rothman, eds., *The Oxford History of the Prison: The Practice of Punishment in Western Society* (New York: Oxford University Press, 1998), pp. 100–116.

115 "Everything passes in the most profound silence": Quoted in Rothman, *The Discovery of the Asylum*, p. 97.

116 Richard Louis Dugdale: Richard Louis Dugdale, *The Jukes: A Study in Crime, Pauperism, Disease, and Heredity* (New York: G. P. Putnam and Sons, 1887).

116 Another relatively early investigation: Thomas Ferguson's study of delinquent boys in Scotland was published as *The Young Delinquent in His Society Setting: A Glasgow Study* (London: Oxford University Press, 1952).

117 "the influence of another convicted member": Ibid., p. 67.

118 It found that half of all the convictions: David P. Farrington et al., "The Concentration of Offenders in Families and Family Criminality in the Prediction of Boys' Delinquency," *Journal of Adolescence* 24 (2001): 580–81.

118 A number of other studies: For the Pittsburgh study, known as the Pittsburgh Youth Study, see Rolf Loeber et al., *Antisocial Behavior and Mental Health Problems: Explanatory Factors in Childhood and Adolescence* (Mahwah, NJ: Lawrence Erlbaum, 1998).

119 the number of children with a parent in prison: See *The Crime Report: Your Criminal Justice Network*, November 21, 2010.

119 The number of children with a parent behind bars: Patrick McCarthy quoted in *The Crime Report: Your Criminal Justice Network*, May 10, 2010.

120 But in a recent book surveying: Interview with Joseph Murray, a criminologist at the University of Cambridge.

120 Bobby wanted to look: Interview with Bobby Bogle and the transcript of the 1993 joint trial of Bobby and Tracey Bogle in Marion County Circuit Court, pp. 136, 720.

121 he extracted a promise: Trial transcript, pp. 393, 407.

121 he listed the shop: Ibid., pp. 436–37.

121 had bought him a tan sport jacket: Ibid., pp. 93–94.

121 Fijalka had bad news: Trial transcript of closing arguments, pp. 132–38, and interview with Tim Bogle.

121 now armed with a .38-caliber revolver: Interview with Tim Bogle.

122 "things got nutso": Trial transcript, pp. 679–81.

122   "Bobby and Tracey were talking nonsense": Trial transcript, p. 689.

122   To calm things down: Ibid., p. 703.

122   "You're sure there's no way": Ibid., p. 720.

122   "This was a chance": Ibid.

123   "They didn't want any trouble": Ibid., p. 97.

123   the brothers barged into the house: This account of Bobby and Tracey's assault on Dave Fijalka and Sandra Jackson is from their testimony in the trial transcript, pp. 102–25. Also, interviews with Bobby and Tracey Bogle.

125   It took Dave Fijalka several hours: Testimony of Willets, California, police officer Blaine Johnson, in the trial transcript, pp. 499–503.

125   might be a stolen car: That Julio Morales called the California Highway Patrol, from his testimony in the trial transcript, pp. 499–503.

126   Officer Johnson sped to the scene: From Officer Blaine Johnson's testimony in the trial transcript, pp. 541–49. Officer Johnson also recalled that Scott Mayo had arrived with a gun in his waistband.

127   At the opening of their trial: Tracey's directive to his lawyer to try to exclude non-Christians from the jury is from Steven Krasik's testimony during motions hearing on the first day of the trial, November 10, 1993.

127   "Tracey feels there is a biblical proscription": Steven Krasik's motions to the judge before the trial began, in trial transcript.

127   At the end of the trial: Tim Bogle's statement to the judge is from an interview with him.

6 Kathy: *"Trailer Trash"*

129   It was Mother's Day: On Kathy Bogle being sad and lonely on Mother's Day, interview with Kathy Bogle.

129   she was charged and then convicted: For Kathy's indictment and conviction for hindering prosecution and custodial interference, see her Oregon Department of Corrections criminal history.

129   Dick Austin had fourteen convictions: From Dick Austin's Washington State Department of Corrections file.

131   "I am recuperating from a long life": Interview with Kathy Bogle.

131   By the end of Mother's Day: Interview with Perrin Damon, then the spokeswoman for the Oregon Department of Corrections.

132   "This is an old story": Interview with Tim Bogle.

132   Her older sister, Bert: Interview with Bertha Wilson.

132   Kaufman County, Texas: That Clyde Barrow broke Bonnie Parker out of jail in Kaufman County, Texas, in Jeff Guinn, *Go Down Together: The True Untold Story of Bonnie and Clyde* (New York: Simon and Schuster, 2009), pp. 92–123.

132 "When he came out": Interview with Deputy Kenneth Garvin of the Kaufman County, Texas, sheriff's office.

132 Both of Kathy's brothers: Interviews with Kathy Bogle and Bertha Wilson.

132 At the time Corey was born: Interview with Bertha Wilson.

133 In July 1990: For a full account of the kidnapping and murder of Sandra Jackson, see the coverage in the local newspaper, the *Terrell Tribune,* July 23, July 25, July 26, July 30, August 2, August 7, August 14, August 16 and September 12, 1990, and February 7 and August 8, 1991. Also see the guilty plea by Corey Lee Wilson on February 1991 in the transcript of his trial for murder in Kaufman County, Texas, pp. 691–763.

133 They were turned in by Lana: On Lana Luna acting as an informant for the sheriff's department and turning in her own son, see the transcript of Corey Lee Wilson's murder trial for his mother's testimony, pp. 442–97.

133 he was released in 2015: According to a spokesman for the Texas Department of Criminal Justice.

133 "When you get right down to it": Interview with Bertha Wilson.

134 She now had to wear false teeth: Interview with Kathy Bogle.

134 "For Kathy there is no need to plan": Interview with Linda Bogle.

134 were arrested at Kathy's trailer home: Ibid.

135 Vickey had numerous arrests: Interview with Vickey Bogle Fowler.

135 she started shouting at her probation agent: Interview with Linda Bogle. Also, Kathy Bogle's Oregon Department of Corrections file.

135 "I'm not a drug addict": See Kathy Bogle's Oregon Department of Corrections file.

135 The case manager immediately contacted: The case manager from the Oregon Home Healthcare Provider checks in to help Kathy in jail, from the Oregon attorney general's press release about Kathy on September 28, 2009.

135 Kathy had claimed for more than two years: Ibid.

136 In September 2008 both women were indicted: See the indictment against Kathy Bogle and Linda Bogle on September 24, 2009, by the Marion County grand jury.

136 Linda was charged with five counts of theft: Ibid.

136 "It was an idea": Interview with Linda Bogle.

136 After being caught: Linda pled guilty and was placed on probation, from the Oregon attorney general's press release about the case, dated September 28, 2009.

137 "She's scammed people": Interview with Linda Bogle.

137 "I think I've lost my mind": Interviews with Kathy Bogle and Judge Albin Norblad.

138 "She can no longer put things together": Interview with Jeannie Kelley.

138 "They have permission to be here": From the transcript of Kathy's trial in Marion County Circuit Court.

139   Kathy Bogle alone had cost: Interview with Judge Albin Norblad.

139   it is virtually impossible to collect: Interview with Derrick Gasperini.

7   Tracey: *A Fateful Compulsion*

141   two-thirds of the 600,000 inmates: Bureau of Justice Statistics report of April 2014 by Howard Snyder et al.

141   "nothing works" doctrine: Robert Martinson, "What Works? Questions and Answers About Prison Reform, *The Public Interest* 35 (Spring 1974): 22–54.

143   symptoms of severe mental illness: Information concerning Tracey's bout with mental illness in prison is from his Oregon Department of Corrections Mental Health File, obtained with his consent.

143   Ann Heath: Ann Heath's observations about Tracey are from a series of interviews with her.

144   Tracey was suffering from paranoid schizophrenia: Heath's diagnosis is in Tracey's Oregon Department of Corrections Mental Health Evaluation report, dated January 15, 1997.

144   Dr. Marvin Fickle: Dr. Fickle's diagnosis of Tracey is in his Oregon Department of Corrections Mental Health Evaluation report, dated October 3, 2001.

145   "I want to do good": Interview with Tracey as I drove him upon his release from prison, August 10, 2009. All that follows that day is from our conversation as we drove around Salem.

147   to register as a sex offender: Tracey's comments at the Oregon State Police office when registering as a sex offender happened while I was driving him to his required appointments after his release from prison.

148   build his dream house: Tracey outlined his plan for building a dream house while we were at Stepping Out Ministries.

149   he would get a gun: Said while we were at Stepping Out Ministries.

149   "Tracey is stunted emotionally": Interview with Tammie Bogle Silver, Tracey's cousin.

150   Tracey was giddy: Interview with Tracey after he had been at Chemeketa Community College.

150   He also bought a car: Interview with Tracey.

151   "The government is robbing me": Ibid.

152   "The kids thought I was really cool": Ibid.

152   "It's kind of boring out here": Ibid.

152   "But that department has been shut down": Ibid.

152   she was now pregnant: Interview with Tim Bogle.

153   "I got a girl pregnant": Interview with Tracey.

154   was accepted for admission that fall: Ibid.

154 "I've done something that no one": Ibid.

154 he could tell Tracey was drinking again: Interview with Tim Bogle.

154 "getting drunk every day": Interview with Bobby Bogle.

155 It finally happened: Interview with Tim Bogle, and Marion County Jail Inmate Roster for May 7, 2011.

155 Tracey got lucky: Marion County Circuit Court criminal cases record for September 11, 2011.

156 to enroll at Portland State University: Interview with Tim Bogle.

157 Giambattista della Porta: See Freda Adler, *Criminology* (Boston: McGraw-Hill, 1991), p. 53, and Nicole Rafter, *The Criminal Brain: Understanding Biological Theories of Crime* (New York: New York University Press, 2008), pp. 20, 44.

157 Cesare Lambroso: Adler, *Criminology,* pp. 54–56, and Rafter, *The Criminal Brain,* pp. 108–10.

157 Ernest Hooten: Adler, *Criminology,* p. 57, and Rafter, *The Criminal Brain,* pp. 150–59.

158 the University of Maryland was forced to call off: Charles Babington, *The Washington Post,* September 5, 1992, and Daniel Goleman, *The New York Times,* September 15, 1992.

158 "It is like the return of the native": Siddhartha Mukherjee, *The Gene: An Intimate History* (New York: Scribner, 2016), p. 380.

158 traits like impulsivity and novelty seeking: Ibid., p. 382.

158 Researchers estimate: Interview with John Laub, professor of criminology at the University of Maryland.

158 Terrie E. Moffitt: Terrie Moffitt, "Role of Genotype in the Cycle of Violence in Maltreated Children," *Science* 297 (August 2, 2002): 851.

159 "It is a complex dance": Interview with Terrie Moffitt.

159 a meta-analysis of twenty-seven studies: Amy L. Byrd et al., "MAOA, Childhood Maltreatment and Antisocial Behavior: Meta Analysis of a Gene-Environment Interaction," *Biological Psychiatry* 75, no. 1 (January 2014).

159 this coincidence of genes and environment: Email from Terrie Moffit to the author, March 18, 2013.

160 "We don't have a lot of studies": Interview with Terrie Moffitt.

160 "a double insult": Interview with John Laub.

8 Tony: *A Murder in Tucson*

161 The local authorities: Tony's marriage to Paula, from Tony's copy of their marriage license.

161 Perhaps because she had been sexually abused: From Paula's presentence report for theft in Pima County, Arizona, in 1992.

161 If the jail officials had looked: Copies of the psychological and psychiatric reports on Tony referred to here are found in the presentence report on Tony, prepared for sentencing him in his later murder trial in Tucson. It included all available criminal and mental-health records on Tony going back to his childhood.

163 They soon moved out to a small: Tony and Paula meeting Chief is from testimony at Tony's later trial for murder in Tucson, Pima County, Arizona, court transcript, pp. 217–25.

164 by announcing soon after they moved in: Murder trial transcript, p. 193.

164 "like a hermit, kind of spacey": Testimony of Robert Trimble, court transcript, pp. 217–25.

164 "He got on top of me": Paula's description of Chief getting on top of her is from the transcript of her testimony in Tony's murder trial, pp. 18–24.

166 Tony and Paula counted their money: Ibid., pp. 25–28.

167 "Tony told me to blame it all on him": Ibid., p. 30.

168 "Tony would not trust anybody": Interview with David Sherman.

168 Chet Hopper: Tony's various stories to Detective Tony Miller are contained in the transcript of Miller's testimony in Tony's murder trial, pp. 130–44.

170 "My wife, man, did not murder anybody": Tony's quote is in Detective Miller's interview with him, introduced as evidence in Tony's trial for murder, in transcript, p. 118.

170 Tony broke and said he alone: Tony's admission is in Detective Miller's interview with him, in trial transcript, p. 173.

170 "Do you have any feelings": Interview by Detective Miller with Tony, in trial transcript, p. 213.

171 "My wife and I gave some false statements": Tony's conversation with the guard is included in the trial transcript, pp 136–84.

171 "Back in Reno all I wanted to do": Tony's conversation with Detective Miller in the Pima County Jail is contained in the trial transcript, pp. 119–44.

172 "Chief tried to rape me": Paula changing her statement about her role in the crime is from Detective Miller's transcript of his interview with her on December 18, 1991, included in the trial transcript for Tony in a separate file, marked "Paula Bogle Video Tape Transcription," pp. 1–84.

173 If Paula had accepted a suggestion: Interview with David Sherman.

174 "He was a cop's prosecutor": Interview with Tony Miller.

174 Peasley had an extraordinary record: See the *Arizona Daily Star,* September 9, 2011, and Jeffrey Toobin's profile of Peasley in *The New Yorker,* January 17, 2005.

174 "It's not fair that my husband": Paula at her trial for theft, *The Arizona Star,* February 10, 1994.

175 "I didn't really need to figure out": Interview with Kenneth Peasley.

175 "An analysis of the statements": This petition by James Cochran, dated January 29, 1992, is in the transcript of Tony's murder trial, as part of a series of loose legal documents filed with Judge Veliz with no page numbers.

175 "During an interview": Affidavit by Richard Bozich, June 17, 1992, in trial transcript, ibid.

176 "his orientation to reality was off": Interview with David Sherman.

177 "Don't worry": Ibid.

177 "Now, let me tell you": Sherman's opening statement to the jury was on the second day of the trial, in transcript, pp. 20–29.

178 "the cause of death": From the testimony by the medical examiner, Dr. Ann Hartsough, on the second day of the trial, in transcript, pp. 104–40.

178 a chance of getting Tony acquitted: Interview with David Sherman.

179 "When you went in the apartment": Peasley's cross-examination of Tony, on the third day of his murder trial, in transcript, pp. 222–64.

180 "We may never know": Sherman, in his closing argument to the jury, on the fifth day of the trial, in transcript, pp. 40–55.

180 "there have been many lies": Judge Veliz speaking to the jury after Tony testified on the third day of the trial, in transcript, pp. 26–28.

180 "the most evil human being": Bert Wilson's testimony, on the fourth day of the trial, in transcript, pp. 12–44.

181 "This man had an unusually disturbing childhood": Report by Dr. Martin Levy, on p. 5 of the Defense's Mitigation Memorandum, in the trial transcript.

181 "If you were going to go out and create": Interview with David Sherman.

182 developed a program of meetings: For a description of the Jacksonville program, see Fox Butterfield, "Aggressive Justice System in Jacksonville, Fla., Intervenes to Ward Off Juvenile Court," *The New York Times*, October 4, 1997.

184 "Flip a coin": Interview with Tony.

9 Tammie: *Walking with Jesus*

188 "Too mean to die": Interview with Louis Bogle.

188 "I asked him who it was": Interview with Tammie.

188 Tammie's three children: Information on Jason, Shannon and Amy is from interviews with Tammie.

189 "I am walking with Jesus": Interview with Tammie.

189 "Jesus is as real to me": Ibid.

189 "Throughout our family": Ibid.

190 "This patient will": Report by Dr. R. F. Hyde, June 17, 1960.

190 "shade-tree mechanic": Interview with Tammie.

190 "We begged our mother": Ibid.

190 "Take off and run": Ibid.

191 He was eventually sent to jail: Ibid.

191 "It was okay to beat me": Ibid.

191 Tammie soon met and married her second husband: Ibid.

191 A Danish criminologist: Lars Hojsgaard Andersen, Rockwell Foundation Research Unit, Study Paper 119, June 2017, Copenhagen, Denmark.

192 His name was Steve Silver: Interviews with Tammie and Steve Silver.

193 "I just laughed at that": Interview with Tammie.

193 He planned to turn: Information about Steve Silver's plans for opening a halfway house for newly released sex offenders is from interviews with him and Tammie.

194 He ended up in prison: The details of Steve Silver's difficult, abused childhood and his teenage crime spree are from interviews with him.

195 Flory Bogle Black: The details of Flory being molested by her father and her troubled life are from interviews with her and Tammie, as well as her Oregon Department of Corrections criminal record.

196 Tammie's other brother, Mark Bogle, and his wife, Lori: Information on Mark's and Lori's criminal histories are from interviews with them and from their Oregon Department of Corrections criminal records.

197 one widely respected academic study: Mark A. Cohen and Alex Piquero, "New Evidence on the Monetary Value of Saving High Risk Youth," Vanderbilt University Law School Law and Economic Working Paper, no. 08-07, and also an interview with Professor Cohen.

197 Her name was Sue Willard: For the dispute between Sue Willard and Steve and Tammie Silver over Stepping Out Ministries, I have relied on extensive interviews with the three of them and a spokesman for the Oregon Department of Corrections.

10 Ashley: *The First to College*

200 Ashley was born into a marriage: This account of the marriage of Tim Bogle and Chris Kanne comes from extended interviews with Tim and Linda Bogle as well as Chris.

203 forge new birth certificates: Tim showed me the forged birth certificates, which he still keeps.

204 the marriage-license application: Tim also showed me their marriage license, issued on March 6, 1989, by Marion County, and their marriage certificate, signed by the Rev. Art Cooper, an old family friend.

204 Tim was charged: The petition against Tim was filed by the Marion County Court Juvenile Division on March 22, 1989.

205 Tim and Chris were taken to juvenile court: Their punishment by Judge Connie Hass is in the records of the Marion County Court Juvenile Division for March 22, 1989. Tim also provided me with a confession he signed on May 15, 1989, and gave to Judge Hass.

205 "You need a job": Rooster's scheme to get Tim a job as a welder and to pass the ironworkers' union test is from an interview with Tim.

206 "When Ashley was born": Interview with Tim.

207 what Sheldon and Eleanor Glueck had discovered: John L. Laub and Robert J. Sampson: *Crime in the Making: Pathways and Turning Points Through Life* (Cambridge, MA: Harvard University Press, 1993).

207 "I always loved going to school": Interview with Ashley Bogle.

207 Ashley's motivation: Interviews with Tim, Linda and Ashley Bogle.

208 "I didn't want to stand out": Interview with Ashley.

208 It was also hard for Ashley: Ibid.

208 eventually diagnosed with bipolar disorder: Interviews with Tim and Linda Bogle.

208 "I was very shy": Interview with Ashley.

209 Ashley had a perfect 4.0 grade-point average: Based on Ashley's high school records.

209 "Fewer than one percent of all high-achieving": From a copy of the invitation, which Tim Bogle provided.

210 "The whole Bogle stigma didn't apply to me": Interview with Ashley.

210 her GPA dropped: From Ashley's final North Salem High School transcript on June 6, 2010.

210 Tim had been caught speeding: That Tim Bogle was arrested for speeding is from the Salem Police Department report on November 4, 2009, and the Marion County Correctional Facility inmate roster on the same date.

211 She soon discovered she was pregnant: Interview with Ashley.

211 Her younger sister, Britney: Interviews with Ashley and Linda Bogle.

211 was soon diagnosed with bipolar disorder: Interviews with Debbie and Linda Bogle.

212 she was kept in jail: Interviews with Debbie and Linda Bogle, and Oregon Department of Corrections file on Debbie, August 13, 2002, and April 27, 2005.

212 Jorden was first sent to prison: From the indictment of Jorden Bogle in Marion County Circuit Court, April 29, 2009, and the Oregon Department of Corrections record on Jorden's admission to prison, April 23, 2009. For Jorden's second prison sentence, see the Oregon Department of Corrections inmate roster for Jorden on April 16, 2017.

212 Kaleb was sentenced to prison: Salem *Statesman Journal*, June 21, 2013. Also see the Oregon Department of Corrections inmate roster for Kaleb on April 17, 2017.

212 Dr. Satyanarayana Chandragiri: Interview with Dr. Chandragiri.
213 "She is still pretty shy": Interview with Tim Bogle.

Epilogue

214 "My brothers always end up here": All the discussion in the epilogue is based on a series of interviews with Bobby Bogle, Jeremy Vanwagner and Bobby's mother, Kathy.

Index